CHRIS PACKHAM'S
Back Garden
Nature Reserve

This book is for all those who have tasted tadpoles.

This edition published in 2010 by New Holland Publishers (UK) Ltd
London • Cape Town • Sydney • Auckland

www.newhollandpublishers.com

86 Edgware Road, London W2 2EA, United Kingdom
80 McKenzie Street, Cape Town 8001, South Africa
Unit 1, 66 Gibbes Street, Chatswood, NSW 2067, Australia
218 Lake Road, Northcote, Auckland, New Zealand

2 4 6 8 10 9 7 5 3 1

First published in 2001 by New Holland Publishers (UK) Ltd
Copyright © 2001 in text: Chris Packham
Copyright © 2001 in photographs: David Cottridge, Chris Packham and other
photographers as credited below
Copyright © 2001 in artwork: New Holland Publishers (UK) Ltd
Copyright © 2001 New Holland Publishers (UK) Ltd

Photographic Acknowledgements

With the exception of those listed below, all the photographs in this book
were taken by David Cottridge:

Colin Carver: p66 • E.A.Janes: p50 (t) • Gordon Langsbury: p34 • George McCarthy: p50 (br); p51
• Chris Packham: front cover (main image and inset cr); p8; p10; p11; p21 (t); p21 (b); p32; p33
(tc); p53; p55; p60; p90; p108 (br); p112; p113; p128; p129 (b); p130; p130 (t); p130 (bl); p131;
p132; p133 (t); 133 (b); 135 • Alan Petty : p49 • Richard Revels: front cover (inset t); p1; p12;
p14; p63 (t); p63 (c); p63 (b); p65; p67; p74 (tl); p74 (bl); p76 (t); p76 (bl); p78; p80; p82 (t);
p82 (bl); p84; p85; p86; p87; p91 (tc); p92 (tr); p92 (c); p92 (bl); p93 (b); p96 (t); p96 (cr);
p100; p104; p106; p107; p108 (tl); p109; p111 (tr); p111 (tl); p111 (b); p116; p117 (c);
p118; p119; p126; p127; p129 (b) • David Tipling: p27 • Chris Whittles: p138 •
The Wildlife Trusts: p7 • Alan Williams: front cover (inset cl); p18; p21; p70; p74 (r); p94

t= top; b=bottom; c=centre; l=left; r=right

Artwork Acknowledgements

Artwork commissioned by Wildlife Art Ltd, www.wildlife-art.co.uk
Artists: Sandra Doyle and Cy Baker

Additional Artwork

Bird illustrations on the following pages by David Daly:
p16; p17; p28; p30; p31; p33; p38; p40; p41; p42; p43; p44;
p45; p46; p47; p48; p49; p136
Line artwork on pages 60 and 69 by Mike Unwin

ISBN 978 1 84773 698 7

Publisher: Simon Papps
Project Editor: Mike Unwin
Copy Editor: Sylvia Sullivan
Designer: Roger Hammond
Cover Design: Frank Ideas
Diagrams: William Smuts
Index: Janet Dudley
Production: Joan Woodroffe
Publishing Director: Rosemary Wilkinson

Reproduction by Modern Age Repro Co. Ltd, Hong Kong
Printed and bound in Malaysia by Times Offset (M) Sdn Bhd

CHRIS PACKHAM'S
Back Garden
Nature Reserve

NEW HOLLAND

CONTENTS

MAMMALS 52

INVERTEBRATES 70

PONDS

PLANTS

PHOTOGRAPHY

AFTER THOUGHTS

THE WILDLIFE TRUSTS

By the late 1960s, in response to the widespread devastation of our natural habitats, Wildlife Trusts had been formed across the length and breadth of the UK. Ancient woodlands, wildflower meadows, lakes, mosses, moors, islands, estuaries and beaches were all rescued in an urgent drive to save our natural heritage for future generations.

There are now 47 individual Wildlife Trusts covering the whole of the UK and the Isle of Man and Alderney. Together The Wildlife Trusts are the largest UK voluntary organization dedicated to protecting wildlife and wild places everywhere – both on land and at sea. We manage a network of more than 2,280 nature reserves across the UK. These are vital refuges for wildlife and home to many rare and threatened species. They are also fantastic places to visit and millions of people enjoy exploring our nature reserves every year.

Throughout the UK we are putting landscape scale restoration of the natural environment at the centre of The Wildlife Trusts' work. To achieve this we are working together with landowners, partners and businesses to restore, recreate and reconnect large areas of wildlife habitat, and help to safeguard the ecosystems that we depend upon for so much.

Gardening is a great way for people to get close to nature and encourage them to do something positive for wildlife. Gardens also play an important role as parts of a wider network of wildlife-friendly spaces, providing green links across towns and cities.

It is amazing what a difference a few plants, logs or a pond can make for wildlife. Insects, birds, amphibians and mammals can all benefit from simple changes that help to make your garden more welcoming to wildlife.

Thank you for reading *Chris Packham's Back Garden Nature Reserve*. For more wildlife gardening advice and tips, visit our Wild About Gardens website at www.wildaboutgardens.org, which is run in partnership with the Royal Horticultural Society.

If you would like to help protect your local wildlife, support our work, and see the latest news and events, go to www.wildlifetrusts.org where you can identify your local Wildlife Trust and become a member.

All 47 Wildlife Trusts are members of the Royal Society of Wildlife Trusts (Registered charity number 207238).

FOREWORD
BY CHRIS BEARDSHAW

So often overlooked as a genuine resource, our gardens provide a ringside seat to the fantastic theatre and drama continuously played out by wildlife. This complex and extraordinary tapestry, comprised of flora, fauna, habitat, life, passion and death is intimately bound to the seasons, weather patterns and the choreography of sun and moon. Every moment offers unique opportunities to witness nature in all her splendour, from the breath taking acrobatic and aerial displays of Starlings amassed under amber sunset skies to the silent precision placement of feet demonstrated by the predatory harvestmen lurking amidst the discarded foliage of autumn.

There is never a moment when life in the garden pauses or even holds its breath, and although we often consider the solitude apparently offered by our gardens is a great tonic to our frantic existence, we should recognise we are never alone. Step outside with a warm drink to sit for a moment and you will be within sight of a thousand pairs of eyes. Pause here to witness life at its most exciting; granted it may take a while to tune into the detail of ants military discipline, the prima-donna performances of butterflies or the scurrilous behaviour of the Magpie, complete with its pantomime plumage, but patience and an eye for detail are the keys to understanding the elaborately intertwined storyline and extrovert personalities.

Most exciting for me is the relative ease with which flora and fauna are accommodated in our plots and the realisation that the marriage of gardener and nature does not preclude any style, design or fashion since, unlike us, our amiable wildlife guests are not driven by aesthetics but by resources and rewards. Within the pages of this text lies a wealth of passionately portrayed information and ideas on how minor modification of our ideas and actions will produce generous opportunities for wildlife and in so doing create a network of garden spaces throughout the land, the total diversity and scale of which far out-ways even the most generously proportioned nature reserve.

In return we are provided with gardens whose content is more beautiful than our imagination, more dramatic than the best thriller and more diverse than our minds can even begin to understand. Nature never fails to exceed our expectations and we are indeed privileged to share our gardens with such riches.

Happy wildlife gardening.

Chris Beardshaw

INTRODUCTION

It's there, in the dark, in the shadows, waiting. It's watching. It's stalking.

A dry rustle as it shifts among the grass, still hidden, and while we strain to see it, I know it can see us. It's a predator; its eyes are keener than ours, its senses sharper, its jaws sharper still. Again it moves in the deep shade; I remain frozen, suffocating on a long held breath, conscious that just a blink might betray us. I wonder what it would be like to be seized, shaken and crushed, to have it standing over me, its cold and merciless menace staring me in the face. I wonder what I'll think and feel, me the big clever human, me who can drive cars, fire guns, fly in aircraft and write books – me not so clever when I'm just another item of prey.

A bead of sweat runs from my brow into my eye. My vision blurs and, as if it has sensed my instant weakness, now it launches into attack. It moves quickly, twice I see the foliage shiver and feel my body surge as it storms towards me, superior, confident, strong, a natural-born killer with that instinct flaming in its screaming eyes.

"Tea-time", shouts my girlfriend from the balcony as the Violet Ground-beetle scuttles past my wrist and I kneel up in the rank grass that dominates our garden. Megan, aged five, and I trudge up the sunny path to the house to tell mummy how we've just cheated death. We had been crawling around pretending we were Woodlice, taking a closer look at life in our little bit of the real world.

In the kitchen there's a cup of Earl Grey, a cup of orange squash, some biscuits and a programme about tigers on TV. The tea is great, but the TV fails to command our attention. The tigers are in India, not in Netley near Southampton, and we've just had a real encounter with a super predator. We smelled him and felt him. He was un-edited, he lives in our garden, he's part of our community, he's relevant to us. Would you enjoy a cup of Earl Grey if it was on TV?!

Opposite: Simple and stunning. A male Brimstone butterfly competes for brilliance with Knapweed and Ragwort. It's not rare, it's not exotic and with any luck this palette might be on your patch.

Left: At home in our personal reserve. There's lots of work to do yet, but successfully sharing our space with other animals is the goal.

Our society is obsessed with celebrity: Posh and Becks, glamorous gardeners, Manchester United and Coronation Street. And worse, conservation and natural history have fallen under a similar spell. Tigers, gorillas, sharks and the pandas that might mate in San Diego Zoo. Sometimes it's difficult to assess which has least relevance; maybe the pandas could actually sing, perhaps the gorillas wouldn't be sent off at the most crucial moments (I suspect the sharks certainly would!). But seriously, aren't we in danger of ignoring the most exciting species of all – those which we can touch, smell and enjoy every day in our own backyard? Those animals which quite literally help shape the community in which we live, who make our gardens grow or not. And if something is rare, who is better placed to conserve it than the people who live with it? Who is better equipped to effect an immediate and positive influence and, this is the big one, enjoy the fruits of their endeavours first hand? I'm not saying that it isn't worth putting a pound in the pot to save tigers, just that you'll be relying on an Indian, Nepali, Siberian or Sumatran to actually do the work, and if they do, they'll be the ones watching the tiger. Whereas, if you put a pond in your patch you'll get to see the dragonfly that comes with just as much ferocity to prey upon any smaller species. And if that scale bothers you then lie down and pretend to be a Woodlouse. If it does the trick for Megan and myself, then I'm sure it will for you too.

Being an Animal

Imagining that you are invertebrate prey is a good first step in re-assessing yourself in the natural community – just because you know about arithmetic, art, advertising or angina doesn't mean you're not an animal. For all of our consciousness, intellect, technology and religion we are still living, breathing, eating, defecating and reproducing animals. If we had better sense we would ensure that we remained in harmony with the communities of other organisms around us. Because that sense has deserted us, the environment, our environment, is in the state it is today. I blame it on the way we pretend that we are not animals any more, that we are above playing by nature's rules. Well, if you'll forgive the vulgar honesty, ask some cod fishermen if they are above the rules of nature, ask the flooded refugees in Mozambique or the beef farmers who fed sheep to cows or all the increasing number of drought victims all over the world. If you abuse the system too much it breaks. Mending it may still be possible but only if we all make an effort and remember that we're not repairing it just for all the other species of animals but for our own species of animal too.

Ancient Trees

A simple problem that conservationists continually face is that people only seem able to measure natural events in terms of the human life-span. This is an obvious flaw.

Some readers may live near ancient Yew trees. In recent years a Yew tree campaign initiated by Alan Meredith has led to the documentation of these trees and in many cases steps to aid their preservation. Trees are registered, measured and certificates issued. The Conservation Foundation has maps and details if you're interested. Ageing the trees is difficult owing to their growth pattern, naturally hollow, which means counting annual growth rings is impossible. Besides, the girth of one 2.1 m midget was sectioned after

Above: *Urban survivor. An Adder sneaks down some discarded tyres, potent and perfectly patterned. Not an ideal garden guest for many, but a beautiful and valuable addition to any local community.*

the 1987 storm and yielded more than three hundred rings. The growth of Yews is slow; some measure more than 16 m in girth and although it was thought that fifteen hundred years was a realistic estimate (often confirmed by documented historical reference) it is now believed that these trees may live between five and eight thousand years. Sit under one and think about this.

Typically in churchyards, these sacred trees were alive before your gods were born. Before language, before writing, before our species was civilized in any way. These totems of life on Earth defy our petty ideas and arrogance. They stand sentinels to a far greater force and should serve to remind us that, not only our individual existence, but that of our species is a mere spark in the greater line of life past, present and future. We can't imagine eight thousand years because we live for only eighty.

We are small. Small potatoes. What we do is small. Of course, we've done so much in so little time but we've also had an equally rapid and disastrous effect on ourselves and our future which isn't quite so clever. We've run away with ourselves and forgotten the Yew, standing there slowly straining our corpses from the hallowed soil and involving us in its long, long life. Sit for a while beneath its scented boughs and breathe in the age, pick up a twig and know that the world's oldest wooden artefact is a spear made 150,000 years ago and that a similar item was found embedded in the rib cage of a fossilized straight-tusked Mastodon. Think – that tree whispering above you may have been planted by a Neolithic human on a burial ground, that it certainly provided a spiritual focus for Celtic peoples for whom it epitomized a belief in immortality. Gaze out at something redolent of the twenty-first century, a new car, a mobile phone, a skyscraper or jet aircraft and ask yourself if we do justice to that simplicity or have we all forgotten, got lost in big ideas.

Life without a consciousness of nature and its balance will prove to be a gimmick, a fad, a boom bubble that will burst and leave us stranded. We smile, we agonize, we cry today, ours is this present. But yesterday's Yew has tomorrow too and all the things that creep amongst it will crawl and the same smell will seep from its pores and the leaves whisper the same songs in the wind. As you creep from its shade into the sunshine of century twenty-one feel a little more real, a little more animal, a little more aware of those organisms we all but ignore as we speed along. After all, you know what they say about he who laughs last.

Your Resources

But then what's all this sobering reality got to do with wildlife gardening? Well, contrary to some leanings and the title, this is not a book about wildlife gardening in the traditional, dig it, plant it and wait and see mode. It is a book designed to promote the practice of co-existing harmoniously with other species of animal in the places where we live, work and play. It's about modifying your resources, however modest or magnificent, to increase their value to other species of animal and not just the cuddly and glamorous ones either. For instance, you won't see the word 'pest' outside of inverted commas because I do not recognize the term in that context. I see competitors and rivals for a resource that we desire, I see champions and cannot blame other life for trying and succeeding, certainly not in the face of human arrogance. Just like the classroom, on the factory floor, or in the office – in your garden or your community it takes all sorts and, let's face it, if you suddenly open a fully stocked supermarket specializing in the finest ripe vegetable materials you've got to expect a few shoppers.

Natural Chaos

Besides which, the concept of gardening is ecologically 'dodgy' anyway. I haven't checked my dictionary but gardening by definition seems to me to be the enforcement of artificial order over nature's organisation.

Nature can be chaotic, untidy, even ugly through its random complexity. Think of a tree that has twisted under the continual attrition of the wind, that is tilted in an untoward manner. Perhaps a couple of branches have died and it thus appears unbalanced, one-sided and it doesn't complement any grand design for a picturesque environment. In fact, it's a blight upon it. It's a hideous misshapen freak and it's making your garden look bad, offending your sense of symmetry, and even your ideal of the term 'tree'. You want to cut it down, to remove this wart, to be neat and to be tidy.

But the tree is an aged native, a willow, a birch, even an old oak. Within its tatty canopy resides a whole community unconcerned by your alien ideas of order. For them the tree is an essential resource, a little island where they live. That scar on the trunk is not the wound you think it is. That cavity is home to myriad creatures, doing a job, evolving, feeding, surviving alongside you without doing you any harm. They share your time and place in the great grand scheme of things, quite unconcerned by tidiness. And theirs is an organization too complex for us to begin to understand, a functional, dynamic perfection which no gardener

Above: *Submerged in a silvery jacket of air, the magnificent Raft Spider is a pond predator par excellence. A photograph taken in my garden and a V-tank success. (See pages 134–135 for technique).*

could ever aspire too. So bring a more open mind to nature's chaos. Shape it with sensitivity, mould it with consideration, admit its honesty and enjoy its humour. Control is always the alter ego of tolerance in the garden. Relax, let go, get absorbed, share your space. Look in the mirror – you're not symmetrical or perfect either!

But please don't think that I'm anti garden or anti gardening. There are nearly three million acres of gardens in Britain and, paradoxically, as our suburban countryside is systematically ravaged to satisfy our desire to own homes, the accompanying gardens can often be richer than the habitats they are laid over. One important measure of value from the conservationist perspective is biodiversity, and not many habitats can vie with our gardens on this account. In a normal British suburban garden there can be as many as 250 different species of plant. This remarkable figure is far higher than could be recorded anywhere in our countryside and although more than half are probably non-native species. this value as a food source is unrivalled. In fact at the height of summer the blazing beds and borders of a British garden produce a greater array of scents and nectar than you could find in any tropical paradise. Not surprisingly, traditional gardens are havens for insects.

A Closer Look

In the late 1970s an entomologist took a closer look at his garden in the suburbs of Leicester. Quite amazingly he recorded eight of the nineteen species of British bumblebee, eighty-three of the 250 hoverfly and 529 of the two thousand species of Ichnuemon family of parasitic wasp. In this last group he found several species unrecorded in Britain and two tiny chaps previously unknown to science. Don't tell me you need to go to the heart of New Guinea to discover a new species – you may just need to go outside.

In the same garden Dennis Owen found twenty-one of the sixty British species of butterfly. Over ninety-five per cent of his fluttering visitors belonged to just six species: Large White, Small White, Green-veined White, Red Admiral, Small Tortoiseshell and Peacock, but other gems included the White-letter Hairstreak, Small Blue, Painted Lady and Silver-washed Fritillary. His garden was only 4 km from the city centre yet his totals bettered all those recorded on local nature reserves. Indeed, in his relatively tiny garden, he recorded eighty-four per cent of the butterfly species ever recorded in the nine hundred square kilometres of the British Midlands surrounding his home. Pretty impressive, even though he was unhappy about the absence of Holly Blue and Clouded Yellow butterflies. But that was the 1970s, more than thirty years ago, and sadly since then there have been dramatic declines in some species that we took for granted or even considered common.

As far as I can ascertain, from the middle ages through to the beginning of the nineteenth century, gangs of resourceful boys would prowl the lanes in search of those favoured ivy-clad walls where House Sparrows roosted *en masse* each autumn and winter. Caught easily in large soft

Right: *Newts, one of many childhood favourites, but hardly the most enthralling creatures outside the breeding season. They are essential but not exciting pond dwellers.*

nets and by the tens or hundreds, the birds were a welcome addition to any peasant's pot and the practice was encouraged as farmers resented the chirruping competition for their grain stock. I can only remember one such roost as a boy, with maybe fifty to a hundred birds, perhaps enough for one bony meal and now, well I'm glad there are no peasants relying on such a harvest to stave off starvation because House Sparrows, like Skylarks, Partridges and even Starlings, are on the way out. Since 1970 their population has declined by no less than sixty-five per cent.

It's not currently popular to point the finger frankly and precisely, indeed only the most confrontational conservationist will indulge, but the culprits here are not those scruffy lads and their nets. In no uncertain terms those that set and maintain our farming policies have the blood of our bird life on their hands. Too intensive, over too great an area for too long, and lo and behold the finely tuned, beautiful balance of nature has been broken. Herbicides, pesticides, phosphates, nitrates and monocultures. Ponds filled, hedgerows grubbed, woodlands felled, and worst of all everything kept so horribly, so unnaturally tidy.

Farming and Policy

Now of course the farmers aren't the bad guys. A great many farmers like and enjoy wildlife as much as you or I, and many have done far more to help it than we'll ever manage, but the overall management practice is flawed, outdated and in desperate need of reform. Surely we all perceive wine lakes and butter mountains as vile embarrassments, especially when they're paid for in Skylarks and Yellowhammers. But how about the farmer, how does he feel tending the crop he knows is unwanted even before it is planted? Some bemoan his grants and subsidies and the artificial pricing of his produce or harvest, a system alien in most other markets. But what if those subsidies were used to farm countryside instead, to replant hedgerows, to re-dig ponds, who better to do it than those who know how to grow, who know their land – the farmers? This beleaguered industry needs our support and when they get it, it works. The crofting community of the north-west of Scotland have pretty much single-handedly saved the Corncrake from extinction in Britain. The RSPB devised the method, the EU offered some financial incentives, but it was the farmers who actually did the job. So who or what is the problem? The problem is the Common Agricultural Policy, a poorly devised and outdated strategy that is killing our countryside and all the wildlife that lives in it faster than anything else. And guess what, it is managed in Europe and any revision takes place in the face of active opposition from the vociferous French and Spanish farming fraternities – not collectives known for their keen conservation of songbirds.

So the immediate prognosis is not great – too many suits, too few ecologists, too many greedy lobbyists and too few quick and effective decisions. If only they'd listened to Skylarks from their school playgrounds, if only they'd jumped over the fence and searched through the dusty grass for their nests and knelt in awe above those little grassy cups filled with smudged brown eggs, each one a trill, a chorus, a crescendo in waiting. Then perhaps they'd act a little more positively and promptly. But then history reliably shows that we cannot rely upon politicians to enact what we want, even if we vote for them.

Above: *A resplendant cock Pheasant. A paradox, in that because people shoot them, they are surviving. People listen to Skylarks but that's not enough. Our countryside is in a mess so take control.*

Do Something

So if we care, here are our options: moan about it; expect people who don't care to fix it; wait for someone else to motivate them and save the world: or help, do something ourselves. To me the last option seems the best. A little practical, direct action can be satisfying and effective. If you have a garden, in fact if you own anything from a window box to a country estate, then within reason you can manage it. You won't be encouraged to plough it or be paid to poison or pollute it or to discourage everything living from visiting it. And collectively with all of our gardens and all of our resources the potential is staggering. You can help buck the trend and however small your patch is it will make a difference. Even if you can't create a neighbourhood national park or a miniature Minsmere you can offer some small or struggling species a little salvation. The aim of this book is to suggest a few methods, offer a few tips and ignite your enthusiasm and ingenuity. You are the wardens of our 'Back Garden Nature Reserves', arm yourself with information, summon a little energy, come up with a few ideas and enjoy the rewards first hand, not on TV.

In the text that follows I have tried to be pragmatic. I like things that work – I'm not so keen on fantasy. Often though, different practices vary in their effectiveness, so for all of my advice it is down to you to adapt my suggestions to fit your schemes or spaces. I must also fully confess that I am not a gardener by any means, I am an ecologist and a lover of life, of all life. I am also impatient and not alone in this failing, so, many of the ideas proffered are designed for immediate or rapid results. We live dangerously fast lives; few of us have one garden per lifetime so my plans have been drawn to fit feasible reward schedules, most in five years or less. Of course longer term schemes are included and essential but this is not a book full of ideas you'll need to age to enjoy. If you do, then it's a bonus.

I'm sure you'll find a few of my essays a little radical, my love of wasps and tolerance of flies and rats even a little bizarre, but while I tease with extremist humour I have a genuine foundation of intent here and it is one based upon respect. If just one family leaves a wasp nest to fulfil its cycle in their loft, if one wife or husband decides not to spray those flies but to cover their food instead, if one more little boy sneaks out to feed his rats then my trouble would have been worthwhile. I don't expect fan clubs to spring up, I just hope a few folks will think twice.

So let's get down to planning your back garden nature reserve. Every garden is unique, so what you do and where will be peculiar to you. But one fundamental technique that will prove invaluable is assessing what you can offer any species you wish to attract. The best way to progress is to learn a little about its life, its ecology, its requirements and then devise an offer it will not refuse. The first three sections are designed to illustrate this, a mammal (Hedgehog), a bird (Great Tit) and an insect (Small Tortoiseshell butterfly), are defined as a set of sample species. Through analysis of their known requirements we can easily make that offer...

HEDGEHOGS
FLATTENED, HUNGRY AND HOMELESS

We like Hedgehogs. We like the way they snuffle and bumble about like over-clad elderlies at a church bazaar. We like their apparently cuddly but very prickly coats and their neat little black noses flexing about, sniffing and snorting loudly. Their young are undeniably cute and they eat slugs, which, being a lot less popular in the zoological top one hundred, makes them another of the gardeners 'friends'. So why do we squash so many on our roads? Why have gardeners betrayed them by using nasty molluscicides that starve them out or poison them? Like so many animals we have grown up with and taken for granted, Hedgehogs now need our help.

Above and left: *Happy, healthy hogs are a charming addition to any garden's fauna and very easy to attract and satisfy. Sit outside late into the evening and investigate suspicious snufflings stealthily to see if you've got spikey visitors.*

Profile

Hedgehogs are insectivores and thus closely related to moles and shrews with which they share similarities in the dental department – sharp pointed teeth. Spines, each measuring up to 2.2 cm, entirely replace hairs on the back and are moulted irregularly, each lasting at least eighteen months. These offer superb protection to the adults, which can roll into a ball to completely shield all extremities and can erect and relax the spines at will. Sometimes Hedgehogs weigh over a kilogram but their weight varies dramatically as they lose as much as thirty per cent each winter during hibernation, which usually begins in October and ends at the beginning of April. Hedgehogs can slow their heartbeats from one hundred and ninety to twenty beats a minute and chill down to four degrees Centigrade.

Hedgehogs can be found all over Britain and Ireland, and on many islands where they have been introduced. Their favoured habitat is rank grassland adjacent to woodland or hedgerows through meadowland, but they can also be found anywhere where there is enough cover for nesting and adequate food. Beetles, caterpillars, centipedes, spiders, the occasional bird's egg or chick, and earthworms supplement their slug favouring menu. They are said to eat snakes but are not resistant to Adder's venom and would have to rely on their spines for protection from its fangs. If I were a Hedgehog I'd stick to slugs.

Normally five young are born into a specially made nest in mid-summer. They leave after three weeks and after a further three weeks of weaning go their own way. For a short while they may be vulnerable to foxes and badgers but typically they have no more problems other than your Michelins, Pirellis or Dunlops.

You and Hedgehogs

Okay, you didn't break or swerve and you're feeling guilty, what can you do to ease your guilt and help the local hogs? Basically all the information you need to get started is contained in the profile above. By analysing their ecological requirements you can easily deduce how you can adapt your garden to become Hedgehog compatible.

Do you have Hedgehogs in your garden? Well, they are nocturnal so you could easily miss them unless you look and listen for their loud snuffling and sniffing between April and October. Alternatively check for footprints or droppings (black, full of insects, 1 cm diameter, up to 5 cm long and fairly firm) or, sadly, check your gutter for corpses.

If they do visit, then provide them with food and water to guarantee regular sightings. Place the food in semi-lit areas and they'll soon get used to the light. Bread and milk was the staple suggestion for these animals but it probably did for as many as the A1 and M5 ever has. Do not feed these animals cows' milk – it is too rich. Dog and cat food, dusted occasionally with a vitamin powder, is ideal, or you could try a commercial Hedgehog food mix. These feature dried meat, insects, berries and nuts, and need to be accompanied by plenty of fresh water because of their dried nature.

Making Hogs at Home

Okay, now Hedgehogs are visiting regularly, what about offering them a permanent home? All you need is a well drained and quiet corner to build yourself a hibernaculum. At its most basic all that's required is a metre square 'log camp', about 30-40 cm high, packed with dry grass, hay and leaves and covered with a stout plastic tent. This should be further buried beneath more logs and leaves to secure and hide the roof and also provide adequate insulation. A plywood box with a clear ventilation hole and waterproof roof, again filled with dry bedding, is a step up the housing ladder and will obviously last longer, as might either the wooden or plastic commercially available Hedgehog nest boxes. These cost about twenty-five pounds but will require just as much care in siting to become attractive to the homeless hog.

Left : *Don't try this with a wild Hedgehog. It will ball-up, spike you or even give you a non-life-threatening but annoying bite. Even a tame creature like this one can be a handful – a little spine grenade.*

Artificial feeding and housing are immediate solutions and will generally work, but a more constructive and proper course of conservation is habitat management. Don't worry, you won't be needing a tractor, calling in contractors or breaking your back with hard work. In fact the reverse in this instance – it's less work that's required. Fence off a strip of garden 1.5 m wide by as long as you can, say a minimum of 3 m, and clear it of all herbage. Go for a walk in the local countryside and fill a bag with seed heads from big coarse non-lawn grasses and scatter these on your fallow field. Water and nourish. Plant a couple of brambles which will eventually consolidate the emergent tangle and restrict access to nosey foxes and cats. Every few years hack half of it back in summer and allow it to recover. This will create a natural refuge for Hedgehogs and of course a diversity of other life and if there are any complaints from 'er or 'im indoors promise them a blackberry pie. One last word – fleas. Hedgehogs can be heavily infested with fleas, up to five hundred on one animal. The species concerned is *Archaeopsylla erinacei* and it is entirely specific to the Hedgehog. That's to say it will definitely not cross infect your dog, cat, hamster or child. You are not at risk from Hedgehog parasites but should not handle wild hogs through the risk of biting, which is fairly fierce, and the resultant risk of other infections.

Above and right: *Beware bonfires. Please don't unintentionally barbecue nesting or hibernating hogs – check your leaf or log piles, and rake them over before you build your bonfire.*

GREAT TITS

BIG, BRASH, BOLD AND BOLSHY!

The day had begun grey, a pool of smoke the size of England shading half of Sumatra. Now it was raining wet ash and the ground was going grey too. The temperature had fallen and an apocalypse was in progress. As we slid across sludge through the tea plantations and up to the forest edge my disappointment was impossible to hide. This should be paradise, a tropical rain forest with tigers, tapirs, and a myriad other sparkling species. Instead we were entering hell. I waited an hour and then set off to see some birds. It was silent, just the whisper of drizzle on a million leaves. Then, right beside me, I heard a startling call 'teacherr-teacherr'. Startling not because of its volume but because of its familiarity. I looked and yes, here in the distant hell of burning Sumatra, the first bird I saw was a Great Tit, and I liked that! What a species, what a success, what a survivor! I like Great Tits, they're great!

Profile

The Great Tit is, as you might expect, the largest of the seven British tits and clearly the most strikingly marked with its bold black, white and chrome yellow plumage. At the bird feeder it is also the most dominant and demonstrative, regularly striking strange poses to its consspecific co-feeders! Males are markedly brighter than females whereas juveniles are much duller, almost sooty looking.

No other British birds have such a broad repertoire of notes and calls. If you're in the garden and you hear an unfamiliar bird, I bet you a pound it's a Great Tit. 'Chink', 'Tink', 'Tsee', 'Pee' and 'Cha-Cha-Cha' are

Right: *What a pair! Their sulphur yellow breasts and contrasting black stripes and caps make the species a striking little spectacle.*

Left: *Striking a pose. Watch a group of Great Tits on a bird feeder and you're sure to spot some curious antics, but what do they mean?*

typical utterances, but there are thousands more where they come from.

Great Tits are one of Britain's commonest birds and in their favoured native habitat of mature broad-leaved woodland will occur at densities of up to a pair per two acres (0.8 hectares). In groups of gardens with well stocked feeders the densities can be even higher. Because they are heavier and less agile than the remainder of their family they forage lower down on the trunks and even on the ground. The nesting site is a hole and chamber of some kind which is filled with a mound of moss and the cup lined with hair or fur – not feathers like the other tit species. Five to fifteen, normally eight or nine, pale and red spotted eggs are laid in late April, incubated solely by the female whilst the male feeds her, for about fourteen days. The young fledge after nearly three weeks and are independent in less than a month. Like other tits this species feeds primarily on insects in summer and seeds in winter. Of course the Great Tit's larger size means that it can handle larger types of either food. Beetles, bees (stings are removed), butterflies, moths and bugs all feature but there is even a record of a particularly predatory Great Tit killing a Goldcrest and flying off 'hawk-like' with its victim clasped in its feet. In winter its fluctuating vegetarian favourites are beechmast and hazelnuts, and of course peanuts, all of which they will cache for future use. By feeding marked food, scientists have found that Great Tits' memories are not as great as their name and lots of hidden fruits get to enjoy germination.

Above: *Fanned tail, cocked head and flattened cap, this bird is saying something to someone!*

Right: *Groups of the dusky and generally duller juveniles may swamp your feeders after fledging in summer. Be sure to offer plenty of water too.*

a safely sited feeder or loose on a table in the winter and either ensure your garden is rich in insects throughout the summer, or purchase live foods to supplement the natural supply. Because they are bolder and less bashful than their cousins, it's easier to get close to Great Tits. They'll be the first onto any window-placed feeders and can even be trained to pinch peanuts from your hand – a neat, but naughty trick.

Nesting

Now Great Tits have a thing about nest boxes. They'll actually move out of any natural sites in favour of sound and sensibly sited artificial boxes. They're the easiest of all of our birds to encourage to rear a family in proximity to us. The reason that this doesn't happen all over suburbia is simply down to vital statistics – the diameter of the entrance hole and the volume of the chamber. Most of the better boxes you can buy at garden centres or DIY stores are designed for Blue Tits, a species often reticent to take up these proffered residences. Twenty-five millimetres will allow Blue, Coal and even Marsh Tits into the box, but you need a full 32 mm diameter hole for Great Tits – any smaller and the squeeze is simply too much. Also they like more room inside to fill with a minor mountain of moss. The best option is to build your own bigger boxes. Longer term options include planting Beech, Hawthorn and Holly, which will soon bush out and offer cover near your feeder as this added security will guarantee a larger and happier flock of foragers. Trees such as Birch, which support a healthy crop of caterpillars in summer and a nutritious mass of buds in late winter and spring, are also favourites with all the tit species.

You and Great Tits

The best thing about biology is that it all makes sense. It has to or else it wouldn't happen. Nature's intolerance of waste is unrelenting. I think it's easier to be a biologist than any other scientist; all you have to do is watch, listen and think of questions, which you then answer by further observation. If you want to get to grips with Great Tits you simply have to offer them alternatives. It's easy to see whether you have Great Tits. If you're more than two hundred metres from any substantial greenery, bushes or maturing trees the signs won't be good as these birds normally need that sort of cover. Try putting out a feeder for a few weeks and if they appear you won't fail to see them. If they're around offer them the right foods; serve peanuts in

SMALL TORTOISESHELLS

Beneath a gossamer tent in an emerald glow filtering through the serrated panes of the high canopy the larval army is marching. Prickly black and minutely jewelled with white and broken yellow it wobbles and weaves through the forest of glistening spines that jut from each vein and stalk. But the spines are no defence for the marauders. If no path can be picked through stickles they are chomped away, disappearing quickly at the mercy of mechanical jaws into the jet black capsules. High above, spectrums flutter on flashing wings, searching areas to lay a new horde in waiting. It's a Nettle bed in May or June; it could be anywhere from Europe to Japan or in any part of Britain. The species was so familiar that it was largely ignored, although its recent dramatic decline has changed this. However, in many places the spiney armies continue to metamorphose into Small Tortoiseshell butterflies and where would Versace or Hermes or Montana be without them? If you measure glamour as glitz, then your garden ought to be a fashionable haven for these dandies.

Profile

Parks and gardens, wastelands, woodlands, in fact anywhere there are nectar-bearing flowers within the vicinity of Nettles, the only larval food plant, are the habitats of Small Tortoiseshell butterflies. There are two broods a year: one hatches in August, hibernates over winter, emerges in March, mates and lays the second brood, which is on the wing in late May or June. The tiny eggs are pale green and laid in a large batch on the underside of a Nettle leaf. The caterpillars are dark grey to begin with, then blacker. They live in communal webs until they are half grown and then forage singly or in twos and threes in the protection of folded or curled leaves. The pupae are dull brown, washed with a golden sheen and hang head down from a plant stem, usually not that of the food plant. As adult butterflies they have mainly avian predators. I've seen Great Tits, Spotted Flycatchers, Robins and House Sparrows all flying off with Tortoiseshells and once watched Hornets hammering both these, and their larger relatives Red Admirals, in an orchard. The brutal Hornets knock the butterflies to the ground and then pin them down. Dramatic death follows; first the head is nipped off and then the wings, the rest is chewed into a bolus of indiscernible flesh and carried off to the nest. If any meat remains the ever-hungry Hornet will return and carry this off as well. Nothing is wasted and the whole exercise is cruel but rather neat.

As larvae the Small Tortoiseshell is plagued with predators, not least through parasitic Ichneumonid wasps, which lay their eggs directly onto the caterpillars' skin. When they hatch they do so inwards, straight into the living meat. The young wasp is programmed to avoid eating the vital organs so that the caterpillar lives on, sometimes even successfully pupating before the wasp grub does so itself and of course it emerges first, killing the butterfly in the process. Other species of parasite use long ovipositors to lay their eggs inside the larvae whereas others lay them onto the food plant ready to be eaten by the hungry caterpillars. Some are even laid into the butterflies' eggs and don't emerge until the pupal stage. These tiny parasites often appear insignificant but have life histories which make the storylines of our favourite soaps look dull. The parasitic fly *Sturmia bella* has been implicated in the Small Tortoiseshell's recent decline, Crab Spiders are also a menace, as are dragonflies and robberflies.

You and Small Tortoiseshells

Butterflies have even simpler requirements than birds and mammals. Just about all you have to do is feed them. Almost unbelievably I recently found, in an otherwise normally stocked garden centre, a device purporting to be a 'butterfly feeder'. The plastic box was described as a valuable addition to any garden and appeared to contain a liquid nectar substitute, which apparently serves to attract these 'important pollinators'. It comes in red and yellow versions and cost £7.95. Are they mad? Those that made it, those who sell it and those who buy it? I mean artificial flowers are okay for doctors' waiting rooms, your crazy aunt's bathroom, and uninspiring restaurant tables, but the idea of replacing a real flower with a red plastic tub full of sugar water to feed a butterfly is frankly not on. Let's stick to real plants to promote your garden, not only to Tortoiseshells but also a host of other species.

Adult butterflies require fuel not food. They are merely mobile mating machines so they need a high energy activator and that means nectar. Some species of plant produce more nectar than others and replenish it more

The silken web provides a modicum of protection from larger predators but not the insidious attention of parasitic wasps.

Freshly hatched larvae gather in clots beneath the web where they feed furiously on the succulent leaf tips.

Gravid females search the nettle bed for areas free of caterpillars that could compete with her potential brood.

Female Tortoiseshell egg laying onto soft fresh and succulent shoot, an ideal meal for her brood.

More mature larvae forage singly, having left the security of the web and rely on wriggling and dropping from the leaf to escape larger predators.

The cryptic chrysalis hangs in the shade for 2-3 weeks before the adult emerges.

quickly – these are our target species. Because none of them flower throughout the period that the adult insects are on the wing it is necessary to 'organise' a sequence of successive bouquets to deliver the goods. See box on the right for the top ten.

All of these plants grow well in restricted space, in typical garden soils and are low maintenance easy-care species. The Buddleia is the best all rounder but soon gets straggly and unkempt, and thus needs a moderate cut back each winter. Michaelmas Daisy and Ice Plants generally prove to be magnets for Small Tortoiseshells, Red Admirals, Commas and Peacocks in the autumn when all the nectar has drained away from the rest of the garden.

Many butterflies are species specific when it comes to their larval food plant and Small Tortoiseshells are no exception – it's Stinging Nettles (*Urtica dioica*) or bust. I know Nettles are unpopular with the kids because they sting a bit, but you'll need no more than a couple of square metres to get started. Rake a patch of clear soils, put heaps of nitrogen based fertiliser on it, scatter a fair whack of nettle seeds and rake in either in the autumn or

NECTARFUL PLANTS FOR YOUR BORDERS

Spring flowering	Aubrieta (*A. deltoidea*)
	Yellow Alyssum (*A. saxatile*)
	Honesty (*Lunaria* sp)
Summer flowering	Sweet Rocket (*Hesperis matronalis*)
	Valerian (*Centranthus* sp)
Summer/Autumn flowering	Lavender (*Lavandula* sp)
	Buddleia (*Buddleia* sp)
Autumn flowering	Tobacco Plant (*Nicotiana alata*)
	Ice Plant (*Sedum spectabile*)
	Michaelmas Daisy (*Aster novae velgii*)

spring. The species is a fierce competitor and will grow well from bare soils to produce a thick bed of rich green stingers. Not only are they essential to ensure that all stages of this species prosper on your patch but they are also a fantastic environment for a whole community of other non butterfly invertebrates at various valuable levels in the healthier garden's food chain.

Being Realistic about Your Space

Perhaps the greatest enemy of your objectives is idealism. As a child I implored my parents to recreate one of those fashionable gardens, perfectly and quite impractically illustrated in various brightly coloured publications – striped lawns, rosy pergolas, straight fences, lobate borders and neat patios. Naturally our garden was too small, too narrow and cluttered with irritations like garages, coal bunkers, fruit trees, a wood pile, not to mention my camps and my sister's discarded Spacehopper, none of which were ever included in the 'Gardens for you' sections of my grandfather's gardening magazines. So, admit your limitations, analyse them in detail, and turn any negatives into positives by focusing upon what you really can achieve rather than what it would be nice to do.

You could try to plant a grouse moor on the dry soils of a Semi-D in Southwark, or put up an Osprey nesting platform in Truro town centre. Flooding fifty square metres of suburban Inverness and seeding a reedbed

Left: *Chaos, marvellous chaos. A riot of unconstrained growth going wild, and sadly not every gardener's cup of tea.*

won't save the imperilled Bittern, even if it is your favourite bird. In '*Magnum Force*' Clint Eastwood says, 'A man's gotta know his limitations'. Forget the gender directive – it's true. But also in this instance complicated by your neighbours and your neighbourhood's limitations. For instance, if you have the only large garden complete with a few large trees on Brighton sea front, I'd forget about catering for Nuthatches, Hedgehogs, or Pine Martens. But if you have a tiny garden which backs onto extensive broad-leaved woodland in central England, I'd prime the nut feeder and put some cat food out on the lawn each evening. And if your minuscule patch happens to be lost in the ruins of Scotland's ancient Caledonian forest, I'd try a few strawberry jam sandwiches on the bird table – apparently Pine Martens love them. I'm sure you get the picture.

Know Your Neighbourhood

Take a wander out one evening, be a bit nosey, see if the Smeggits in number 10 still have that big ivy-covered sycamore. Peer over the fence, the Bests may have two noisy boys in Man United shirts but they've got a huge pond. And see if Mr Bloveld across the road still has that horrible fluffy cat. How far away exactly is that bramble-strewn wasteland? Is old Barry next door still spending 95% of his pension on slug pellets in a single-handed assault on the Mollusca? Has Sheila's recent appointment at the local concrete company paid dividends in her attempt to fabricate a patio that can be seen from space? Of course, in a country where a house is a castle, none of this is any of your business, but it will have a profound effect on what could be coaxed over your moat and into your keep. Your neighbour's peculiarities are your considerations when it comes to conservation. Have

Above: *Decorative yes, non-native species certainly, but nevertheless a bountiful supply of nectar which is a basic requirement for so many insect species. This alone means that a window box qualifies as a wildlife reserve.*

Above and left: What a fantastic garden. I wish it were mine. Obviously the work of a dedicated wildlife lover, but if yours is a smaller patch don't worry. The habitat adjacent to the blocks below will be a rich source of species which could easily be attracted to lower floor window boxes.

Sunshine hours and aspect you might have dwelt upon when placing barbecues, patios, conservatories, or merely deckchairs. Unfortunately, all these 'secondaries' do need a modicum or more of thought. Some important plants have uncompromising requirements in terms of the soil and its drainage where they are rooted, and light and shade where their leaves hang. The good news is twofold: one, many of these requirements and their intricacies are known and the information is relatively accessible. Thus you can choose and cultivate successfully. Two, if you have a small garden or a small area you can probably modify it by draining or flooding, and or by digging out and replacing the soil. But beware, this could be a big, messy, unpopular and expensive initial step. But then if you want heather because you want lizards, who am I to dampen your desire for dry well drained and impoverished acidic soil by the truckload?

a word with Barry though, try to slow up his genocide, show him photos of happy Hedgehogs and smiling Slow-worms – and if all this fails, tell him about the lottery!

Right, now you've considered the surface topography you'll have to get a bit more physical. Soil types, are not a fascination for many, nor are drainage patterns, hydrology, and the acidity/alkalinity of your potential pondwater.

ALL AROUND YOUR PLACE

A great distance from the nearest 'big trees' may also be limiting when it comes to attracting woodland birds such as the tits, nuthatches and woodpeckers

Lots of 'sterile' housing with very little greenery between you and the wider countryside will not help. Some of the stronger flying, bolder or tenacious species will reach you but too much concrete will slow them up or rule them out altogether.

Spread the word. Try and involve your neighbours and community in conservation by gently persuading them to consider the impact they can really have on their environment. The best way to get someone to feed the birds is to invite them round and show them what you've got over a coffee, a beer or a barbecue. Enthusiasm is often infectious.

Unfortunately a neighbour's cat will have a profound effect on your garden's fauna and how you seek to encourage and manage it. There is no doubt that a cat-free garden is a healthier environment all round but achieving this is not easy. Try some of the ultrasonic deterrents and at the very least politely enquire if the animal might be collared with a double bell or new techno alarm collar: maybe this would be an ideal Christmas present for the moggy's owner.

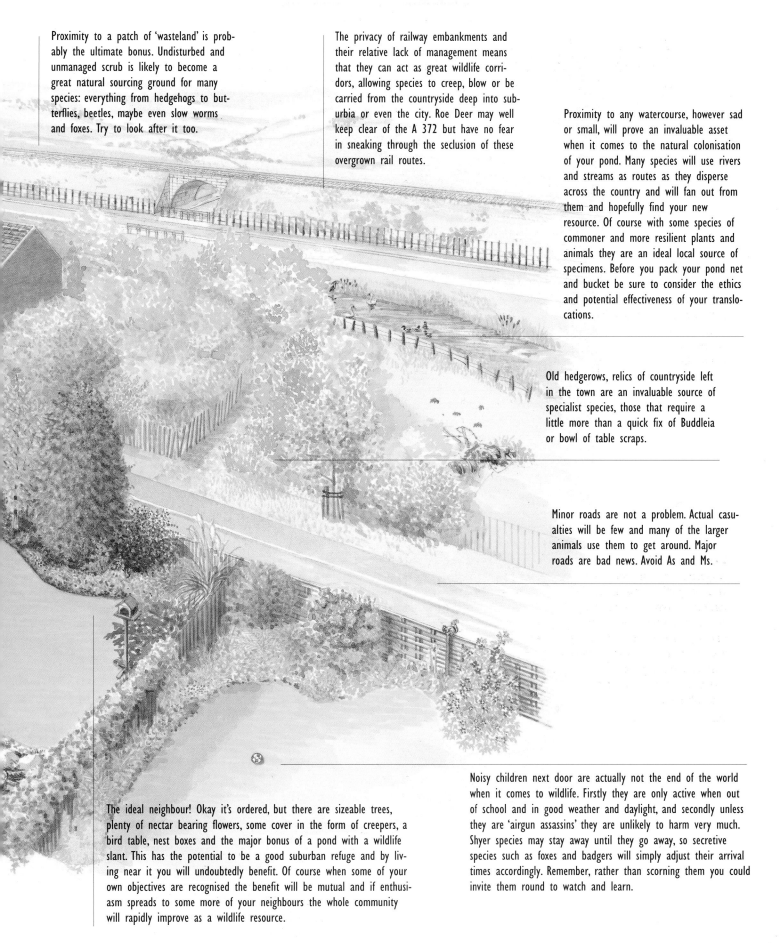

Proximity to a patch of 'wasteland' is probably the ultimate bonus. Undisturbed and unmanaged scrub is likely to become a great natural sourcing ground for many species: everything from hedgehogs to butterflies, beetles, maybe even slow worms and foxes. Try to look after it too.

The privacy of railway embankments and their relative lack of management means that they can act as great wildlife corridors, allowing species to creep, blow or be carried from the countryside deep into suburbia or even the city. Roe Deer may well keep clear of the A 372 but have no fear in sneaking through the seclusion of these overgrown rail routes.

Proximity to any watercourse, however sad or small, will prove an invaluable asset when it comes to the natural colonisation of your pond. Many species will use rivers and streams as routes as they disperse across the country and will fan out from them and hopefully find your new resource. Of course with some species of commoner and more resilient plants and animals they are an ideal local source of specimens. Before you pack your pond net and bucket be sure to consider the ethics and potential effectiveness of your translocations.

Old hedgerows, relics of countryside left in the town are an invaluable source of specialist species, those that require a little more than a quick fix of Buddleia or bowl of table scraps.

Minor roads are not a problem. Actual casualties will be few and many of the larger animals use them to get around. Major roads are bad news. Avoid As and Ms.

The ideal neighbour! Okay it's ordered, but there are sizeable trees, plenty of nectar bearing flowers, some cover in the form of creepers, a bird table, nest boxes and the major bonus of a pond with a wildlife slant. This has the potential to be a good suburban refuge and by living near it you will undoubtedly benefit. Of course when some of your own objectives are recognised the benefit will be mutual and if enthusiasm spreads to some more of your neighbours the whole community will rapidly improve as a wildlife resource.

Noisy children next door are actually not the end of the world when it comes to wildlife. Firstly they are only active when out of school and in good weather and daylight, and secondly unless they are 'airgun assassins' they are unlikely to harm very much. Shyer species may stay away until they go away, so secretive species such as foxes and badgers will simply adjust their arrival times accordingly. Remember, rather than scorning them you could invite them round to watch and learn.

CONSIDER YOUR ASPECT

Consider your aspect. Now there's some advice! But when it's followed with a suggestion that before you get started with any wildlife gardening you think about drainage, soil type, slope and position relative to neighbours, the postulation becomes practical rather than philosophical.

The single most important external influence upon your future plans is sunlight. Thus the direction that your house and/or garden faces relative to the sun will have a profound effect upon many things, not least heat and light for growth. There's is no point in planting sunflowers in the shade, but if shade is what you've got there are plenty of equally productive species that will attract and provide for a similar range of animals.

If you would like insects – bugs, beetles, bees and butterflies – to buzz around your place then you'll need to set them up with a few nectar-filled suntraps. A buddleia bush in the shade would not only be a little straggly but also deserted of life. When you're planning or planting consider this carefully; it is unlikely that your resource will be in shade all day long. You may need a 'morning bush' and an 'afternoon bush' and remember that other creatures such as lizards and some birds also have a keen affinity for our big yellow star.

Other considerations are soil type and drainage. It's normally easier to make it drier than wetter which is a shame because a mosaic of soil moisture could be highly desirable

Left: My mother says, 'There's rarely any substitute for hard work'. Unfortunately, my mother's rarely wrong.

if you plan for a pond and accompanying marshy fringes. Most modern gardens of average size will be well or too well drained, an artefact of the building process, and to get water back into the ground will almost certainly require an external source, that is a tap with a flow organized or paid for by you. If you are not on a meter then consider this and don't feel too guilty about it being a 'waste'. You can also conserve a lot of useful 'garden-water' by installing water butts under all of your drainpipes and if you're fanatical and do it with a series of butts you could store enough to see a modest garden through summer droughts. If you plan major drainage I'd advise liaison with a hydrologist.

Soil type is more easily manipulated as you can buy a few cubic metres of almost all soils from alkaline to acidic and put it wher-

Above: Put peat in your garden and I'll never speak to you again!

ever you like. Thus it is easy to alter the soil profile of your garden and there are few gardens that wouldn't benefit from this. Many new houses have a very thin, indeed a mean layer of top soil spread over gravel and builders' rubble. You'll be better off by raking this away, digging the rubbish out and shifting a lot more and a lot better soil in. It will be messy and back breaking, but will certainly pay dividends in the end.

Improving your soil with peat is of course a complete non starter. Peat bogs are incredibly endangered habitats and due to gardeners' demand for peat nearly all have been destroyed in the UK. Peat-free composting materials are widely available. The B & Q chain is very active with this initiative but the Wildlife Trusts will provide details of where to buy peat-free products (see page 140).

Above: Phone 'soil supplies' immediately – or get a few cacti and a rattlesnake – this ground needs help.

PLANNING PERMISSION

Okay, it's teatime, and you've made a special effort rejecting microchips for something actually cookable and possibly even edible from Delia's latest. It's gone down well. Now is the time to tell them.

The lawn's going. It's going to be a wild flower meadow. The patio is set to be a six point feeding station for birds, so sorry, 'Tibbles' is retiring to the Blue Cross. The shed, well, that's a nettle bed waiting to happen. Aunt Vera's Magnolia doesn't have a preservation order, and nor do the two 'non-native' borders. The barbecue is in the balance: it's a good spot for the swamp. The nation's wildlife needs us, we must unite to save the newt.

Expect a public enquiry. Or sit-ins. Your partner chained to the aforementioned Magnolia won't look good if the boss sees it in the local Press. Thus I must advise discourse, diplomacy, and democracy. In reality we all share spaces. So sue for the best amenable compromise, don't confuse 10 feet with 10 metres when it comes to the cut, tolerate the few begonias (great slug food anyhow!) and try to win any opponents over with stonking views of your first successes. Give them full on male Great Spotted Woodpeckers ten feet from the dining room table. Show them frolicking fox cubs for supper. See them enthuse, see the barbecue fall, watch gleefully as they flood the vegetable patch in anticipation of a plague of amphibians. Or pray they tolerate your eccentricities.

Above: *Pit bulls in a china shop? Not really, because ball games rarely last the full ninety minutes in the garden, and by tea-time the wildlife will have its day. And to be fair, like it or not, it's their space too.*

Follow the Rules

Of course, on a moderately more serious note are the legal planning constraints imposed by your local council. Tree preservation orders are under used and over abused – be careful when chainsawing a glade, in some places the maximum fine is £20,000 per tree. Conservation areas are popular and can be a useful method of unifying the appearance of a neighbourhood in which they apply. They are not actually a nuisance, but act as a guideline to try to maintain the aspect of an area, both in terms of its architecture, its aesthetic resource and its environmental value. Indeed, even some environmental improvements can counter the rules here, but such problems are easily overcome for the trouble

of a phone call to the planning officers in charge. They will generally politely discuss your proposals, and if they are perceived as in any way radical pay a visit to understand the reality. When all is straight, you apply for permission, and if your neighbours don't disapprove too violently and your plan fits in the general scheme of things, you progress. Please don't let fear of this process tempt you to plough ahead without notification. Aside from simply not being fair, it would be a real misery to have to undo all your hard work. If your plans are on the 'Grand Scale' then so must be your preparatory work. Drainage changes might sink your neighbour's foundations, and earth-moving equipment wake their baby. As usual consult experts and use a combination of common sense and good manners to combat any potential conflict. It will always help if your neighbours learn to enjoy your wildlife as much as you do. If you annoy them in the process it may be very counter-productive in the long run.

BIRDS

BACK GARDEN BIRDING

A curious and unfortunate affliction, which grips many serious ornithologists, is the need to keep lists. Not content to document all the birds they've seen in Britain, or indeed the world, some fanatics even keep lists of birds they've seen on television or in zoological collections. Whilst such obsessions border on lunacy, I think it's fairly reasonable to keep a note of all the species that one encounters in the garden. And over a few years you'll be surprised by quite how many different types of birds you might be able to find. One acquaintance of mine who keeps such a garden list has spotted Buzzard, Hobby, Merlin, Bewick's Swan, Red-breasted Merganser and Yellow-browed Warbler. He lives no more than a mile and a half from the centre of Southampton in a densely populated suburb. Bill Oddie once had a garden that over looked the ponds on Hampstead Heath and watched Greenshank flying over. Within his fenced boundaries he also enjoyed Redstart, Pied Flycatcher and, quite extraordinarily, a singing Wood Warbler. For my part I once had the good fortune to have a flat which over looked a river and during the dreary second half of an FA Cup Final, glanced out of the window to notice an Osprey. The real highlight however was a Nightjar which one evening flew up the river at low tide and was quite evidently lost, flying as it was north when it should have been flying south to Africa.

Of course these are exotic exceptions, the real gems of lists which have taken between five and ten years to note. But most city gardens should over a period of time produce somewhere between fifty and eighty different species. Many garden species are refugees from woodland clearings and edges and they successfully endure a noisy cat ridden existence in our gardens because the structure of these often closely matches the vegetational layers found in woodland. Ground, herb and shrub layers, understoreys and canopies even composed of introduced species, provide a replica of their natural foraging and nesting grounds. What's more, any food shortages can be alleviated by one of our national obsessions: the great British bird table.

Left: *The perfect antidote to a nil-nil draw, a view of an Osprey out of the dining room window (sadly it didn't stay for extra time).*

As you might expect eccentricity runs riot, not only through the design of bird tables, everything from gothic castle, Tudor and thatched cottages, post modernist blocks and even a few 'monstrous carbunkles', but also with regard to their menus. Fish and chips for Starlings, haggis for Crested Tits, hot-cross buns for Mute Swans and egg custards for Moorhens. The national cuisine is stretched to the limits. The best bird I ever saw coming to a table was no less than a Water Rail, a customer to one avian restaurant *par excellence*; a floating feeding platform on someone's garden pond. Generally bread is the most frequently provided food, but it has one third of the energy of fat and you should be careful about feeding dry, stale bread to breeding birds; it can easily become stuck in the throats of their young. Always provide plenty of water as well as food. The same applies to desiccated coconut, although fresh bisected coconuts hung upside down provide a welcome alternative to some of the more acrobatic visitors, perhaps the most common of which are the tits. Some of these species spend up to 97% of their winter's daylight just searching for food, obviously a critical factor affecting their survival. Bird tables are also very valuable as a whole, because believe or not, more than fifty individual Blue Tits probably visit your platform or your feeders. A maximum of 148 have been recorded and many of these are actually entirely dependant on bird table food. Without it, it's thought that up to fifty percent of garden birds would probably die.

So recognize your responsibility, consider the options in terms of diets and methods of delivering them. Keep your binoculars and notebooks at the ready, and stray no further than your dining room or kitchen window to enjoy the best things in life – birds.

DELIVERING THE DIET

As I write, there are about ten to fifteen Great Tits, a similar number of Blue Tits, at least one Marsh or Willow Tit, a couple of Coal Tits, eight Chaffinches, five or six Greenfinches, a pair of Goldfinches, two Robins, a Dunnock, a Blackbird, a single Collared Dove and at least three Nuthatches on or around our patio. Every ten minutes a Jay pops up for some loose peanuts, and normally once a day a Sparrowhawk tries its luck. I have to say that these birds are not personal friends of mine, I am not living in a Technicolor Disney cartoon where all the birds, bees and beasts love me. No, the cold cruel facts are that they're all here because I feed them every day of the year. Our rectangle of concrete is the neighbourhood's McDonalds for birds. They know the menu, the prices and the best seats. The regularity of opening hours always guarantees a packed restaurant, there's no door policy – squirrels, of which there are currently two – are welcome on the ground but not on the feeders which they destroy. The Sparrowhawk is welcome too – I am happy to lose a few customers to anything that beautiful.

Fundamentally a bird feeder equates to a permanently fruiting tree. If it's filled all year and not only enriched for a short period it is, in all honesty, better than that which nature provided. What's more it's an instantly mature tree. You buy, fill, and site it and it's ready for action. No seedling, maturing or years of waiting for five or six berries. No, it's Wham – Big Food Source – wherever you want it! With a modicum of ingenuity you can place your feeder wherever it's best for the birds and for you. Safe from predators but easy to see. And of course for a few pounds more you can appeal to different species

Left: *A commercially available peanut feeder that will ensure that only the birds get the food. Narrow gaps between the bars also selects which species can squeeze through. Yes to tits, no to Starlings.*

Above: *A little twee, but at least it is delivering the goods. At the end of the day it doesn't matter how smart or how scruffy a bird table is: so long as it is safely sited and regularly loaded with grub, no birds will turn up their bills.*

by getting a second feeder and filling it with a different food, maybe up-market types such as Siskins, Long-tailed Tits, Woodpeckers or those dapper Nuthatches – my favourites.

Ground or Table

The simplest feeding station is the ground, but there are two problems with scattering food on your lawn. Firstly, not only birds will be able to access the food. Dogs, cats, foxes, badgers, squirrels, hedgehogs and, less savoury for some, rats and mice, will all have free access to your fare. Secondly, not all birds like to feed on the ground – thrushes, finches, pigeons, robins, magpies and jays regularly do, and tits will, but they prefer not to. They are tree-feeding types and don't feel safe down that low.

The simplest solution is the bird table, a flat platform which is raised to reduce the mammalian interest. Cover it and the food will last longer in the relative dry; make a tray of it and the food won't all blow onto the ground in the wind.

Again a range of species will use it, but some won't enjoy it, and if they don't then you won't either. Faced with a plate of peanuts or sunflower seeds all the tit species will fly up, pinch one and then fly off to some cover to eat it – all you'll see is a flash of blue and a whirr of wings. The answer is to shop for specialist feeders and there are hundreds to choose from.

From a Feeder

Traditionally, the peanut basket is a favourite. This wire mesh tube prevents the removal of the whole nut and ensures that the clientele stick around pecking at it whilst you get to watch them. Feeders and baskets come in all shapes and sizes, but must be protected from squirrels which easily gnaw them open to feast on the feast that falls. Plastic shields beneath supporting poles or slippery domes suspended above those that hang will normally do the trick, as will the heavy duty caging that surrounds the interior nut dispenser of some models, (see opposite) Nevertheless, never underestimate the persistence, the ingenuity, or the damnable destructive capability of Mr Nutkin.

Other Options

Various essentially similar devices dispense seeds or mixes through port holes in the sides and come in simple, easy to maintain utilitarian plastic or rustic or posh ceramic forms, some too decorative to effectively dispense anything other than pretension.

Some of the better models also come in a choice of colours, typically silver, black, red, green and blue. This is not to match the patio paintwork but has been proven to attract different species at different times of the year. Regional differences seem to apply, so if you fancy some really simple science get yourself a notebook, a pencil, stopwatch, calculator and a few pots of paint. You never know, you might prove that some Blue Tits are colour blind.

If like me, you believe that the best things in life are birds, then you'll need to think big. Big feeders stock more food so they need to be less regularly filled and will satisfy a bigger flock. Mine, he says bragging, can hold 6.4 kg, that's 14 lb. of food and it's got sixteen feeding ports and basically it's a case of, 'Go ahead Greenfinch – make my day.' Needless to say, these monster feeders need a good heavy base for support. But you know when it comes to feeders, big is still not the best.

Plastic suckers are the tops when it comes to feeding birds. No longer attached to toy arrows or Garfield's feet (think about it), they now serve to stick peanut, seed, multipurpose and live food feeders to your window, which means that the diners are all but in the room with you. Birds take a little while to get used to them but if you stand still you'll not get better views of your best friends. A few tips: 1) Don't economise on the quality of sticker, if they don't stick you'll be forever sweeping up seed on the windowsill, and the birds will never feel safely perched; 2) Don't go for those which have a water trough as well as a food tray. The first dirty bather to squeeze in and shake off renders everything else invisible, and 3) Beware of Collared Doves. They are too heavy and too flappy for even the strongest suckers and will tear your feeders from the glass. Stick it where they won't or can't reach.

Left: *A fully loaded feeder complete with five fans no doubt a little fatter for their endeavours.*

Below: *The fanatic in action – if they can't get enough, then nor can I, and remember regularity is the key to keeping them coming.*

WHEN, WHAT AND WHO TO FEED

I am always being asked: 'Should we feed our birds all year?' At some time it must have been frowned upon to do so, but not now. Our garden birds have become sorry refugees from a ruined countryside. In the last thirty-five years the intensification of agriculture has ravaged our rural bird populations – Skylarks down by 53%, Tree Sparrows by 93%, even House Sparrow numbers have collapsed by 65%. Combine this with the urbanizing of the countryside, building around our town and city fringes, with pollution through the overuse of pest and herbicides, plus over extraction of water, and it is clear that rural Britain has become a difficult place for wildlife to prosper. It's not an overstatement to say, 'Your birds need you'. If we all stopped feeding the birds tomorrow the effect would be catastrophic. If twice as many of us put food out it would be remarkable. So yes, yes, yes – please feed the birds all year round.

Let's consider the benefits to the birds. Firstly, because they are small and have high metabolic rates most garden birds need to consume between twenty-five and fifty per cent of their body weight every day. In winter, when foraging time is restricted by the shorter day length, Blue Tits need to find food every twelve to fifteen seconds. Things are tough out there on the patio, so it's

Left: Naughty boy's appetite for apple produces a guilty look. Still, share and share alike?

important that the right choices are made. They need it fast, but 'burgers and fries' are not enough for our birds; they need balanced diets.

Peanuts
Peanuts are not actually nuts - they grow in the ground and are more like lentils and peas. High in proteins, oils and calories, they are ideal for the smaller species such as Blue and Coal Tits. In recent years somewhat exaggerated reports have appeared in the Press about peanut poisoning. Aflatoxin is the problem and while it is rare it's also real, so buy good quality peanuts. If you wouldn't eat them yourself maybe you shouldn't offer them to the birds.

Sunflower Seeds
Sunflower seeds have a very high oil content, and de-husked sunflower hearts are tops in terms of calories. Black sunflower seeds are even better than the standard 'striped seeds' as they have even more oil. Again these are great for the little burners of the bird table, Blue and Coal Tits.

Cereals
Oats, normally rolled, or even de-husked and crushed into pinhead oats are high in carbohydrates but not so oily or so rich in calories. Mixed corn is what many ground-feeding birds used to get in our farmed fields. It's okay as a staple, but even with maize added doesn't rival the oil-rich sunflower seeds.

Left: Water is often in shorter supply than food, so both drinking and bathing water are essential and should be regularly replenished all year round. Here a heater prevents winter freezing and keeps a bathing Song Thrush happy.

Raisins and Sultanas

Moderate energy for fruit-favouring species. Best scattered onto the ground or piled onto the bird table as they are too sticky to go in a feeder.

Nyjer Seeds

This finds its way into many seed mixes where it is a valuable oil-rich energy-giving item. Sometimes it's called 'thistle seed' which it isn't, but it can be used to attract Goldfinches to specialized feeders – that's if the more resourceful Greenfinches don't get in first.

Seed Mixes

These products are the best option by far as they combine all of the above items in a balanced formula to attract a wide range of birds to a single feeder. The best brands contain black sunflower seeds, sunflower hearts, peanut granules, kibbled maize, pinhead oatmeal, canary seed, millet and hemp.

Table Scraps

Don't waste these and never leave a restaurant without a Foxie or Birdie bag. (These were formerly known as Doggie bags, but since some restaurants probably seat dogs themselves these days they are no longer required for our canine friends.) There will be something in your scraps to suit something outside, even if it's mice, slugs, or next door's cat. I put all ours on a raised platform each night; this keeps the 'mess' in one place and allows me to see what's eating them, either by watching or checking for footprints. Feeding on a raised table may also reduce the likelihood of attracting rats, whereas if you throw everything directly to the ground you are inviting these rodents to dinner.

Fat Products

Suet is not cool. Lard is now laughable! No darlings, it's Extra Virgin Olive Oil for us. But the birds like the old-fashioned stuff. Lard and suet cakes infused with peanut flour, seeds or whatever you've got, hung up on bits of string, are a Blue Peter regular and they work brilliantly. Fat is a superb source of concentrated energy. Aside from the usual tits and greedy Starlings you'll stand a chance of attracting Nuthatches and even Treecreepers, Long-tailed tits and Goldcrests. If your kids are growing up and not making 'bird cakes' they are being deprived, and so are the birds.

Live Foods

Most garden birds are omnivores, enjoying both animal and plant food depending on availability, season and taste. Mealworms and Waxworms are standard commercial wrigglies and they are not as expensive, as difficult or as messy as you'd imagine. For twenty-five pounds you can dispense twelve thousand mealworms to smiling robins, dunnocks, wrens, blackbirds, plus all the usual suspects from the feeders above. All you need is a smooth-sided bowl to prevent invertebrate escapees.

Practicalities

Shop for bird food to combine value for money with ease of collection. Mail Order is the best option because you can arrange deliveries of specific foods at competitive prices, and this will allow you to keep a ready stock of food, which is very important.

I once ran out of bird food. It took me ten to fourteen days to organize new stock and refill the feeders, and nearly two months for the number of birds to recover. My Nuthatches vanished until the next winter, no doubt having located another more reliable feeder elsewhere. A disaster.

Of course stock means storage. I use plastic dustbins, although if your dry storage space is not rodent proof I'd go for the metal equivalent to prevent mice from being too tempted. Dryness is essential because any moisture seems to increase the risk of mite infestation.

Cleanliness is critical and incidences of *Salmonella* and *E.coli* seem to be on the up. Large concentrations of birds sharing the same feeders mean infections spread rapidly and soon dead or dying birds will litter the garden. Avoid such unpleasantness by cleaning beneath feeders, sweeping the bird table and disinfecting it and all the feeders and water dispensers, at least three or four times a year. If food remains uneaten or goes mouldy, dispose of it carefully and quickly.

THE COST OF FINDING FOOD

It's very difficult for us humans to imagine just how critical it is for some of our smaller garden bird species to find, tackle and consume their food in an optimal manner – especially in winter when literally every second counts. They are so small and expend so much energy staying warm through the long cold nights that their daily survival depends upon them being able to locate food every few seconds during the day. So how do they do it?

Firstly they have to find it, and to make this easier they develop what we call a 'search image'. Through practice and reward they learn to spot their food more efficiently than if they were just looking for anything else. It's just like when we say that we are 'getting our eye in', and it is critical to winter survival. Without it birds just wouldn't be able to find food efficiently enough and as a result they would die.

It's not just about finding food, though. Choices need to be made about which food to find and where, because there is no point in spending more energy locating and eating something than can be recovered from it. Thus decisions are made about how far to fly to get a reward, about the best size to collect and how long it's worth to spend eating it. The technical name for this phenomenon is 'optimal foraging' and there are plenty of human parallels. For instance, you wouldn't run all the way to the supermarket, collect one

Above: *Keeping feeders well stocked is essential for your garden birds.*

stick of celery, carry it back home and then eat it. It would cost you far more energy than you would recover and would be a horrible waste of time and effort. But it's about the packaging too. Imagine if the celery were wrapped in a steel case – it simply wouldn't be worth the energy expenditure to access the reward. And it's the same for the birds on your feeders.

Removing a sunflower husk takes time and has an energy cost. Some species have evolved tools to reduce this, such as Greenfinches whose bills are adept at snipping the covering off, tweezering out the kernel and swallowing the booty without too much trouble. Now imagine a Long-tailed Tit doing the same. Its beak is simply not adapted to this task, and yet in some places this species has become a regular visitor to feeders. For the tit, the difference between normal and de-husked sunflower seeds could be the difference between life and death if things get really tough.

In fact for all the birds that visit your feeders it could be a disaster if they arrive to find them empty. Two or three hops around the neighbourhood with no reward will cost a lot of valuable energy that cannot be wasted in the bleak mid-winter. And think of this – if you went all the way to the supermarket only to find all the shelves empty, how many times would you go back before abandoning it as a viable source of food? Not many, and this is why you will 'lose' your birds if you have too many 'empty days'.

FEEDING EXOTICS

Not satisfied with Nuthatches? Bored with Blue Tits? Great Tits not grabbing your fancy? Then you need some exotic interests and if you're lucky there might be something in the neighbourhood for you.

In recent years a number of new species have been tempted to the bird table. Blackcaps, now known to over-winter here regularly, will nick morsels from the table or even perch on the fat-cake. Bullfinches, starved out of the countryside, have started to nibble seeds and peanuts as have Goldfinches, Yellowhammers and Linnets. Long-tailed Tits, Goldcrests and even those dinky little jewels, Firecrests, have said yes to the ambitious chef, but then once ambition gets started, it knows no bounds.

Ring-necked Parakeets, those escaped pets and former residents of Asia and aviaries from South London to Kent, now roam widely from Henley to Margate and south to Hampshire, Surrey, Sussex and Southern Kent, not to mention most of London. Initially they were held in check by a few stiff winters but now noisy flocks of five hundred plus can be seen flying to roost and also descending onto a few select bird tables. I visited a lady's garden in Sandwich in Kent where every day for the price of some Granny Smiths and a couple of over-ripe Coxes a colourful cabaret of these brilliant green and rose-pink exotics descended to brighten the winter's gloom. It was a fabulous treat, and one that could be available to millions of southern bird lovers.

Even more ambitious are those raptor enthusiasts who have invested in a large freezer and filled it full of 'hatchery offal', the rather ungracious name for all the dead male day-old chicks that will never 'enjoy' life in the battery farms of Britain. These become a valuable food source for many zoos and falconers and make a neat bite size treat for everything from Buzzards,

Left: Tawny Owls are quite common suburban predators – go on, impress your friends.

Sparrowhawks, Kestrels and Tawny Owls, all of which I've seen visiting special feeding platforms across the UK. The Buzzards were daily guests at a ten-metre high table which was loaded by a rope pulley and bucket system, thus avoiding the need for extending the ladder. Six chicks, defrosted at dawn and served at nine-thirty a.m. led to a despicable display of table manners between the mild but more minor male and a fatter foul-tempered female – great value!

Another gentleman in Berkshire has a similar table, albeit lacking in a dumb waiter, something he's made up for with the practised ability to pitch a yellow fluffy chick with pinpoint accuracy. Its particular nifty addition is a forty watt, well weather-proofed lamp. Here it's not breakfast for Buzzards, but a case of supper for the local Tawny Owls which arrive and depart quickly, silently but no doubt gratefully after their free first course of the evening. It's all over in an instant but his photographs are superb.

Pheasants, Fieldfares, Green Woodpeckers, even Crested Tits and Grey Wagtails have been tempted onto tables across the UK. See what you've got in the neighbourhood, pick up the book to check what it eats and devise a realistic alternative to its diet, followed by a means of preparing and presenting the dish. All you have to do then is sit back and wait. Remember, few of us will say no to a free meal!

Right: A Fieldfare on apples, if you don't have a tree try scrounging some seconds from the greengrocer.

Left: Ring-necked Parakeets – noisy, greedy and funky.

BIRD NESTING BOXES

All your attention is focused on a small black hole cut in the front of a little wooden box pinned onto the garage. Did you see a bird go in, or did you just imagine it? The trouble is you really want to see a bird going in, in fact you may want it so much you might imagine it. Minutes tick by and you're still focused on that tiny black circle. You turn around to get a biscuit and – Oh, what was that? No, was that a bird that flew out? Damn! You'll have to keep watching, you can't go out and lift the lid, because if there is a Blue Tit in that nest box it might fly off and not come back and you don't want to imagine anything as bad as that.

There is something intrinsically satisfying about building a home for a bird, waiting to see it chosen and then watching a family raised and fledged from it. Something fascinating about the birds' speed and tenacity throughout the process and something simply awesome about their dedication and energy. And from a bird's point of view it's a bonus too. I mean, you've been feeding them all winter, you've lured them into suburbia with an endless diet of top treats, but now, when the business starts, when they get the essential urge, where are they going to do it? The problem, as ever, is the 'too tidy' phenomenon.

New Niches Needed

Because so many of our 'garden birds' are woodland species that have gone over to the 'urban side', and because in food-rich areas their population can increase to higher levels than those found in their native habitats, there will always be a shortage of nesting sites. The avian housing problem is exacerbated by our preoccupation with 'over-gardening' and removing too much dead wood, our misplaced hatred of ivy with its sheltering and secret niche forming habits, and our sterile modern house building styles that leave no cracks in the eves or crannies in the brick work. And it's not just our gardens, it's all around the neighbourhood – in our parks, public areas, patches of 'wasteland' or whatev-

Above left, above and below: *Some species prefer a little secrecy – Tawny Owls and Robins are cases in point – whilst Blue Tits can be brazen box fillers and do the business right in front of your window. Here a fledgling*

er. With an obvious shortage of mature trees what hope is there for a Blue Tit finding an unoccupied hole, a Robin finding a crack beneath a bough, a Flycatcher discovering a cleft in the ivy, let alone a Starling squeezing under a loose roof tile or a Swift skimming into an entrance to a nice dry loft. That's why when last spring I put up eighteen nest boxes in our garden, super saturation I might add as it's not that large, by the end of the breeding season nine had been used, eight successfully. That's nine nest sites that weren't previously available, immediately snapped up by the homeless of Netley, Southampton. More importantly, it's twenty-seven more Blue Tits, nine more Great Tits and four more Robins than fledged in our garden the year before we moved in.

Over the years enthusiasts have designed nest boxes and platforms for almost every species you can think of. From Willow Tits to Ospreys; from Little Terns to Long-eared Owls; from Goldeneyes to Goldcrests. And it continues.

While Jim Flegg's *Nest Boxes* first published by the BTO in 1971 is still an industry standard, more recently the Hawk and Owl Trust's *Boxes, Baskets and Platforms* has helped raptor enthusiasts, and an increasingly ingenious array of commercially available boxes has provided the DIY–challenged amateur with an instant answer to the dearth of natural nesting sites.

Wood or Not?

Traditionally nest boxes have always been wooden affairs, some over indulging design and of little use to any bird, others being so rustic that rustic was rapidly replaced by rotten. With today's pressure-treated timbers there is no excuse for the latter, so simply shop for a sturdy, practical and easy to clean box and expect to spend somewhere between seven and twenty pounds. If you're cool you'll make sure the timber came from sustainably harvested forests – otherwise it simply means you're indirectly doing someone else out of a home somewhere else in the world. However, purists would say that wood has had its day. Increasingly popular are wood-crete boxes. These 'prefab' homes are made from a secret mix of concrete and sawdust which allows the box to breathe and thus reduces both condensation and humidity. It's said that research has shown that birds prefer these boxes, that more young are fledged and that they'll last a lifetime. I once plagiarised Prince Charles on national television and called these boxes 'monstrous carbuncles' and as a consequence was much chastised. Call me old fashioned but I think they look awful, so I'll stick with my DIY pine plank, my Spear and Jackson ripsaw, a few screws and some scentless creosote, thank you, and anyway nine out of eighteen in one year isn't bad is it?

Siting nest boxes is critical and yet very difficult to provide precise guidelines for. This is simply because no two gardens are the same and aside from the basic common sense required you'll just have to experiment. Two things to remember are shelter from wind, rain and strong sunlight, and safety in terms of predators, particularly cats. You should combine consideration based upon these

Left and below: No cavities in your neat brick work? Then give a flycatcher, wagtail, robin or sparrow a little space filler at the cost of twenty-five minutes of DIY.

requirements with your desire to witness the breeding show and a need to clean out the box. The latter couldn't be simpler – pull out all the old nesting material in the autumn, scrape or brush out any residues and effect any external repairs. If you do get a problem with cats then there are some specially made products available to discourage them, such as a stout plastic tube which clips into, and tightens onto the nest hole, to effectively stop cats clawing at the entrance. If squirrels or Great Spotted Woodpeckers are the foe, steel plates with holes of an identical diameter screwed onto the face of the box will at least slow, if not stifle an attack on the occupants. One last tip, if a box is not used in one year don't be afraid to move it in the winter and try a new spot the next spring, a few feet can sometimes make all the difference to our more fickle feathered friends.

Left: All systems go in the Packham 'Tit rehabilitation programme'. My girlfriend's dad, Richard, made this beauty and the Great Tits were in after ten minutes.

Below: Try for Treecreepers with this specialized design.

BIRD NESTING BOXES

Top Tips

- Pressure-treated timber largely negates the need to paint the finished box with any wood preservative. However, most pressure-treated timbers seem to be honey-coloured or green, so if you wish your boxes to blend in a little more an extra coat of staining preservative in dark oak or chestnut may be necessary, but remember only treat the exterior of the box, never the inside.

- Make sure the timber is at least 2 cm thick to provide good insulation and to avoid warping and splitting.

- Use brass or plated screws and clips to facilitate repair or maintenance.

- With the exception of the entrance hole diameters these dimensions are only a guide; they do not need to be religiously adhered to, cut your box according to what you have available, the birds are not often that discerning.

- Screwing or nailing a box to a tree is not a sensible option if the tree is ever likely to be felled. When chainsaw meets metal, catastrophe and serious injury can result. An alternative is to use wooden pegs or dowels. Usually made from teak, beech or oak, these can be hammered into slightly undersized holes drilled in the tree. Fixing to walls, wooden or brick, should be done as solidly as possible. Birds don't like wobbly boxes.

- Most boxes should be sited between two and five metres in height, but of course their position should be predominantly determined by inaccessibility to predators (cats, squirrels, mice and rats), and the local climate. Do not place it in too exposed a position or with the entrance hole facing the wind or tilted upwards, or too close to another box — leave a distance of about 10 m.

OPEN-FRONTED

HOLE NESTERS

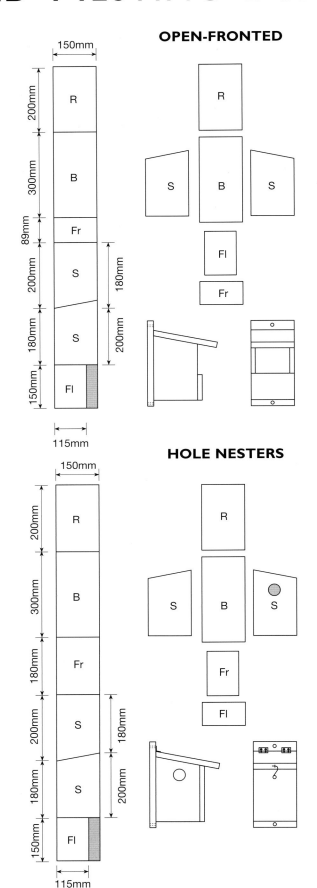

Size of hole	Species
25mm	Blue Tit, Coal Tit, Marsh Tit
32mm	Pied Flycatcher, Great Tit, Nuthatch, Tree Sparrow
200mm	Stock Dove, Tawny Owl, Jackdaw, Goldeneye, Goosander
Open	Robin, Spotted Flycatcher

TAWNY OWL

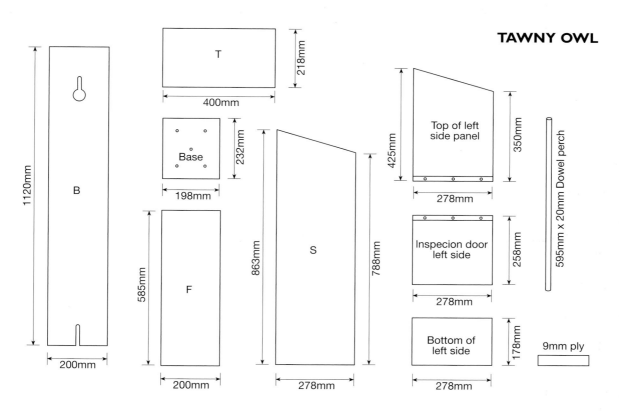

T
218mm
400mm

Base
232mm
198mm

B
1120mm
200mm

F
585mm
200mm

S
863mm
788mm
278mm

Top of left side panel
425mm
350mm
278mm

Inspecion door left side
258mm
278mm

Bottom of left side
178mm
278mm

595mm x 20mm Dowel perch

9mm ply

TREECREEPER
SWIFT

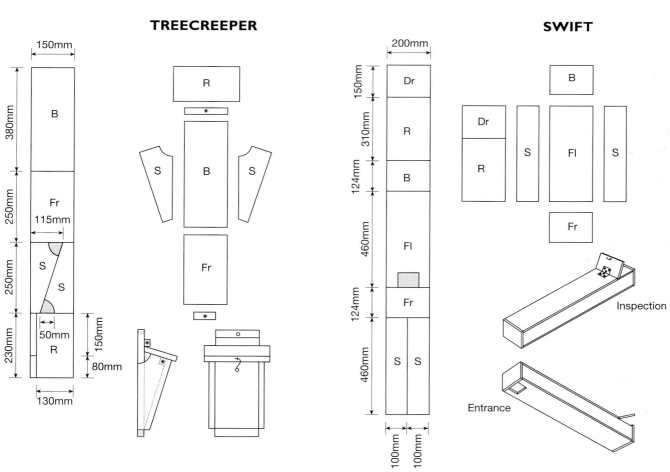

150mm
B
380mm
Fr
250mm
115mm
S
S
250mm
50mm
R
230mm
150mm
80mm
130mm

R
B
Fr

S
S

200mm
Dr
150mm
R
310mm
B
124mm
Fl
460mm
Fr
124mm
S S
460mm
100mm 100mm

B
Dr
R
S
Fl
S
Fr

Inspection

Entrance

37

ROBINS

Every time you open an envelope wishing you a Merry Christmas there is a thirty-five percent chance that a big-breasted bird is there to endorse the gesture. Big, red, cherubic, cheerful and smiling – not quite like the real thing, for robins are not always endowed with such a friendly demeanour.

A woodland species, Robins have side-stepped into suburbia with comfortable alacrity and flown into favour with romantic gardeners and bird lovers alike. Of course, they'll sit on your spade as it rests in an idyllic vegetable patch whilst you treat them to a few worms and instruct them to rid your produce of pests. Yes, they'll set up home in an old kettle, a hat, a bicycle basket, paint pot or some other amusing or decorative spot, and yes if you go looking on a Christmas morning they'll have a red breast to remind you of the blood of Christ. But if you take a closer look in spring you'll see the same loveable sweeties beating nine bells out of one another. Robins are fiercely territorial and males can be excited enough to attack anything red if it appears in the wrong place. They'll quite literally peck and claw it to pieces in a flurry of shrieking and squawking – quite good fun if you're into gladiatorial baiting with birds. A stuffed Robin makes an ideal decoy but a red feather or even a twist of red tissue can get one of the most aggravated specimens going.

But hey. We like Robins because they like us, and yes they are often very confiding, allowing close approach and even with patience coming to the hand to feed on tasty titbits with mealworms being an ideal treat. This habit however is largely confined to the UK race, as on mainland Europe they usually shun any human association and are far more shy and skulking. Strangely they are also extremely sensitive when they begin nesting and will readily desert the nest if you disturb them too early in the egg laying process. I was sadly reminded of this last spring when allowing my four year old a squint into a nestbox at home. For this reason, site your boxes or kettles

Above: 'Oi, you lookin at me?' Robins belong to the hooligan element, always looking for a scrap – or for a few that you throw out.

with caution and privacy. Of course it is nice to watch the adults delivering beakfuls of goodies to their brood, but if you are going to enjoy this spectacle, the predators will almost certainly be exploiting it. If you think you have hidden it well enough – hide it twice as well.

Estimates for our British population range between one and five million pairs, but they are always checked by a hard winter and of course by cats who too easily prey upon their cheeky, forgiving nature. A ripe old age for a robin, if it's able to escape the jaws and claws, might be between eight and ten years.

In the spring and summer robins feed principally on invertebrates. Almost anything of the right size can be on the menu, from ants, beetles, spiders, millipedes, slugs and snails – even small fish and lizards. In winter they'll turn their attention to fruit and again almost anything goes - bramble, elder, rowan, spindle, buckthorn and yew to name but a few. Throughout the year they'll come to bird tables to scavenge the peanut and sunflower seed crumbs or any other minor morsels overlooked by the more specialist species. In lab tests, however, birds fed on fruit alone lost weight and died. So if it gets cold and you love your robins, splash out on some mealworms – just three grams a day is enough to keep them going through the winter.

Left: *The scalloped plumage of the fledgling Robin has evolved for camouflage.*

your door to hear a burst of such cheer.

If you've got Robins, try to look after them. They are not on the slide yet, but who knows what's around the corner. Often there's a cat lurking, so make sure your scraps are placed well away from cover to give these ground feeders a chance of escaping the

Robins will choose almost any kind of hollow to site their nest, a bulky structure of dead leaves topped with a grassy cup lined with finer materials such as hair and very occasionally feathers. Between four and six eggs are laid and these are incubated for about two weeks by the female alone. Males return to help feed the young, which fledge after a further two weeks and are independent within a month. The youngsters' tanned, scalloped, brown plumage is exchanged for the classic red breast within three months, and by the spring they are ready for a bit of 'argie bargie' and 'how's your father' if they can find a vacant territory.

The real bonus of a robin residing in your garden is its song. A bittersweet melody, a warble with a few shrill notes. Males deliver it typically loudly in all months bar July and in winter the females chip in too. They are famed for singing under street lamps, or at night and on cold evenings it's always welcome as you dash to the warmth of

hidden pounce of death. If it gets tough in winter – persistent cold or prolonged ice and snow – then shop for emergency rations of mealworms to boost their diet. Hide nestboxes very well and again think cat, think mischief, think safety. Don't bother with too many boxes – unless your garden is very large, it's unlikely that a pair will tolerate another pair nesting so close, so concentrate instead on appropriate siting rather than numbers. If your offer isn't taken up in the first year, move the box – re-advertising it around Christmastime, because these little red-breasted charmers are pre-occupied with fighting for your attention on the doormat before they get down to the serious springtime business of fighting for a nest site in the garden.

Below: *Small, secretive and skulking, a contender for Britain's least sexy bird? Yes, until it starts to sing, because the Dunnock is a sweeter songster still and has similar requirements to the Robin – peace and catless quiet.*

FIVE FAVOURITE FINCHES

I'm not so much a tit man as a finch fancier. You see finches are less fidgety, they'll actually sit still and allow you more than a quick flash of their fashionable colours. There are ten resident British species of these small, primarily seed-eating birds. While Linnets, Twite, Redpolls, Crossbills and Hawfinches should only be considered as garden rarities, there are five members of the group which you should be able to attract if you and your neighbours have a few mature shrubs or trees in the garden.

The somewhat everyday **Chaffinch** is the most numerous British finch throughout the year and it breeds country-wide. From April onwards, it builds a charming little moss-covered nest holding up to five pink eggs. The male is brightly coloured and the female drabber, both easily distinguished by their olive-green rumps and very conspicuous double white wing bars. A monotonous 'pink' call is also diagnostic. In winter our native population is swollen by an influx of visitors from Scandinavia and Northern Europe and it's then that they'll be most apparent. Chaffinches very rarely land on seed feeders and never on the nuts. Instead they are content to hop around on the ground beneath feeding stations, picking up the crumbs that fall from above. They'll eat almost anything from bread and biscuit upwards, but relish commercial ground seed mixes, which if you have a large flock are well worth supplying, and, of course, if you're lucky you may find a Brambling among them. These winter migrants always appear washed out and have a conspicuous white rump.

The next finch up the ladder will sit and hog the ports of some seed feeders all day. They're the stout, greedy, bolshy and big-billed **Greenfinches** and they'll arrive in pairs, families or small flocks. The males are fairly splendid in their yellow-green finery and the flashing yellow markings on their wings and tail are really conspicuous when they fly away. Again widespread in Britain, Greenfinches like to perch high up to sing and scan about so they too prefer fairly mature shrubberies. If you hear their twittering song with its terminal drawn-out 'swee' you will have little trouble coaxing them down to a seed feeder loaded with black sunflower seeds. They go mad for them and will clean you out repeatedly. They'll also produce a huge dirty pile of the husks, which should be swept up immediately before they begin to meld into a horrible stinking slime. Our balcony is currently flooded with this noxious mess as our Greenfinches still prefer 'husks on' to the far easier for them, and cleaner for us, sunflower hearts. Choosy, eh?

Often a pair of **Goldfinches** will arrive in winter and stay until April before they disappear to breed. Wasteland, rough grassland or roadsides are their favoured 'native' habitats where thistle, groundsel, dandelion, dock and a host of similar seeds secure their favour. These birds are pretty special. Gaudy admittedly, but dainty too, and I'm always pleased to see their red, white and black faces peering at me through the kitchen window. Nyjer seed is the key to their hearts, although sunflowers come a close second. If you have the space then plant a few teasels each year and these birds will delight in perching on top of each of the prickly, egg-shaped seed heads and helping themselves to the kernels. When all the teasel seeds have gone you can always reload the heads with sunflowers by simply pushing them into the bracts. This might well give you a great photo opportunity too.

Left: Bullfinch is a top ten British bird and no doubt about it. It has declined by more than 50% since 1970, so let's hope that our remaining residents copy their continental cousins and start visiting feeders in earnest.

40

Left: *A bit flash – the chronically overcoloured Goldfinch. Who says we don't have natural exotics?*

Above: *Siskins in typical aerobatic antics on Alder, they'll also rampage through suburbia often in flocks of a hundred or more. All you need is seeds.*

Siskins are very small finches, distinctively yellow, green and black in colour with a deeply forked tail and squeaking 'tsy-zii' call. You'll be fortunate to be visited in summer but in winter, when their numbers can often be greatly increased by overseas visitors, they are fairly regularly feeders in large or more open gardens. Siskins are highly acrobatic and will swarm onto seed and nut dispensers and show a definite preference for those with red fittings. This became apparent years ago when retailers began offering peanuts in orange-red plastic ready to hang bags. They still do, so if you fancy trying for Siskins start with a couple of these, but take care, it requires less than a nano-second for squirrels to bite open the bags and shed their load to the ground, and these flighty little birds won't go for them down there.

At the pinnacle of the British finch list is the wonderful **Bullfinch**. One night after school when

I was twelve or thirteen I cycled around the neighbourhood and found no fewer than four Bullfinch nests. Today, I've yet to see or hear one in our garden and have not glimpsed that glowing white rump disappearing into cover for many months. The decline in Bullfinches has been dramatic and sad because they are simply stunning. Plump and neckless they might be but the male's pink breast almost fluoresces and contrasts marvellously with his velvety black cap. The female, who's never far away, is almost as nice with her mauvy-brown chest and each has a short stubby bill strong enough to split sloe stones and nibble through buds and seeds of many kinds. On the mainland of Europe where they are generally commoner, Bullfinches have been visiting bird tables for years but this is a habit which is only now beginning to be seen in the UK. Sunflower seeds loose on the table, but also on less busy feeders, seem to attract them but it's something I've yet to witness myself.

With the exception of Chaffinches, all these species like to nest in thick cover. Goldfinches and occasionally Greenfinches even choose the enveloping darkness of ornamental Cyprus trees, so Hawthorns, Beech, Elder or Privet are on the long-term planting list. Keep the bush dense, as it will restrict access to predators such as cats and Magpies.

Planting natural food-bearing bushes is also a fairly long-term option but you could sow a border with sunflowers, teasel and thistles and edge it with some honesty. In winter all of these species have seed heads which would attract finches but I'm afraid that two or three stems of each may not be enough to pull the birds in. Many finches like fields so think as big as you can.

Left: *Bickering on the bag – male Siskins get possessive over peanuts but it's not this which leads them to see red. They seem to have a genuine fondness for the colour itself.*

BLACKBIRDS
BUSKING BEAUTIES ARE TOP OF THE POPS

The day decays into a deep purple and the street lights switch to red and then glow through to orange. As the chill sets in from the clear sky and televisions flicker inside rooms waiting for tea-time, the virtuoso takes his stand on the silhouetted aerial. A fluent symphony of beautiful flutey notes is warbled in a liquid contralto, which lasts only eight or ten seconds, but is repeated gloriously several times in a minute. The Blackbird is the supreme suburban songster, blowing the Robin or the late-lamented Song Thrush clean out of the avian charts. And Blackbirds are newcomers; during the nineteenth century they were solitary and elusive birds of dense thickets, much as they are today in parts of mainland Europe. It was only really after the First World War that they shed their shy and retiring habits and stormed into suburbia.

Our humble Blackbird occupies most of Europe, North Africa and a band that stretches from Turkey to China. Britain's Blackbirds are sedentary but in winter are joined by continentals, many of which continue down to central Spain. In most parts of the UK they will be the commonest breeding species in gardens, and their rough grass nests can be hidden almost anywhere, from a cleft in an apple tree, to a roll of wire behind the shed. The substantial cup holds up to six eggs from March onwards, although clutches can be found in any month of the year. The female alone incubates for two weeks and the young fledge in another two. In two more she starts all over again. In the meantime all the males in the area will be at war; they strike mad postures when disputing territories, fanning tails, stretching necks and puffing themselves up, even fighting – not quite to the death.

Blackbirds are true omnivores, and having the biggest bill of all our resident thrushes, they focus upon the larger items in each class of food. Earthworms are fundamentally important to their ecology, and their head cocked, peering-down-and-listening posture, followed by a hop-see-swallow can be seen on lawns country-wide.

Left: *Stunning – a male Blackbird with a beak to die for. Which savages still put these in pies? Show me the whites of their eyes!*

A huge diversity of invertebrate prey is consumed and an even greater variety of fruits, berries and seeds. Yew, holly, hawthorn, rowan, apple and elder are favourites, but they'll gobble up whatever's there.

Consequently, catering for Blackbirds couldn't be easier – offer whatever you've got in the way of fruits and dry scraps. Maintain a well aerated and drained lawn to provide an earthworm supply, and ban insecticides. When it comes to planting food-bearing bushes, yew is an impossibly slow-growing species and holly not very speedy either. Go for rowan and especially elder, which produces huge flower heads that attract loads of insects, and lots of berries to satisfy all tastes. It also produces good nesting cover before it reaches maturity and 'opens-up' inside. Ivy is good for nest sites too and should be allowed to riot along a fence or a wall. For years we had such a resource in my parents' cat-ridden garden but no nests. As soon as a dog was taken in, several successful Blackbird broods a year were fledged, a fact that has always suggested to me that Blackbirds are keen on secrecy and security when it comes to breeding.

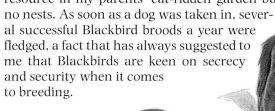

Left: A *speckly juvenile gobbles rowan berries.* Right: *Here a pair get to grips with elderberries, another favourite on the menu.*

SONG THRUSHES

A late snow had fallen one April and I slipped and skidded on my Clark's shiny soles all the way to the school grounds where two Song Thrush nests were hidden in a tangle of elder and old man's beard. The birds slipped silently away as I crept through the caves beneath the bushes. What they left on that crisp Saturday I shall never forget. A bowl of pale brown, perfectly smooth mud, ringed with grass, and lying in this archetypal nest were five sky-blue eggs each dotted with purple, almost black, spots. The other held two miniature 'freak eggs', each the size of a Malteser, but still perfectly marked.

Song Thrushes were never as visibly common as Blackbirds but it was a rarity if, in any spring and summer, I pushed my bike back into its shed without having been stirred by just such a sight. In fact I became complacent, writing only 'S.T' in my nature note books. Had I only known what was to come. Now it's at least three years since I last pulled myself into a hedge and glimpsed that little cameo. Our thrushes have declined considerably.

Let's not pretend we don't know why – our farmland is a rolled expanse of chemically ravaged wilderness and our gardens are pest-free plots where we are obsessed with tidiness. Okay, that may sound confrontational, but you get my point.

Like Blackbirds, Song Thrushes are principally dependent upon earthworms to shore up their diet. It is only when worms are in short supply that they turn to snails, the prey to which they have become inextricably linked owing to their habit of bashing them against stones to access the soft body of the animal. Song Thrushes are also less cosmopolitan in their choice of vegetable matter, it seems that being able to turn to snails is the way they typically survive. So it's in our hands, probably literally. Dump the slug pellets safely in the bin and accept a few holes in your prized green-stuffs and your local Song Thrushes might make it, but if we continue to effect a 'molluscan

Right and below: *Rich and varied is the song - a great start to an early day in suburbia.*

genocide' across suburbia, it might be that the last snail becomes the last straw.

Branch Bundles and Stick Piles

Years ago, I remember reading in a pamphlet about gardening for wildlife that if you were short of bushes, you might encourage birds to nest in your garden by suspending loose bundles of branches on your walls and fences. Because I could imagine nothing but a few sparrows sitting in them and thought that it would look ridiculous I dismissed this as an 'armchair' idea and forgot about it. But during the autumn before last we felled a willow and a storm-blown birch in the garden, and piled all of the brash at the base of a dead oak trunk. By spring a pair of Robins had taken up residence in the impenetrable tangle. Then a Dunnock joined in, then a Blackbird and then the Robins again and then the Dunnocks again. Five successful broods flew out of our huge heap of branches! So now it's going to stay. I've had to promise to move it and 'house' it more neatly behind a fence in the corner. If you have the space, why not give it a go?

Right: *Unfortunately the French eat both, which doesn't help when a species is in decline.*

HOUSE SPARROWS
SHOCK HORROR! SPADGERS IN RARITY SCARE

In 2009 the Royal Society for the Protection of Birds, the British Trust for Ornithology and other conservation groups published *The State of the UK's Birds 2007*, a definitive index of population trends for many British species. According to figures collected over the last thirty-seven years the House Sparrow and Starling populations in the UK had fallen by 65% and 73% respectively. That's close enough to seven out of ten sparrows and Starlings less than when Man landed on the moon. In 2007 both were listed in the Government's Biodiversity Action Plan, meaning that their conservation is now a priority.

Now I could grind out in detail the reasons for this sorry state and apportion blame accordingly, but I am sure no readers of this text are responsible for these genocides, and the obvious problem lies in farming policies, and the outdated and urgently in need of reform Common Agricultural Policy. Still, I doubt you sit on the appropriate European Committee to effect immediate change, so what can we do to help our sparrows? Well, I know someone who had a really good idea....

David White is a bird photographer and also a bit of an all-round ornithological whiz. In 1998 David recognized, like many people, that most modern houses have no gaps to allow cavity nesting birds inside, the difference is that he came up with a practical solution in the form of a prototype nest box.

Initially, all three holes were in the front and while the two outer entrances were occupied within two weeks there was a lot of bickering before the middle box was taken up. Mark II had the holes in the ends and only one in the centre of the front. This did the trick immediately. It seems that although House Sparrows are a communal nesting species they don't like to see too much of each other's private lives. The preferred size of the entrance hole is 32 mm – just too small to allow Starlings access. Dowel perches are also necessary as male sparrows love to sit outside their nest and chirp about things, a behaviour that probably serves some social service and may be important to a colony's establishment and success. David feels that 'multi-boxes' are necessary to lure sparrows into new neighbourhoods, as single detached residences are never as popular, a lack of 'confidence' in solitary nesting being the cause. There is no reason why boxes with five or six or even more chambers couldn't be erected other than the manhandling at the top of the ladder. Don't let your ideas and ambitions compromise safety.

Upright nesting tiers work extremely well in the United States for a species called the Purple Martin. Essentially a large House Martin, this species chooses natural cavities instead of making mud cup nests and takes well to boxes, a great many of which are erected on its behalf. David plans such a structure for House Sparrows, alternating holes from side to front all the way up to prevent 'white caps'. I plan to erect one of his horizontal designs to see if I can encourage a few local spadgers to join us. It would be nice to see residents' groups erecting a few in new estates or British Telecom hanging them on urban telegraph poles? Just an idea.

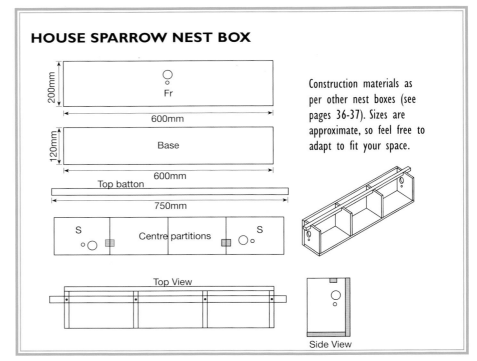

HOUSE SPARROW NEST BOX

Construction materials as per other nest boxes (see pages 36-37). Sizes are approximate, so feel free to adapt to fit your space.

200mm / Fr / 600mm

120mm / Base / 600mm

Top batton / 750mm

S / S / Centre partitions

Top View

Side View

STARLINGS
COCKINESS FADES FOR THESE URBAN LEGENDS

Starlings should be born survivors. Stocky, omnivorous, with a taste for anything – however tasteless – there was a time when they were ascendant avians. One key to that past success was their protractor muscles. Attached to the top part of their beak are the muscles that provide the strength to open the beak rather than close it. Unusual when you think of it, but highly effective when probing in soil for invertebrate larvae such as leatherjackets, as the widening of the hole facilitates a more effective removal of the wriggling and retreating grub. Starlings can rotate their eyes to the front of their skull to give them binocular vision into the hole without having to remove the beak and peep in sideways and they have good low light vision. They are highly vocal, excellent mimics and also practise 'brood parasitism'. (Basically, females lay eggs into other females' nests.)

So how can a bird with such a fascinating ecology, extensive behavioural repertoire and striking appearance be so generally reviled?

Well, in the past our resident Starlings were joined by vast numbers of wintering vagrants from the continent and flocks and roosts in excess of a million birds were not uncommon. Of course the resultant noise and mess offended those obsessed with silence and hygiene and the spectacular swirling clouds of birds, undoubtedly one of the most exciting sights of birdlife, left such folks unmoved. But not the Starlings, which in many places were gassed, harried or even dynamited.

Our breeding Starlings were also dubbed 'pests' because of the attentions they afforded fruit orchards, particularly cherries. Here too they were terrified, albeit briefly, with tapes of their own alarm calls, shot at, and poisoned. Not surprisingly, Starlings have fared even worse than House Sparrows and have declined by 73% in the last thirty-five years. So what can we do?

Well, as usual, feeding and providing nest sites are the practical answers. Starlings will eat almost anything, so scatter what you've got onto the ground where they'll be out of the way of the other hanging or table-feeding species. They can be a bit of a nuisance on fat cakes, but really all you can do is grin and bear it, while remembering that Blue Tits have actually increased by 33%, Great Tits by 91%, and Great Spotted Woodpeckers by a marvellous 314% in the same period of the Starlings' decline. It is clear to see which species needs help, even if it's not your favourite, and if you do live on a new estate in an impregnable house you might think of putting up a couple of boxes. Simply scale up a 'tit-type' box and make sure it has an entrance hole of at least 7-8 cm diameter.

If the nation made a concerted effort we might make a difference, but what is really needed here is a change in agricultural policy. So when you put down your saw and screwdriver, for once pick up a pen and write to your own MP. Tell him or her you are frightened that your children won't hear the twitter of sparrows outside their windows as they wake, or Starlings pretending to be Tawny Owls, and that a life without these urban legends will be like a life without the FA Cup Final on BBC1 – once unthinkable but now horribly inevitable.

Above: *'Open-beak probing': the key to starlings success as great grubbers.*

Right: *Not so sparky, the juvenile birds are plain brown, but not for long.*

GREAT SPOTTED WOODPECKERS
ENOUGH TO MAKE YOU ANTHROPOMORPHIC

Few creatures are so cartoon, so much caricatures of themselves and so basically exciting as woodpeckers. They are essentially funny; anything that regularly hammers its head against hard wood is bound to carry the burden of humour. And 'Great Spots' are naughty too, always looking over their shoulders expecting a telling off for nothing more than going about their rather mad business. They're brightly marked and brash, with a laugh fit for a dockside tavern at closing time. It's true, and once in a while there's nothing wrong with anthropomorphism.

Although these birds prefer stands of timber with more than a few mature trees, using hedgerows, railway embankments, copses and parklands, they are able to penetrate deep into urban environments. You're unlikely to mistake their striking pied plumage or red undertail coverts or their harsh and far-carrying 'tchack' call. But drumming is best. In spring, males advertise their territories by striking an appropriately resonant branch rapidly and repeatedly with their beak. A short but powerful burst of sonic fire results and no doubt excites the females. The nesting hole is excavated in trunks or branches and a chamber holds up to six eggs which both parents incubate for just over two weeks. The appallingly ugly young emerge about three weeks later and proceed to make a horrendous din for the rest of the summer.

Great Spotted Woodpeckers have relatively short, stout beaks with squared-off chisel-shaped tips and use these to both hammer and prise apart dead wood in pursuit of grubs and bugs. Fruit, seeds and nuts are also on the menu, as are the nestlings of other birds and often they will either cunningly catch them inside their nest boxes, by pretending to be their parents outside, or by battering a hole through the front of the box. The luckless fledglings are dragged out and be pecked to bits on a nearby branch. Nature raw, in beak and claw. Fortunately, you can tempt them with less bloodthirsty bait - fat, suet and peanuts, particularly in winter when it's not so necessary to focus on a protein-rich diet to rear their young. If

Left: Remember when Woody was still a woodpecker? With some of these guys on your feeder you won't need animated astronauts to help the story along.

you make 'birdcakes' from fat mixes and hang them up you may encounter a couple of problems. Firstly, other birds, especially Starlings, also love them and will steal most of your woodpecker's food before these slightly shyer birds can take advantage of it. Secondly, once familiarized, the 'peckers themselves will soon learn to sever the string and send the whole thing tumbling to the ground where it's easier for them to eat it but also easier for rats to discover it, you to tread in it, and worst of all, miss all of the action. An alternative design to suit primarily 'peckers is to take a heavy log complete with bark and drill or cut holes in it, say 2 cm diameter and 3 cm deep, at regular intervals along its length. Then plug these with your fat mixture while it's still malleable and hang or stand it in position. It won't prove exclusive but it's slightly more natural and as such, might, if you've chosen creatively, offer a photographic opportunity. If you become a major fan of *Dendrocopos major* then treat them by including mealworms in your fat mix. They'll love you, albeit anthropomorphically!

Above: The sexes are separable. Males have a crimson nape – something that is only really conspicuous when they are at rest.

THREE TREATS!
TWO NUTTERS AND SOME FAT FELLOWS

Nuthatch

My friend Ian says that Nuthatches look 'hard' but I think they simply lack any sense of humour or for that matter many social graces. I am sorry to anthropomorphize again but it's true. They bark their snappy and aggressive calls to each other with little decorum and seem to consistently bear grudges, posturing and bickering over a few old nuts.

Casting such notions aside, Nuthatches are almost mini woodpeckers, equipped with large, dagger-shaped bills. They climb the bark with similar alacrity but focus instead on gleaning insects from the surface or from cracks, and feed on smaller seeds such as beechmast and soft hazelnuts. These they wedge into crevasses in trees or walls before they hammer them apart to peck out the kernels. They'll do the same to any loose peanuts you provide as they loathe spending any time away from the security of the tree trunk when feeding. They'll hang on to nut feeders for sure, but seem to resent it and invariably upset all the other birds, so I feed them with a separate pile of their own loose peanuts. If you have any local, mature or even old oak, beech or hazel woodland you should try for them. Tolerate their anti-social antics and should they deign to nest in your garden you will witness a work of great artistry as they neatly plaster up the entrance to any cavity with mud until precisely the diameter they favour is achieved. Curiously, when using nest boxes they'll also cement around the lid from inside – mad, eh?

Jay

Another woodlander that might sneak into your garden is the exotic-looking Jay. Jays will stealthily approach bird tables loaded with loose food, particularly peanuts, and then only land for as long as it take to stuff up their especially large throat sacks. Typically, this adaptation is used to carry up to nine acorns, which they hoard in their private larders. Exceptionally they'll secrete these up to two miles away and being crows, and thus among the most 'intelligent' of birds they actually remember where the large majority are hidden. Of course, those that they forget germinate and may go on to become trees. Jays are probably the most important method by which oaks spread uphill. Trivial Pursuit – my middle name.

Woodpigeon

Okay, I know, you're thinking 'Three Treats' Nuthatch, Jay and... Woodpigeon! What the...? But look, what else do you get in your garden that isn't covered somewhere in this book? I mean, yes, Treecreepers, Hawfinches and Woodcock are interesting birds, but not regular in most gardens. So let's get real and enjoy what we've got: Woodpigeons.

I once read somewhere that the damage to crops, combined with the size of their population, made Woodpigeons the most serious bird pests in Britain. Apparently they cause more than a million pounds worth of damage to clover, brassicas, lettuce and peas. Can you tell me how much damage we do to the environment each year and quantify it in pounds sterling? In my garden 'Woodies' are welcome. They come to feed on acorns and recently I spied no fewer than sixteen on the lawn. When the acorns run out I shall feed them a cheap cereal-based ground food mix and if one nests in one of our trees I shall enjoy its gentle and therapeutic cooing.

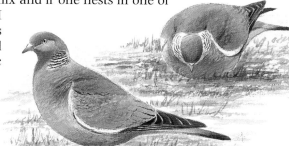

THE TRUTH ABOUT SPARROWHAWKS AND MAGPIES

It's sad but true, that like a lovelorn soldier I carry a small collection of photographs in my wallet. I'm away from home a lot and it's good to put a favourite face to a crackling voice on a satellite phone. But sandwiched between my girlfriend, little girl, a Ferrari 246 GT Dino, Audrey Hepburn on a bicycle and Stirling Moss's autographed business card is a flimsy picture of a male **Sparrowhawk** cut from a magazine. He stares with fixed fury, his chrome yellow eyes blazing over his burnished blue back, his trousers fluffing over his lengthy legs, standing in a puddle reflecting the neat barring on his breast. When it comes to loved ones, pin-ups, fantasies and heroes he scores in all four categories – for me at least, the best bird in Britain and a contender for the world title. Sparrowhawks tease us with their jet fighter fly-bys, their flashes of dun shadow going away in silence through the wood. They tantalise us by leaving fresh kills on the footpath, the flesh still warm, the feathers still floating on the wind, or with their delicate whinneying call, close behind a cloak of birch rendering them invisible. Sparrowhawks – you've always just missed them.

Above: If you can't face the truth, don't look – death is essential to all life

But now after years of waiting we are all in with a chance. After more than a century of senseless persecution by gamekeepers and two decades of pesticide poisoning, the population of these dainty little raptors lay in ruins. In many parts they were a rarity or absent altogether, but gradually over the last thirty years they have spread back to their old haunts and into a few new neighbourhoods too. And because so many of the farmland refugees have concentrated in our gardens then so have their predators. In many places Sparrowhawks have joined Kestrels as an urban species. Who can blame them? All that food, buzzing around feeders and on tables, rearing broods in boxes, is a veritable bonanza.

I hope that most of us enjoy the Sparrowhawk's brief visits; some people even get great views occasionally. That Sparrowhawks snatch a few tits is, of course, perfectly natural, and we should be no less disturbed than when we watch a fly struggling in a spider's web. Predation makes the natural world and your garden go round. Thus it saddens me to read in magazines, or to receive mail from those who hate these raiders, who want them 'controlled', who blame them for falling songbird numbers. Look, they had a tough time, you forgot they existed, now you feed the birds and by so doing so you feed them. This is nature, it's self-regulating, if there weren't enough small birds in your garden there wouldn't be any Sparrowhawks. They'd produce less young, stop breeding altogether, or fly off somewhere else. If Nightingales enjoyed a similarly remarkable recovery would you complain that they kept you awake at night? Probably. Get a life, and stop letting your human emotions get in the way of good biology.

This brings us neatly from the raider to the bandit, the burglar, the vandal, the current all-round-bad guy of the bird world: the wonderful **Magpie**.

If I had a pound for every gripe I've heard about the mischievous murdering Magpie I wouldn't be writing this book, I'd be looking for Shoe-billed Storks in a swamp in Uganda. Magpies have become complete scapegoats, if a bird can be anything to do with a goat, and are widely, and sadly seriously, believed to be responsible for the dramatic decline in songbird numbers, particularly in suburbia. Let's get a few things straight.

Magpies are adept at raiding birds' nests and eating either the eggs or the young. They do not often kill adult birds. Thus they exert their impact on small bird populations from late March through to June, for perhaps three or three and a half months of the year. The eggs and young are not part of the all-important breeding base of any species population, and are thus less important in the potential recruitment of new individuals.

Left and above: If you can't face the truth, don't look – Magpies do raid nests but who accounts for all the rest?

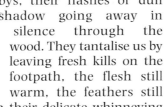

Above: *Noisy and obvious, like American G.I.s in World War II, Magpies beg for trouble.*

Left: *Oh yes. Even Audrey Hepburn struggles against beauties like this enduring favourite.*

And don't forget that Magpies are omnivores, that will scavenge anything at some times of the year. They're not strict carnivores that must have meat. Ask yourself, when was the last time you saw a cat eating a salad?

Yes, Magpies have increased; they've tripled their numbers in the last twenty years, probably because of a relaxation in persecution, although we've yet to understand all the nuances that have allowed them to expand their niche so quickly. But it must have occurred in response to something, a new or changed opportunity. So it's strange therefore that the Magpie started to expand pretty much when the really dramatic decline started to occur in farmland bird populations. Ask yourself, which animal do you know that increases its numbers when there's less of its 'food' available, and continues to do so until there is nearly no 'food' left? Perhaps small birds are not its 'food' at all, or at least not the part of its diet that influences its own population changes. It seems likely that the increase and decline are not linked, and thankfully both the RSPB and BTO agree with me.

A study of twenty-three songbird species using data collected since 1962 and published in 1998 showed no correlation between the relative increases in Sparrowhawks and Magpies and decreases in smaller birds. Indeed, in some areas songbirds thrived in spite of the increased predator numbers. The most respected and informed juries have considered the accusations. Result – Not Guilty. Case Closed.

Yours or your neighbour's cat kills adult birds, the breeders, the incubating or gravid females, the territory holding fittest males for twelve full months of the year. And their chicks too. Which do you think exerts a greater impact on the bird population?

Next up. Magpies are bluey green, black and white, noisy birds with long tails. They sit on tree tops, roofs, and readily fly across roads in front of cars. They are highly apparent in the environment. Dunnocks on the other hand are dowdy little brown birds which skulk like mice beneath bushes and are relatively timid, even in suburbia. Ask yourself, do I see more magpies than I see Dunnocks, and does that mean there are really more Magpies than Dunnocks where I live? You see, drive by, or walking to the paper-shop bird censusing techniques are not without their flaws.

BIRDS ON CAMERA
DO-IT-YOURSELF WILDLIFE TELEVISION

There are a couple of recent inventions which have helped our garden birds into the video age. Spurred on by the enormous success of series like *Springwatch* on BBC TV, and enabled by the rise in quality and decline in cost of small security type video cameras, a number of companies offer a neat package which allows you to witness all the shenanigans that unfold as a brood of birds, typically Blue Tits, are reared in a nest box. Their standard kit comes complete with a nest box, some with a choice of Blue Tit or Great Tit sized entrance hole, a tiny infra-red camera and a ten to twenty metre lead which runs into your television, video or computer.

The cameras are normally fixed focus, but of a sufficiently wide angle that everything is sharp from the entrance hole down to the bottom of the nest cup. The image is black and white but surprisingly good; though because the camera is placed in the roof of the box one limitation is the single top view which sometimes means you get a lot of chicks' crowns and not much else. The benefit is that the lens remains relatively clean through the early stages of the brood stay. As they begin to get

Left: *Take One – fresh from 'costume' and 'make-up', a Great Tit poses nicely for a repositioned camera. Less privacy than Hello Magazine!*

'feathered up' the lens gets pretty dusty and may need cleaning. In the three that I have investigated this is quick and easy and shouldn't disturb the birds too much, as it is facilitated by unclipping and raising the hinged lid, removing the camera from its socket, wiping and replacing it, something that can be done in two minutes or less. Note that this also means that there is no need to leave the camera in the box when it's not in use. When you are sure the birds have settled, preferably when the clutch is complete or even after hatching, you can quickly slip the camera in and begin viewing. Some even have a microphone so you don't miss out on any of the squeaking. It's never quite as high quality picture as on TV, but they are your birds, there's never a shortage of activity and on this account the show is particularly enjoyed by children.

At least one of the manufacturers offers an alternative box suitable for Starlings, which I can only imagine would be as much fun as tits. The starter kits cost around one hundred and fifty pounds and they get my vote because although that's a big outlay for fourteen days of birdwatching a year, they reveal a little bit of secret bird life that you never otherwise see.

Also on offer are bird boxes where the camera is pointing out of the hole, or bird tables with a similarly hidden device. The former you site in range of your feeding facilities, the latter you erect, load with food, connect up and sit back to watch. These cameras supply colour images and to be honest they suffer in strong sunlight. as the currently available cheaper video cameras fail to deal with contrast as well. Often under such conditions the subject is dark and the background washed out. Of course you can maximise the quality by repositioning the set-up to reduce the difference in relative lighting intensity, but they never quite make it, providing as they do merely a close-up of something you can see more clearly through your binoculars or telescope.

Recently I have invested in a wireless CCD security system. This consists of a colour digital camera about the

Above: *Take Two – top view of the finished clutch, the ideal time to introduce the camera, thus minimising disturbance.*

Above: *Take Three – action. Here comes the caterpillar, and the fledgling Blue Tits are clamouring for more.*

size of a chunky TV remote controller fitted with a wide angle lens. A flap on top folds up and can be angled to transmit via microwave the image and sound over a distance of three hundred metres to the receiver, which sits on top of the television or video. This means it can be used anywhere in the garden without any cabling. It simply screws on top of a normal camera tripod and you can site it at will, preferably with a reasonably clear line of sight to the receiver, glass not reducing the quality of reception. The pictures are excellent; they suffer in strong sunlight, but in low light and with a black and white camera they come into their own. Two little rows of infra-red LRDs either side of the lens seem to throw out enough light to produce quite acceptable images in near darkness.

The camera is not water- or squirrel-proof so I intend to make up a metal box to house it, then I'll feel more confident about leaving it outside in all weathers and in all positions. The wireless benefits are obvious; it's quick and easy to move. In one quite expensive swoop most of the diurnal and nocturnal wildlife in the garden is on Channel Six in the kitchen, and if I don't feel like waiting up I stick in a three-hour tape and simply rewind for the action in the morning, all the while perfecting my David Attenborough impersonation.

Recently I had the good fortune of visiting Graham Roberts at his home in Havant, Hampshire. He had cannibalised a Blue Tit camera box to sneak unique views of a pair of swifts that were nesting in his loft. He showed me some fascinating tape of the birds' nesting process including delicate mutual preening, egg turning, the constant addition of feathers to the unsubstantial nest and the sleeping adults cuddling all night. One regularly puts its young over the other's back in an embrace. Graham's genius for getting 'into' nests knows few bounds, he's done the same for Peregrines too and the pictures are great. Anyone for Treecreepers?

MAMMALS

FOXES
A FEW HOME TRUTHS

He is neither cunning nor crafty, nor even very quick or brown. He has never killed indiscriminately or wantonly and I'd put a pound on the fact that he's never harmed a cat. Okay, he used to pull your dustbin over before the introduction of the wildlife unfriendly wheelie bin, and yes, he'll dig up lawns and flowerbeds and even the shallow graves of your late beloved hamsters. Okay, he'll leave his bitter scent on your trees and clusters of faeces in prominent places and in the winter time his mate will let out a blood curdling cough and scream throughout the night. If you're lucky, you might live in a neighbourhood where every day you are afforded views of one of the most attractive characters in our fauna, the Red Fox.

In low, late autumn sun when foxes have grown their winter coats, to see one anywhere, let alone in your garden is a very special treat. They are exquisitely marked on the head and face and too perfectly proportioned to qualify for the 'pretty' tag. They are simply beautiful.

I've had my property damaged by foxes – in fact *I've* been damaged by foxes and still have the scars to prove it. I used to keep them as a boy, but despite bloody set backs and ripped and chewed clothes they remain a very firm favourite. The fox is a creature that comes to us young but always with baggage – generally a poor representation based on equally poor biology. For instance; foxes will break in to somebody's chicken run and go mad killing all the chickens. To the fox the hen-house is a supermarket and when you visit the human version do you only come home with enough food for one meal? No, and nor would the fox if, as under natural conditions, it were allowed to repeatedly return to the shop each night to pick up another ready to eat fowl. This isn't a psychopathic animal – it's an efficient shopper. And this is the twenty-first century, if smallholders and farmers alike will not implement the incredibly cheap and effective means of fox proofing their poultry, then *vive le fox*.

Foxes are omnivores and will turn their noses up at very little you might offer. Ours get kitchen scraps of all kinds

Above and below: *Not just a pretty face. Radar-dish ears – all the better to hear you with – a nose to die for and eyes that can see in near darkness. Simply beautiful evolution.*

and the occasional meat treats. They are not perturbed by oriental fare or by hot curries, but to date have not acquired a taste for prawn crackers! We feed all year round and I have no doubt that this is of some dietary use to our foxes, particularly in the winter and spring when reduced foraging time and care of their cubs are considerations. I've spent many evenings watching foxes, badgers and cats together in gardens. There is a clear hierarchy; foxes are at the bottom of the pecking order with cats very securely at the top – if they want to be. Many cats are curious about these visitors but unless there are any titbits they fancy for themselves they don't bother to get involved. If fresh chicken is on the menu then your cuddly Tibbles easily chases off Reynard and Brock with a bit of hissing and hackle raising. Thus true stories of cats as fox prey I would say are largely unfounded, if not extremely rare.

LIVING WITH URBAN FOXES

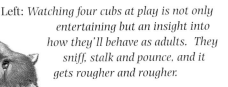

Trevor Williams's uncle had a farm. He didn't really like foxes but he reckoned the hunt did more damage than they were worth, and that it wasn't worth giving up one day to chase one fox because it had pinched one chicken. 'Nature's burglars' he called them, and young Trevor fell for their mischievous charms and has never fallen for another. In the early 1990s he started the Fox Project in Tonbridge in Kent, and now each year sees him caring and rehabilitating hundreds of injured adults and abandoned fox cubs. He employs four part-time staff and is helped by a team of ninety volunteers. Paradoxically, the other side of the charity is concerned with people who don't like foxes, or don't want anything to do with them. When it comes to knowing what the public think about foxes I figure Trevor knows best, so I asked him a few questions.

Left: Watching four cubs at play is not only entertaining but an insight into how they'll behave as adults. They sniff, stalk and pounce, and it gets rougher and rougher.

Question: So what don't people like about foxes?

Answer: Well, it's all sorts, everything from noise, particularly in January when they are beginning to mate, through to fear of them attacking their pets. If it's the noise, we tell them to just close their windows and turn up the stereo – even if they succeed in chasing the fox from their property, they'll hear it from next door. There's not much you can do about noise.

Question: And the pet issue, that's nonsense too. isn't it?

Answer: Yes and no. I know of one attack on a dog, a Jack Russell that was trying to get at a den with cubs. The vixen bit him on the nose. As for cats, I have no personal evidence of foxes ever killing cats, but I've heard of a half a dozen cases which I might give some credence to, probably a result of the cats again harrying fox cubs. If people complain about rabbits and guinea pigs going missing then we say, 'They're natural prey – house them properly and they'll be totally safe'.

Question: What about garden damage – digging, etc.

Answer: We get hundreds of calls about this, in fact we run a taped advice line. Basically it's about deterrents. The problems are nuisance damage, such as digging holes, scent marking, which many people find offensive, and territorial

Left: 'Get lost vole-breath, I've got a head-ache' – or a moment of tenderness between a pair of suburban beauties.

marking with faeces. Not surprisingly, people object to having their lawns covered in fox pooh and they can also worry about health and hygiene problems, the *Toxocara* parasite that can cause blindness in children. Firstly, we tell people to pick it up, pooper scoop it, and then if the faeces are on grass we recommend using a product called 'Scoot'. Used as directed, this works; rather than get caught out foxes just stay away. If the mess is on soil or concrete then we recommend using 'Renardine', which if you decant onto a small pile of sharp-sand will stay active longer and not drain away into the ground. Planter Bags also seem to be favourite sites for this sort of action. Try 'Get-my-garden' here – it's safe, based on citronella, but its jelly pellets don't last as long as the others. Lastly, we always suggest that repellants are placed where the animal can be found entering the garden. Check for paw prints on fences, footprints, hairs. We've tried the ultra-sonic deterrents, but found them only eighty two per cent effective, compared to the chemicals at ninety four. You'll never create a fox-free zone, but you can definitely reduce their activity.

left: *When very young, fox cubs are more 'kitten' than 'puppy' but they already have that distinctive odour as Trevor betrays here.*

dripped on. You've got to persevere and it's slow, but it definitely works.

Question: **Dare I mention rabies?**
Answer: Well imagine the paranoia that will result when eventually a 'bona fide' case appears over here. It's going to be horrible. The disease is hugely exaggerated. Anyway, it's on the decline in Europe, there hasn't been a human fatality since 1972, and the vaccines and treatments for us are up to date.

Question: **Historically the Fox swings to and fro in favour – what's the current score?**
Answer: Lots of short-lived, loud shouting by a few people, while the vast majority secretly enjoy them. I don't think mange or anything else has made them unpopular, people like foxes in suburbia. One day last year I skidded to a halt to get a better view of a fox in a field, then I sat there thinking, 'Hey you've got hundreds of these things in your care at home'. Once foxes have gripped you it takes more than a little nuisance to put you off.

Question: **You haven't mentioned mange?**
Answer: In the seventies we hardly saw any mange, but now it's spread almost everywhere. Bristol is the worst area, and because it is canine mange people do fear that it could spread to their pets. No one knows how easily this might happen – the research is ambiguous, it might need direct contact, or it could be windborn. It might survive in the grass. If your dog does contract mange it is easy to treat and cure and there is no reason for your pet to end up looking as scabby as some of the poor foxes.

Question: **So can we treat it ourselves?**
Answer: Yes, definitely and effectively, but never pharmaceutically. The chemicals work well in captivity where you can inject them but dripping them onto bait is too risky. They can kill other animals including pets if they steal the bait first, and besides we are having great success with a completely harmless homeopathic treatment, which is cheaper too. Arsenicum and Sulphur can be crushed from tablets and dusted onto food, or the liquid

Question: **What's the Fox Project's opinion on feeding foxes.**
Answer: We say if you want to feed them, then do it, but make sure the food is a bonus, not a new life style. Feed them two or three times a week, randomly and don't try to domesticate them. Don't feed them too close to the house, let alone indoors, and never by hand. No sloppy dog food – give them kitchen scraps.

Trevor Williams is my kind of conservationist – pragmatic, realistic, and efficient. The Fox Project offers information and advice to local authorities country-wide. It helps Environmental Health Officers, parks personnel and the public, providing up to date advice. They won't like the tag but Trevor and his team are experts. For more information see the website www.foxproject.org.uk, or call the advice line on 01892 826222 (pre-recorded message lasting four minutes, standard call charges apply).

BRING ON THE BADGERS

Despite the efforts of Defra, the Badger enjoys widespread popularity as a cuddly amicable, nocturnal, nice, all round mammal. Not the vector of an insidious disease which has dairy farmers on the brink of ruin. Both are wrong – cuddly, amicable and bumbling, Badgers are not. Territorial and ferocious sometimes, they are always far from bumbling – Badgers are highly efficient, opportunistic omnivores. They can and do eat almost anything fleshy or fruity, from acorns to birds, from apples to beetles, from corn to young rabbits. But for all its cosmopolitan taste the Badger is actually a specialist with one real meal on its mind – earthworms. Badgers' whole ecology, the sites of their setts, their social lives, their territories and reproduction all depend on the availability of worms. They can and do survive in worm-deprived areas, but they are probably always dreaming of worms. They get worm withdrawal syndrome, they start raiding dustbins, eating slugs, sandwiches, peanuts and Kellogg's Ricicles, because increasingly these maverick melids are taking to this crazy lifestyle and thriving in suburbia. Our lawns yield a few of their old favourites, but then who wants to suck up a wet noodle filled with dirt, when some generous home owner has thrown sweet treats and chicken pieces all over the grass?

Dennis Chapman loved his Badgers. He secretly procured (from a local supermarket) huge volumes of food, no longer fit for human consumption on account of the mysterious 'sell by date' and laid on a spread second to none. He did this every night for more than fifteen years. His reward was quite simply the best Badger show in the world. Eleven animals, we called them Newcastle United, appeared regularly, but seventeen was his record. They would come right up to the open french window and peacefully munch away while an audience of privileged people enjoyed the show. Then he moved and apparently the new residents preferred Coronation Street and cheaped out on the Rice Crispies.

Unwittingly Dennis had probably encouraged a dependency in this clan of Badgers and as his removal van pulled away it left them with a problem. Being terri-

torial and having a complex social hierarchy means that it's not easy for Badgers to move onto fresh foraging areas. I spoke to Pauline Kidner, a wildlife rehabilitator based at Secret World near Burnham-on-Sea in Somerset, a lady with lots of 'hands on' experience with Badgers, and she echoed Trevor Williams's Fox comments. Feed titbits occasionally as an additive to their diets, not as a replacement for all natural foods. She feared for Dennis's team and thought that his neighbour's gardens may have been attacked when he left, something she sees as an increasing trend. Infilling, in housing terms, by building on every scrap of suburban 'wasteland' has robbed these animals of the little space they needed for privacy. Now they've been forced to live right alongside us and even in our gardens. So it's not just lawn holing or bulb digging, it's major earth moving activities which plague people. The former symptoms can be treated by supplementary feeding in other parts of the garden, i.e. scattering peanuts away from the borders whenever the raiders display a taste for tubers. The latter problem is more difficult to rectify. Badgers are protected by law, you may not harm them, and it once took Pauline and her team four years to tempt a family of particularly tenacious animals into an artificial sett.

If you feed loose peanuts for birds or squirrels you may inadvertently attract Badgers. The squirrels will cache any excess in the garden and this in turn leads to late night excavations. Peanut Butter is another item that most Badger feeders swear by but cheap, cereal-based dog foods may be closer to a natural diet.

Pauline doesn't encourage indoor or hand feeding. Badgers are wild animals and very powerful in the jaw and claw department. They are not dangerous, just need a little obvious respect. Oh yes, there's currently a paranoia about the risk of contracting TB from Badger's dung-pits. It's nonsense, a mean piece of propaganda perpetrated by those who wish these charming creatures harm.

As a university student I studied Badgers for five years. Thus I have had more 'Badgery' than 'boogie nights' and have an expansive network of 'Badgery' mates. I was once invited to watch a particularly resourceful Brock scale a 2.5 m high fencepost to dislodge a peanut feeder. The prospective performance clashed with the Cup Winners Cup Final. Shortly after Nayim's spectacular goal sunk Arsenal in injury time, the Badger was celebrating his own success and performing a lap of honour with the nuts. It was a great evening. I've also had the pleasure of Mr Alistair Kilburn's company of Badgers. His exquisite garden in the New Forest has a sett and the show is not to be missed. Badgers inches from your cosseted nose, no mosquitoes, no worries about them getting your scent and an excellent commentary from Alistair. All for a few pounds. If you are based too far from any woods to ever attract these funky favourites to your patch, book early for the New Forest Badger Watch when you are in the area.

I don't think you would be able to encourage Badgers to site a full blown sett in your garden whatever it's like. If it was their choice of site they'd have built it already. They are also necessarily strict in their requirements. Sandy, diggable soil, a slope principally to assist with the ventilation of the tunnels and chambers and the all-important vegetation cover to hide the area. A healthy sett is pretty big and busy so unless your taste is for a 'Somme' garden, all craters and dirt, it's the last thing you'd want.

Another acquaintance, the pioneer wildlife filmmaker and lifelong Badger lover, Mr Eric Ashby, has built a small 'outlier sett' in his garden, where Badgers visit and stop over for short periods. A hole leading directly to a length of concrete drainpiping some 30 cm in diameter and onto a well drained cement chamber have done the trick. He has a viewing window which is, of course, a real bonus for the dedicated fan or photographer.

So if you are keen, adapt and apply Plan A to a quiet corner and encourage some bracken or similar shrubbery to grow between you and the entrances. You won't be able to see any curious squatters, but they'll feel safer and settle quicker if they can't see you – until you slowly and surreptitiously snip away some of the foliage to improve the view.

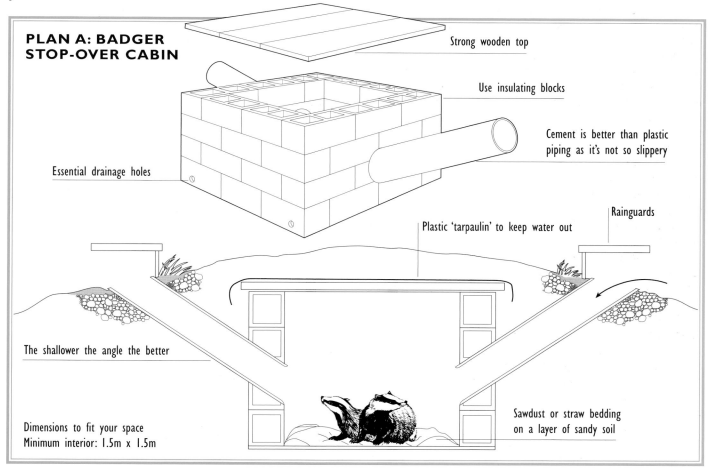

PLAN A: BADGER STOP-OVER CABIN

Strong wooden top

Use insulating blocks

Cement is better than plastic piping as it's not so slippery

Essential drainage holes

Rainguards

Plastic 'tarpaulin' to keep water out

The shallower the angle the better

Sawdust or straw bedding on a layer of sandy soil

Dimensions to fit your space
Minimum interior: 1.5m x 1.5m

GREY SQUIRRELS – VALUE OR VILLAINS?

In 1876 the native Americans Sitting Bull and his war chief Crazy Horse dealt a justified blow to George Armstrong Custer and his misled seventh cavalry at the Little Big Horn in Montana. No one got out alive. In the same year another pair of native Americans collaborated with a Mr T V Brocklehurst at Henbury Park near Macclesfield in Cheshire, and unfortunately both got out alive. They rarely sit but they have driven many crazy, and it's definitely too late for the cavalry. Brocklehurst must rank as one of the foremost eco-traitor because his charges were no less than Grey Squirrels. In the years that followed through to 1929 the list of fellow lunatics is long and distinguished, the releases couldn't have been worse timed, our native Red Squirrels had been in a low ebb owing to their susceptibility to viruses and by the time they started to recover in the 1920s the Greys had entrenched themselves.

Between 1945 and 1955 bounties of one shilling per head were offered, and free cartridges handed out to squirrel hunting clubs; no less than £100,000 was paid out. But the scheme didn't work and by the time I was born it was over.

I once conducted a public opinion poll for national television on the popularity of Grey Squirrels. I asked young and old alike on a number of southern shopping precincts what they thought. To a man and a woman they loved them. They had their own favourite squirrels, they fed them, nursed sick squirrels, named them. We went to a couple of garden centres to find some negativity, but found none. At an arboretum a forester said that yes, they could be a nuisance but they generally weren't worth worrying about.

Grey Squirrels are one of a successful group of arboreal herbivores with more than 200 species world-wide. Their bones are relatively light, their hind limbs heavier and longer and their feet equipped with long curved claws

Left: *"Gosh, I couldn't pinch another peanut... Hmm, a pool of sparkling fresh cyanide. The Joneses are too kind!"*

for greater grip. Their bushy tails are useful balancing aids and the relatively loose skin on their flanks helps them parachute when leaping from tree to tree. They're diurnal, not very keen on high winds, nor heavy rains, but capable of running at speeds of eighteen miles an hour and swimming well. Acorns, beech-mast, nuts of all kinds, shoots, bark, pollen, roots, bulbs, tubers and fungi are the veggie choice; insects and birds' eggs and their young form the opportunistic meat menu. Basically Grey Squirrels are an all round rodent action hero. And they are not slow in the sex stakes either. Males can mate in every month of the year and mature females produce two litters a year in February and June. Between one and eight young, typically three, are born in their tree nest or drey and they are independent between thirteen and sixteen weeks. Lastly, being arboreal, squirrels escape the attentions of all but the luckiest foxes and quickest cats, and are safe in the trees from all but the bravest Tawny Owls, a few Buzzards, and Goshawks, and there aren't many of these hiding behind the maisonettes.

So what do we do with our squirrels? You can loathe them if you like. You could quite legally shoot a few, but that would only tempt others into their vacant territories, and probably make you unpopular with the neighbours. My advice is to learn how to live with them, even enjoy them if you can.

Squirrels are not intelligent, let's get that straight. But what they can do is persist, learn and remember, thus if they feel the need to reach the nuts they will keep trying until they accidentally find a way of doing so and then never forget it. And because they are naturally inquisitive

Above: *American Psycho. The real 'Barstardos' – a bandit legend with a price on his head, the price of peanuts.*

Left: *Give him an inch and he'll chew your nuts off. The painful price of insufficient security, and you'll get a bad back picking up the ruined feeder too.*

they will explore every opportunity in the process, and because they are highly agile and apparently fearless they will leap, scale, or scurry into the most inaccessible places and thus they appear to be intelligent.

Now if you underestimate any of the above aspects they will beat you. You will lose every time and wind up with chewed up bird feeders. I should know. Last summer Nutkin and his pals perfected a new maneouvre to reach my favourite feeder and gnawed it to pieces. It was definitely out of leaping reach and fitted with an effective squirrel guard, so how did they do that? Well, the remarkable 'Barstardos', an athlete of neighbourhood reknown, ran down the balcony handrail, leapt at forty five degrees onto a second feeder, bounced off its squirrel guard and catapaulted himself onto the tray of the aforementioned food dispenser, a total flight distance of maybe 6.5 m. He deserved Air Miles. The guile, the skill, the inventiveness,

the supreme sportiness. An extra metre between the two feeders did the trick. So much for 'Barstardos!'

Commercial squirrel guards or squirrel proof feeders are generally very good if used with common sense. I invest in them because they are generally a lot less ugly than the homemade deterrents. You see, a slippery plastic drainpipe surrounding the supporting pole of a bird table will stop them. My girlfriend's Dad has encased his bird table in a cage that would safely secure Hannibal Lecter. (Actually the squirrels do get in. I've seen them. But I haven't told him!) But bits of drainpipe or cages look so awful I'd rather just feed the rascals and be done with it.

What a good idea. Hazel nuts, peanuts, pine nuts, whole maize, black sunflower seeds and wheat are squirrels' favourites in decreasing order of preference. Splash out on little 'Squidgie'; get him or her some hazelnut kernels at around thirty five pounds for 5 kg, and put them in a birdproof squirrel feeder. Yes, it's true, it has a little shelf for 'Squidgie' to sit on and a flap which will take it five minutes to figure out how to lift up, and none of those nasty dirty garden birds will get in. Yours for fifteen pounds! Sarcasm aside, it's a good idea. It keeps food off the ground, discouraging 'Squidgie's' cousin 'Ratty', keeps it dry and should keep him off the feeders for a while.

Finally, why not let the squirrels that plague you entertain you? Simply test their ingenuity with a succession of different tasks, each rewarded with a bowl of nuts. Ropes, tubes, water jumps, ladders, slippery poles, flaps, traps, flaming hoops, pits with spikes at the bottom? No forget the last two. For ideas watch Indiana Jones and James Bond movies and think secret squirrel instead of secret agent.

TRICKS FOR TREATS
— A SQUIRREL ASSAULT COURSE

The plans below outline a few ideas that might test the squirrels in your garden. Adapt them and combine them with your own cunning conundrums, to almost thwart the rodent agents. Remember that entertainment is the name of this game and the delicate balance between difficulty and impossibility must always tilt to the former. If your clowns don't get paid, they will stop performing. To this end always bait the course well with nuts during the learning process and take care that they're not all pinched by the birds in the meantime. Once the squirrels can overcome your obstacles also take care to ensure that their reward bowl is filled regularly, a few days without treats and they'll get bored and maybe start chewing. Lastly, remember the fun will only result if you prevent the squirrels from 'cheating'. Thus you will have to site your contraptions away from any trees or fences, and of course out of pouncing reach of those real devils — the cats.

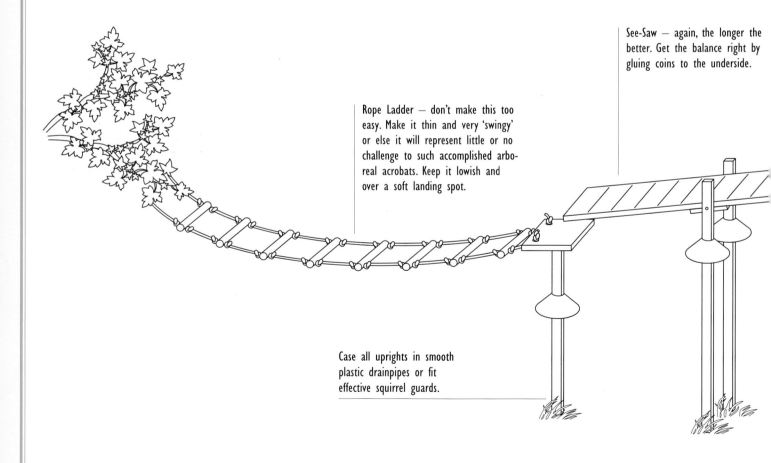

See-Saw — again, the longer the better. Get the balance right by gluing coins to the underside.

Rope Ladder — don't make this too easy. Make it thin and very 'swingy' or else it will represent little or no challenge to such accomplished arboreal acrobats. Keep it lowish and over a soft landing spot.

Case all uprights in smooth plastic drainpipes or fit effective squirrel guards.

Water-jump — this requires very thin sides to prevent sneaky cheating and an ideal tray might be provided by greenhouse gravel trays. As for the jump, 1 metre is easy, 1.5 not too much trouble and 2 easily doable for the squirrel but a little ungainly for you to construct. Whatever, it will amaze and enthrall the kids.

Loop the loop — make from flexible piping, the main difficulty is getting the competitors to go through it. Complicated and ungainly baffles are one way, but filling it with food is another. Cut holes for this purpose.

The Reward — the final leap needs to be flexible so keep the post movable, then you can increase the gap as the athleticism of your squirrels increases.

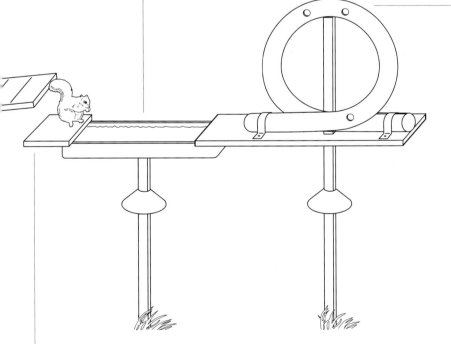

Make the platform large enough to allow a soft landing.

Important — Secure the bowl or else they'll it knock onto the floor to pinch all the prizes.

RATS
PLEASE GIVE THESE RODENTS REFUGE

We should recognize the rat as the most important animate factor in the social, intellectual and artistic development of the western world. This beaten, trapped, poisoned and hated little rodent has influenced the course of civilization and the way we all exist. Without the rat one third of Europe's population would not have been exterminated in the 1340s, and the 'Pied Piper' would have been short of a few children.

Left: Brown Rat – a global champion, one of nature's most adaptable and successful survivors who will triumph in spite of all our prejudice.

The Bubonic or Pneumonic plagues were once a pestilence of some potential. Celebrated highlights include the Great Plague of 1665, which killed 98,000 Londoners; the actions of the Kipchak army who, disgruntled with a boring three-year siege, catapulted plague corpses into the town in the Crimea; and the heroism of Eyam, a tiny suicidal hamlet in England. The last great pandemic swept across Asia in the 1890s, probably killing thirty to forty million a year until about 1917. And you know, it wasn't really the rat that was the vector of all this misery; it was the tiny flea that rode on its back.

The plague apart, rats, still do enormous damage – to our crops. The US loses three per cent, India fifty per cent, and the planet as a whole gives up ten per cent of its grain produce to rats every year. Big, bad and black, is there any hope for the rat?

Not much, because the Black Rat is now a very rare animal in Britain and may even be extinct on the mainland. Of Indian origin, this ship-loving species spread the first plagues when it established here between 1100 and 1200. It's a neat, attractive animal with a tail as long as its body, large eyes and ears and a nifty little nose. The larger, 'rattier' Brown Rat is a more recent invader, only arriving on the British mainland in the 1720s. Another eastern immigrant, it travelled via Russia and Europe and immediately routed Black Rats from most of their haunts. It breeds more rapidly, producing up to six litters a year with about ten young in each, giving a mathematical potential of 350 million descendants from a single pair in three years. Under the oppression that man inflicts upon rats, Brown Rats fare better because of their ability to live outside our homes and workplaces. Black rats always appear in buildings, not in countryside hedgerows, woodlands, sewers or rubbish tips. Thus they make a much easier target for human poisoning campaigns.

However, rats have found some favour since 1850 when Jack Black, the official rat catcher to Queen Victoria, began to breed the albinos and other coloured varieties he removed from his traps. The National Fancy Rat Society continues this interest today. These are mutant forms of Brown Rats, which actually make very good pets. They're not prone to biting or 'going for your throat' when cornered, instead contenting themselves by running up to twenty-seven miles a day in their exercise wheels. This insane statistic belies their 'intelligence' which sees them rapidly solving puzzles, sprinting through mazes and pressing the correct buttons for scientists. In fact they can be even be trained to sniff out TNT and heroin, so it's high time we forgive the Rat his past ills and protect him if he's black and tolerate him if he's brown.

And I do tolerate them, in fact I offer them safe refuge in our roof space and food in the garden. It strikes me as no different from feeding squirrels, both animals are rodents, of a similar size and eat pretty similar things. The poor rat is simply burdened with an out-of-date reputation and I've never been a sucker for poor propaganda. It's also very easy to prevent any in-house visits, which obviously wouldn't be tolerable, and if they chew through the TV aerial cables – so what, I don't want to be a millionaire or give a damn what unpleasantness is abroad in Albert Square. Rats play an important role in our community – that's why they're there in the first place. Prejudice is fuelled by ignorance and intolerance and neither should be acceptable to a rational person. If you can't accept them as interesting or valuable then at least turn a blind eye, and after all if you can't outwit a rodent without killing it – you're in trouble.

A MOUSE IN THE HOUSE

House Mice

The patter of tiny feet, a pause, a little scratch, then a scurry or a nibble, was for hundreds a years the last thing we'd hear before falling asleep, because House Mice shared our houses. They were a part of our lives, so it strikes me as a shame that today we are too readily a party to their deaths. Many people have an irrational fear of mice, normally House Mice. As usual I'm preaching tolerance. I'm not suggesting that you invite the 'Mices' to your dinner parties, just that you don't panic when you see one and dial M for murder courtesy of 'Pest Control'.

Feeding mice is easy – they'll eat almost anything. The one problem is their sex drive. They are remarkably fecund. Females can produce ten litters of between four and eight young a year. That's a maximum of forty extra mouths to feed and its no good thinking that 'Tibbles' will keep them in check, because, contrary to legend and anecdote, cats are not effective at curbing thriving mouse populations. In fact in many urban settings it's the Brown Rat which is this species principal predator. So I admit, living in harmony with House Mice is tricky, but how can you resist their little pink twitching noses, their twinkling whiskers and their audacity? With a trap I expect. Bah!

Wood Mouse

Wood Mice are a different kettle of mice and can be clearly distinguished from House Mice by their far larger ears and eyes and their warm-brown coat. Surprisingly they do not produce the classic musky 'mousey' odour associated with the House Mouse. They are

From top to bottom: *House Mouse – naughty but nice, a city dweller and kitchen burglar if you don't keep a clean kitchen. Wood Mouse – big-eyed, big-eared garden beauty who will sneak in during the winter. Remember – no holes equals no access. Yellow-necked Mouse – bigger, brasher and a lover of garages and outbuildings – a bonus to be enjoyed.*

undoubtedly the most widespread of our small mammals and can be found in any habitat where there is suitable food. Seeds are their principal diet – oak, beech, ash, lime, hawthorn and sycamore are complemented with buds, fungi and a taste for small invertebrates. In late spring and summer, caterpillars, snails and beetles are a common diet supplement. Like so many species of small mammals, the population of Wood Mice fluctuates through an annual cycle. Although they can breed in every month of the year, it is typically between April and September that females produce litters of up to nine young which themselves are able to begin breeding after only seven or eight weeks. Consequently their capacity to respond to any unusual abundance of seeds is phenomenal.

Yellow-necked Mouse

Closely related to, but larger than the Wood Mouse, this species weighs up to 45g (the Wood Mouse is about 25g). It is difficult to distinguish the two in the field but on the cat's 'trophy mat' the Yellow-necked can be seen to have a large patch of orange-yellow fur on its chest. A small streak is present on many Wood Mice but the distinct collar is diagnostic. Yellow-necked Mice can be quite keen to invade houses and if you have a mouse in the house, and live in the south-east or south and west of England, you might just be fortunate enough to be entertaining a Yellow-necked Mouse. Before you wedge that cheese on the bait hook and flex the trap, you may wish to identify the living creature. It would be such a shame to murder one of these wonderful mice.

MAMMAL VIEWING BOXES

We tolerate rats in our loft each winter and feed them alongside the stream in our garden because they play an important role in the community where we live. If they didn't they simply wouldn't be there. We have taken minor steps to prevent them entering the body of the house and grown to ignore their nocturnal scratching and scurrying. As yet they've not managed to chew through the TV cables – big deal if they do. Of course rats will eat anything but corn and maize are our favourites and easy to store as dry foods. Feed in pipes or under cover to keep the pigeons off but do so secretly. Please do not draw these wonderful creatures to the attention of your probably less rational neighbours who might still blame the Spanish for sending that nasty armada or the French for Waterloo. Wood Mice are also regular visitors to our home. We don't often see them indoors but recognize their lesser noises and occasional squeaks. These animals are worth getting to see though. Their huge bat ears, lovely golden coats, pretty white tummies and gleaming black eyes make them an extremely attractive animal subject to entice into view. But they are very nervous and need regular training to make the best of. Small mammal feeding boxes are very easily constructed and placed against a window and best fitted with a low wattage bulb attached to a dimmer switch. Bait them each evening with pet store rodent mix or more enticing delights and, when something is regularly cleaning the plate, gradually begin to increase the level of light. Do it over weeks rather than minutes and be sure to keep the lights of the viewing room off – with any luck this will allow you to see them, without them seeing you. If you keep quiet and keep up the feeding, in the end you'll be rewarded with great views of the more tolerant individuals. House Mice and Bank Voles are other potential visitors. The plan (below) is not precise, merely an idealized guide – feel free to adapt sizes and positions to fit your home. For instance, ours is strapped against a garage window and has two drain pipes as entrances each with a carpet base to allow the rodents to climb up to the chest height box.

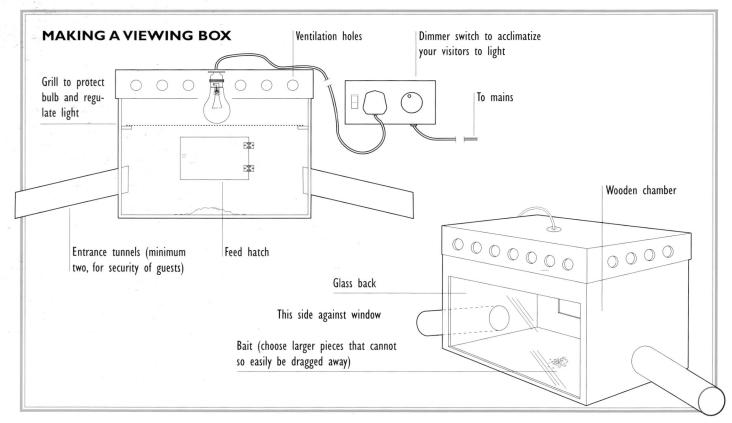

MAKING A VIEWING BOX

Ventilation holes

Dimmer switch to acclimatize your visitors to light

Grill to protect bulb and regulate light

To mains

Entrance tunnels (minimum two, for security of guests)

Feed hatch

Wooden chamber

Glass back

This side against window

Bait (choose larger pieces that cannot so easily be dragged away)

EXOTIC MAMMALS

Left: *This Roe buck is about to lick all the aphids from this rose. Honest.*

Roe Deer

A silhouette shivers in the shade, a patch of brown slowly steps forward and a big black nose shines nearly as brightly as the two large eyes that appear from beyond the brambles. Stealth itself is lurking in your midst. Nimble, quick and shy, the Roe Deer is now very much a part of our suburban fauna – even a curse on the well tended allotment. Their one requirement is cover, thick bushes or brambles in which to hide during the day and secrete their fawns. Unless they're brave and you're sharp-eyed the only sign to betray the nocturnal nibbling culprits will be their distinctive hoof slots in the soil. Check the size of these, 4.5 cm long and 3 cm wide is almost certainly Roe; Fallow and Sika are deer of a different disposition and are far rarer visitors to town gardens. But if the track is as small as 3 cm in length the Muntjac might be your marigold muncher. This tiny dog-like deer was introduced to the UK in the early part of the last century and prospers in many parts of the south and east.

So what can you do if Roe are denuding the dahlias? Give up gardening and enjoy the visitors by getting up early is the first option. Erecting 2.5 m high wire fence all around your garden is more expensive and an eyesore inducing second. If you really prefer begonias to Bambi the problem is apt to become a difficult one. Try tempting them with more tasty alternative foods. Potatoes, turnips, sugar beet or deer pellets might do the trick for a while, but it is equally likely to encourage them to forage further and even focus upon your neighbours' foliage.

Pine Marten

Just two hundred years ago Pine Martens raced around most British woodlands. Now they're sadly restricted to the more remote parts of Scotland, the Lake District and through introductions to isolated pockets in Ayrshire and Yorkshire. A fantastic climber and jumper with a lithe and supple body, the Pine Marten is closely related to the Weasel and Stoat, but its fluffier coat and richer colours make this a real cutie and its taste for non-meaty dishes means it can be tempted into the gardens of the wilder north. I'd go so far as to say that if you live in a Pine Marten's range and you're not feeding it you must be mad.

Pine Martens are about the size of a cat so a good stout feeding platform is required, and, like the Badger, they have a sweet tooth. I've only once seen them well and this was on a 'bird table' attacking a pile of strawberry jam sandwiches. The host assured me that they couldn't get enough and were equally partial to marmalade and treacle. These wonderful animals are making a slow spread south through Scotland, so, if you live in the countryside and near some fairly sizable woodlands or forests keep your eyes open for their characteristic five-toed paw prints and shiny mucus-covered droppings. If you manage to encourage a visitor they may bring the family along at the end of summer which would be fabulous and you might also make a friend for life as they live up to twenty years.

Above: *Simply stunning in the cuddly stakes, and a serious contender for Britain's most beautiful mammals, Pine Martens are in fact fierce predators and normally extremely shy. A lot of patience will be required to get good regular views.*

MORE EXOTIC MAMMALS

Dormice

The Mad Hatter was right. The dullest mammal in Britain is the Dormouse. Despicably dozy, sleeping at least five months of the year, strictly nocturnal and always arboreal, and thus impossible to see, it is, in my opinion, grossly overrated on account of its large twinkling eyes, furred and thus un-rat like tail and extremely, nay stupidly, long whiskers. For me this conservation icon is a very superficial-furry-animal. And the likelihood of it occurring in your garden is next to nil. However, its cousin the Fat or Edible Dormouse, a species allegedly introduced by the Romans as an esteemed delicacy, is not as cute. It is regarded as a non-native invader, but nevertheless might be a long shot as a garden visitor if you live in the Chilterns. Legends persist in naturalists' tales that these creatures like to hibernate in lofts and raid apple stores. Well, since most of us no longer store apples, and as modern houses are mostly impregnable at loft level, I fear that this could now be no more than nostalgic nonsense and the likelihood of you harbouring a plump, bushy-tailed fugitive in the roof-space is equally zero. Just as well – this creature is even duller than its cousin, sleeping for up to seven months. If you ask me they're both best left to conservationists to lose sleep over, which strikes me as an ironic and amusing paradox.

Above and below: *Caught in a brief moment of consciousness* (above), *the not-so-common Common Dormouse in a typical postcard pose. Red and not yet dead* (below), *the Red Squirrel still clings on to a few precarious footholds across southern England.*

Red Squirrels

When I visited the Isle of Wight recently to meet a man who feeds Red Squirrels outside his lounge window I'd forgotten quite how red they actually are. Their coat colour is variable, both between individuals and seasonally, but these animals were virtually glowing. They were glorious, flaming in the sunshine and I'm embarrassed to admit that they made our back-garden Greys look rather dowdy. They also have a reputation for being the shyer of the two species, but they scaled the rope ladders that led them from the trees to the tables and sat munching Hazelnut kernels only a few feet away from us with little concern, accustomed by years of kindness, perhaps.

The relic distribution of these delightful things is a complex affair, with lots of little pockets hanging on away from the main strongholds of Scotland, Northumberland, The Lake District, East Anglia, North Wales, and most of Northern Ireland and Eire. In the south, Jersey, the aforementioned Isle of Wight and Brownsea Island are secure havens. Red Squirrels dwell in coniferous forests where cones, shoots, bark and sap form the bulk of the diet, but peanuts or hazelnuts are an easier treat to supply on your feeding station. Red Squirrels are even more arboreal than Greys so if you wish to lure them out of the branches you'll need to provide a route. Thick, natural, non-nylon rope seems to do the trick and will be easier to erect and maintain than fixed wooden walkways. As ever, the regularity of their reward is the key to your own.

LEGEND OF THE BAT BOX

Left: *A Noctule having hysterics: it's just seen your bat box and can't contain itself. Rather apt, since your bat box is unlikely to contain it!*

Young and expectant eyes gaze up in the dark. The focus of their hope is a small box nailed on a naked face of bricks and the event so desired is that a bat, or better a swarm of bats, should pour out of this little wooden Tardis. The moon rises and the heart sinks. Final score: Cold disappointed child -1 Bats - 0, and I bet it's the same everywhere because, I here boldly postulate that bat boxes in suburbia are a waste of time and effort. Not only have I never seen one used, I've asked nearly every warden on every urban nature reserve that I've visited across the UK in the last couple of years if they have. The result – hundreds of embarrassed 'Nos', with only a damaged handful of exceptions.

And should this surprise us? Not really, because bats have extremely high metabolic rates which they moderate through periods of reduced activity. Basically, they can shut down, by aestivating during the summer and by hibernating in the winter when their insect food is absent. Now, if you are going to become inert you risk becoming vulnerable, not only to predation, but also to the elements. Thus choice of the roost site is critical.

In the seventies we all learned that bats had declined, and we all wanted to do something to help. Rather than nailing

Right: *In your dreams? Probably, because bat boxes in an urban setting do not seem to work. Re-direct your children's enthusiasm into something that does.*

together pieces of pine planking, we should have been lobbying farmers to moderate their use of insecticides. If there are no bats where you live, or only a tiny fraction of their former population, it is far more likely to be a result of diminished or absent food supplies than a shortage of safe roosting sites. So put away your tenons, rips and band saws and pick up your pens and pencil. There are no plans for a bat box in this book. False hopes for you and your children are not on my agenda.

And they are not on the agenda of the Bat Conservation Trust, who produce an excellent bat box leaflet and do not endorse all of my negativity regarding these devices. Tony Hutson of the BCT admits that a single, poorly constructed, leaky wooden box set up in suburbia is not going to be an attractive proposition to even the most wayward bat. From his experience boxes work best where there's plenty of food but no roost sites, such as hazel coppice or coniferous woodlands, and also in areas where large numbers of boxes are erected and well maintained. On this account he suggests that good quality boxes are far more likely to be used if a scheme is implemented to erect a number throughout a community.

The BCT and People's Trust For Endangered Species collected data on the use of bat boxes in 2004 from 12 areas of England, Wales and Ireland. Occupancy levels ranged from 20% to 90%. Wedge-shaped wooden boxes were reported by bat groups to be the most successful type. Bat boxes were found to be used to varying degrees by all but two British species. A few species formed maternity colonies in them, but mostly they were occupied by small groups of males, mating groups and solitary bats.

Tony told me that those ugly woodcrete boxes appear to be far more effective than traditional wooden types, a benefit to bats but a blot on back garden beautification perhaps. The choice is yours.

WHAT'S THERE?

Way past bedtime, aged nine, there was little more exciting than the prospect of borrowing Dad's torch and being allowed to crouch at the bedroom window in the hope of casting some faint light on those creatures which stole across our little lawn in the dark. And also little more less rewarding. A few glimpses of next door's ginger moggie were not really highlights. Eric Ashby, Graham Dangerfield and occasionally Tony Soper were overrun with badgers, foxes, hedgehogs, rats and mice.

Above: Barn Owl pellets – the young naturalist detective can pull them apart to identify the victim.

Chris Packham saw cats and Mrs Slaney putting her milk bottles out. And it's not surprising because it generally takes a long time and quite a bit of patience to successfully introduce nocturnal animals to lights and even then some are impossibly shy. So what's the short-term solution, how can you discover what stalks in your garden after dark without sitting up and not seeing it? Well, in those days when all the technology was going in Neil Armstrong's direction, I came up with a simple plan, here modernised. Visit a garden centre and purchase one or more large, shallow plastic gravel trays of the type used on greenhouse shelves. Purchase the appropriate volume of fine grain sand to fill the aforementioned to their brims. Place the trays in the garden load with the sand and level with a bit of 'four by two'. Moisten to ensure the crumb texture of the grains will receive a thumbprint and remain firm. Place assorted baits on and around the trays, retire indoors, watch football, news or soaps, and sleep.

Leaping into the modern age means replacing Tonto's skills with techno frills. If you bait your garden regularly, eventually something will take advantage, so once you find yourself waking to empty plates introduce a low wattage light, preferably powered through a dimmer switch. Using this, you can gradually increase the illumination, taking care to correlate *lux* with the disappearance of your treats.

Candid Camera

Now, if your garden is relatively secluded or quiet you might find the visitors arrive early in the evening. If not, the mysterious raiders will probably sneak in when you prefer to be snoring. Solution – a camcorder and an auto timer. Night one: set up the camera sighted firmly on the food in its usual place and switch on when you turn in. The tape will run for at least an hour afterwards and you can rewind and fast forward it easily and quickly the next day. Try it a few times. If you get blank lawns, then set an auto timer to switch the camera on an hour after you go to bed, and so on until you find out what is accepting your hospitality and when. Try a range of foods in different sites to determine the exact mammal fauna of the garden. You may only see next door's ginger moggie, but you may be surprised.

Sighting the Evidence

But you don't have to see an animal to know that it's there. Footprints and other signs can precisely betray a presence even in its absence. Feeding signs are frequent and many species have characteristic ways of handling their food so if you study what they leave over you can identify the donor. Pine cones and nuts are nibbled in quite different styles by squirrels and other rodents and pecked by woodpeckers – an artefact of their different definitions and relative strengths.

Even predators handle their prey differently. Mammals such as foxes or Badgers chew feathers from any bird they eat, leaving quills with torn ends. Hawks and falcons pluck the feathers out leaving the ends intact. Indigestible matter such as feathers and bones are also regurgitated in the form of pellets by a great range of avian carnivores, not just by owls and hawks. Crows, gulls, Magpies, even Blackbirds produce pellets and consideration of their content and location should fairly simply identify the producer. The prize in my pellet collection is a tiny white, extremely fragile tablet of fishbones which was left by a Kingfisher on a riverside fencepost. Those produced by larger species, especially owls who swallow their prey whole or in big chunks, can be broken open to reveal all the bones of their victims which also are fairly easily identified.

Least savoury but equally useful are faeces. By taking a look at the colour and shape most can be traced to the creatures that deposited them. My favourite are those produced by Green Woodpeckers. Pale beige and white cylinders about 2-5 cm long, they can be crumbled in the palm of a hand to reveal the dried remains of hundreds of ants – a most satisfying experience and one which always impresses young naturalists but distresses mothers.

COMMON OR GARDEN FOOTPRINTS
– PLUS A FEW SPECIAL SPECIES

The footprints and trails of our common visitors are all easy to discern. You don't need to be much of a Sherlock to deduce what's sneaking around your homes, just get a guide to animal tracks. After a few nights you'll find identifiable spoors and see who's chomping on the chicken or nibbling the nuts. Next door's ginger moggie more than likely! The illustrations on this page are roughly to scale.

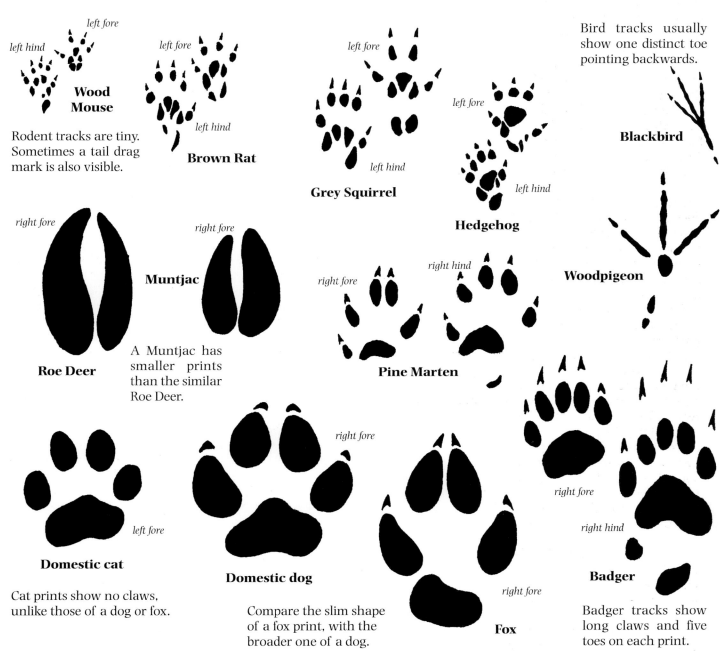

left hind *left fore*
Wood Mouse

Rodent tracks are tiny. Sometimes a tail drag mark is also visible.

left fore *left hind*
Brown Rat

left fore *left hind*
Grey Squirrel

left fore *left hind*
Hedgehog

Bird tracks usually show one distinct toe pointing backwards.

Blackbird

Woodpigeon

right fore
Muntjac

right fore
Roe Deer

A Muntjac has smaller prints than the similar Roe Deer.

right fore *right hind*
Pine Marten

left fore
Domestic cat

Cat prints show no claws, unlike those of a dog or fox.

right fore
Domestic dog

Compare the slim shape of a fox print, with the broader one of a dog.

right fore
Fox

right fore *right hind*
Badger

Badger tracks show long claws and five toes on each print.

INVERTEBRATES

THE RISE OF THE MINIBEAST

When I was four, sometimes all I needed was a matchbox with a few holes punched in the top. My mother typically used the outside tine of a table fork for this and sometimes the sweet-smelling, paper-covered pine would splinter and I'd have to wait for another box to empty. Sometimes she'd have the patience to swap all the matches into the damaged carton and let me have the other. As you can tell, detail was important to me – that's because I was a young entomologist. For my fifth and maybe my best ever birthday I received the *Observers' Book of Common Insects and Spiders*. I still have it. The dustjacket is fairly intact, it smells more like a book than most books do these days, and I can still remember every illustration, even lines from the poetry that it included. Today I'd say that it appears as a charming but rather old-fashioned book, not like this one! But in the hands of a five-year-old in the year that England won the World Cup it was brilliant. You see, it was a grown-ups' insect book, a veritable treatise with diagrams and scientific names. While ladybirds continued to fascinate me, the books by the same name were consigned to the baby-book-bin, and I rose to the challenge of recognizing a *Chrysopa carnea* when I found one.

Now you may surmise that I was precocious little swot, but if that's the case, I've met lots more. Children whose single-minded interest leads them to focus in such an obsessive way that their narrow field of knowledge rivals that of many adults. That's why I don't like 'minibeasts'. It's a naff catch phrase, a dumbing down which isn't necessary. You don't, in my opinion, need to 'sell' ladybirds and stag beetles to children. What could sell itself better than a beautiful little red beetle with countable spots, that tickles as it runs up your finger to hesitate thrice before it wafts away like a fairy. Or than the armoured robo-creature with massive horns and attitude enough to threaten giants like five-year-olds. Maybe I'm being pedantic, but I still get a bigger buzz when some kid wanders up and asks me what I think of his or her *Dytiscus* than when another whines on about the 'feelers' on their 'creepy-crawly'. They are antennae and it's an invertebrate and kids like knowing more than us. Please don't offend them.

But now I must eat some humble pie, because the best book I've ever had about finding, catching and housing invertebrates was written by Roma Oxford and published by the Yorkshire Wildlife Trust. Yorkshire Electricity very kindly sponsored it and it's called: *Minibeast Magic* (ouch!). It has no rival; no more serious tome, is, or could be as useful. It's wonderfully practical and resourceful. It's also delightfully illustrated. Frankly, if you or your family have an iota of interest in minibeasts (argggghhh) then get hold of this book. There, it hasn't got shiny red elytra with twin or other spots so I've given it a hard sell.

Wherever you live and whatever your garden is like, it will have hundreds, if not thousands, if not tens of thousands of invertebrates living in it. Insects, Spiders, Crustaceans, Molluscs, Millipedes, Centipedes, and Annelids, not to mention Protozoans, Rotifers, and

Right: *'The diversity of form and function in common invertebrate life should provide no end of wonder for juvenile humans'.*
A. J. C. Feggit,
Entomologist and Sociologist (imaginary)

Nematodes. The vast majority of these life forms are microscopic and we'll all live our lives without ever seeing them or knowing their names, let alone understanding how they keep our gardens going in the great scheme of things. It's the bigger terrestrial invertebrates which we can more easily get to know or know better, and either process is fascinating because these are the creatures that could not be less human, more alien than any others on earth. Look at a snail winding up a stem, what could be more different than you in structure? Consider a beetle scuttling beneath the bark, what can it be seeing, sensing, what is its life like? And the dragonfly hanging on sparkling wings, what does it see, what does it feel as it arcs skywards to snatch a fly? You see, it's impossible but we have to try, and when we fail we must just wonder.

Compared with the birds and mammals that we love so much, there is a truly awesome diversity of invertebrate life on, under or just beyond our doorsteps. To ignore it is a waste, to harm it is ignorant, and to exterminate it dangerous. If you do one thing this summer, pull on some old jeans and a jumper, and go and lie in the garden flat out, face down and peer about until you discover a 'new' species. Play Darwin, pretend to be Attenborough, make up a name for it, call it *Fastcrawlerii smithus*. Please don't miss out on the magic of minibeasts (or invertebrates, as they really are).

Over the next few spreads this book covers just a few of these animals. Not all are 'popular', a few are much maligned, some loathed. In contrast, others are lauded and loved, celebrated in art and literature, endowed with almost spiritual significance. Whatever, they are creatures that try to live with us and therefore deserve a break.

Above: *Shop for or manufacture soft muslin nets. Cheap coarse nylon newsagent specials will soon destroy or dismember any bugs or butterflies.*

Taking a closer look

Direct observation is always the best way of learning about the behaviour of any animal, watching from a non-intrusive distance. But this can be very difficult with small creatures, especially invertebrates; after a few seconds of manic scuttling, they disappear under a leaf or into a crevice never to be seen again. So to get to grips with the antics of ants, the behaviour of beetles or the habits of

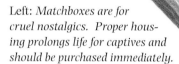

Left: *The perfect birthday treat – a good quality robust glass hand lens that will focus fresh eyes upon a superior detail than toyshop plastic items.*

Left: *Matchboxes are for cruel nostalgics. Proper housing prolongs life for captives and should be purchased immediately.*

harvestmen, it is best to capture them and make observations over a few hours or days in a suitable vivarium. Trained, gentle and fearless fingers can be very good for carefully collecting many robust species – Stag Beetles, Cockchafers, large snails, slugs or earthworms. But others are more tricky. Have you ever tried picking up a centipede?

Pooters

Most simply a tablespoon and a soft watercolour paintbrush make a fine combination, the brush for chivvying or teasing from cracks and the spoon as the carrier. However, for fast-moving or very small animals the humble pooter is the best tool. These suction traps can be bought from entomological suppliers, or easily constructed at home.

A few simple guidelines: no ants, nothing else likes their formic acid which they will undoubtedly discharge upon pooting; no slugs, everything small gets stuck in their slime; no spiders in mixed bags, they'll eat everything else; don't overcrowd your pooter, empty it regularly, transferring by paintbrush those animals you intend to keep, and always suck gently, many creatures are fragile, and the pinging of a dizzy beetle richocheting around your pooter is not acceptable.

Many other invertebrate species are normally invisible to us so 'trapping' will increase the scope of your collecting. Dig out your partner's or parents' umbrella or better still get hold of an intact old one! Find a large stick and proceed beneath the low boughs of an oak. Hold the 'brolly upside down by its spike over your head and gently tap the overhanging branches. A myriad bugs, beetles, caterpillars and spiders will tumble down and you can paintbrush or poot them out accordingly.

Pit-fall traps

Pit-fall traps are great for catching nocturnal species. Thoroughly clean a 2-litre clear plastic soft drinks bottle, dry it and then cut around its sides about 15-20 cm from the base and again 2 cm below the neck. Discard the middle tube, invert the top and fit it snuggly into the cup base. Staple the two together with four paper staples, bury it in the ground so that the lip is flush with the soil's surface and cover with a loose fitting piece of bark.

Check for captives at least daily and remove from the ground when not in use.

The young naturalist's favourite method of housing insects – the jam-jar – might be better known as the torture chamber. A few holes punched in its lid are not enough for adequate ventilation. Always replace with a mesh cover; a square of fabric cut from old tights held in place with an elastic band is an improvement, but a clear plastic sweet jar or a wider topped tank will be more successful in terms of climate control. Entomological suppliers provide tanks, tubs or boxes for adults and larvae of all kinds of invertebrate, so if you're serious it's worth the spend.

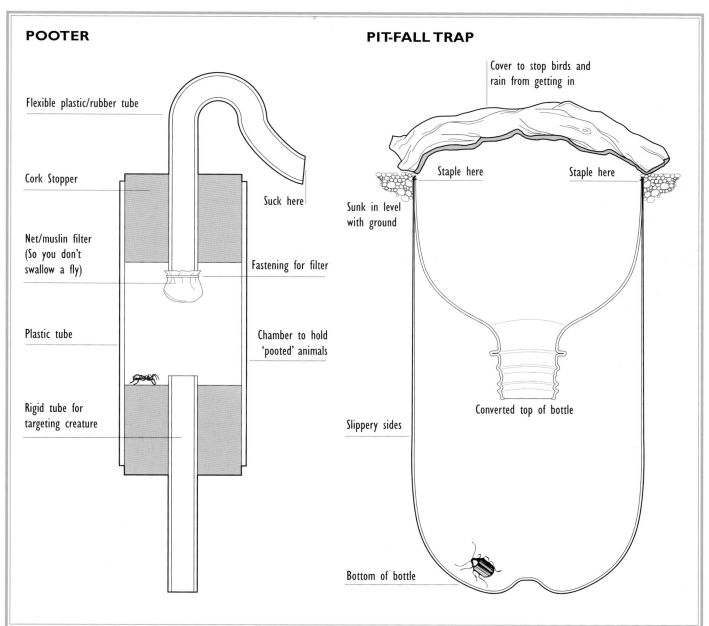

POOTER

Flexible plastic/rubber tube

Cork Stopper

Net/muslin filter
(So you don't
swallow a fly)

Plastic tube

Rigid tube for
targeting creature

Suck here

Fastening for filter

Chamber to hold
'pooted' animals

PIT-FALL TRAP

Cover to stop birds and
rain from getting in

Staple here   Staple here

Sunk in level
with ground

Slippery sides

Converted top of bottle

Bottom of bottle

BUTTERFLIES
WHY SHEER WONDER DOESN'T NEED A NAME

On the page opposite are eight butterflies with which I hope you are largely familiar, if not by name then by sight, as these are all the species that are almost guaranteed as garden visitors. However, for me, butterflies are a perfect example of a group of animals that encourage both complacency and distracted obsession with nomenclature.

You see, whilst it is essential to be able to name something to effectively communicate, to become preoccupied with recognition and naming is a tragic waste of a naturalist's interest, an interest which is hopefully fuelled by the wonder of the thing he or she observes. Peacock or Comma, Brimstone or Orange Tip – so what? Consider those fragile planes of dusty tissue, veins so delicate – coloured so beautifully, those wings that flutter so crazily to keep these things airborne. Imagine those eyes – nearly half a head – each complex containing thousands of lenses. What do they see? How do they see? Do they see a thousand little different views or build all the images into one composite picture? And what about that mouth? No lips, no teeth, just a long coiled tongue – a watch spring with a nectar seeking tip – and the antennae, those two clubs, what do they sense? We can only imagine. And that's the key – get close to a butterfly, hold your breath, watch your shadow, creep in until your nose is ticklingly close and then look at it as you did all

Above, top left: Holly Blue female in repose, perhaps the daintiest darling. Left: Small Copper, glimmering glitz that's definitely not as common. Above: Painted Lady, a migrant from southern summers for whom Buddleia is a veritable magnet.

those years ago as a child. Don't ask its name, just ask questions you can't answer, and be in awe.

The butterfly bush

Buddleia is an easy to grow and prolific garden plant and is always a draw for many species of butterfly, including including all the Vannessids, the browns and the whites, not to mention a host of moths, flies, bees and wasps. Rotting fruit is also popular, especially in the autumn, so if you're orchardless try some Cox's apples, carved open and left in a sunny spot on the lawn. If no butterflies show up, at least my friends the wasps will have a feast.

Many species of animal and plant have different requirements throughout their lives, not just those that metamorphose such as butterflies. Nevertheless, careful consideration will need to be applied to cater for all stages, something that is often impossible on a garden-sized reserve. This is certainly the case for many butterflies particularly those woodland or grassland species that require maturity or miles of open space to prosper. Fortunately, the adult stages rarely refuse nectar so Buddleia will be a welcome refreshment centre.

COMMA

The ragged wings are an effective camouflage when the Comma is at rest. This species has become more common in the last ten years. They always strike me as a little more cautious than Small Tortoiseshells when you are stalking them on their autumn favourites, Michaelmas Daisies.

SMALL TORTOISESHELL

Small Tortoiseshells overwinter as adults here in the UK, typically hanging upside down in dry roofs, garages or sheds, emerging in March. They have seriously declined in recent years. Their rich orange jerkins are nothing to be sneezed at, especially when a gang get going on a suitably nectarful clump.

WHITES

The Whites are blighted with 'pest' status and discourtesy, being overlooked as obvious, common and plain. But for myself the Cuckoo is a poor harbinger of spring, compared with the flaming, sulphurous wings of a male Brimstone (top) bouncing across suburbia, setting March ablaze with simple colour. Large and Small Whites (middle) have larvae that nourish themselves upon cabbages and their allies, but a little hole here and there is a small price to pay for a garden full of these aerial blossoms, fluttering prettily from the vegetable patch to the patio. Green-veined Whites are more partial to Charlock and Rape, so they're someone else's problem. Orange Tips (bottom) are simply beautiful, a colour-by-numbers painting set from a six year old's fairytale.

PEACOCK

Peacock butterflies have two prominent 'eyes' on their forewings, similar to those that emblazon the tail feathers of the Peacock itself. This is another reason to pay only passing attention to the biological naming process. It is almost totally devoid of humour and imagination.

RED ADMIRAL

With its broad scarlet ribbons and thick velvety body, the Red Admiral is a favourite summer migrant to the UK, having escaped the fierce Mediterranean sun. Individual insects may frequent the same flowers at the same time each day before flying off to roost in a tree for the night.

SPECKLED WOOD

Speckled Woods are pretty dowdy but terribly exciting because they actually fight for the sunspots in glades and clearings. Males will repeatedly rise in the twinkling duels, jostling with each other until somehow one of them decides who has won. Whilst the victor settles in the sun, the loser languishes in the shade, out of heat and out of favour with any passing females.

CATERPILLARS

Left: *The banded brigade in action: Cinnabar larvae gnawing Ragwort into a stump. When it's all chewed out they'll troll off to the next.*

It may seem perverse to you, but there is something therapeutic about a chunky caterpillar marching up ones finger. Perhaps it's the rhythmic massage of its pairs of sticky feet; perhaps it's the tickle of its coat of fluffy hairs; or merely the cheerful disposition of the little wandering larvae. Or perhaps I'm mad. But caterpillars do have an appeal, they have potential, they are going to turn into something completely new, and many are brilliant marked with stripes, spots and bands of colour, or bedecked with flamboyant tufts of hair or thick minky coats. From punk rock to Ascot, there's always a little caterpillar fashion to be seen. Others, of course, are masters of disguise, pieces of leaf, bark, strips of twig or even bird droppings. Some are solitary, some unite to build webs, or race about in lines. Fat, thin, short and long, they've all evolved strategies to help them survive whilst they achieve their one task – to eat like crazy and pupate. Favourites include the groovy stripey Lackey moth caterpillars which race up and down fruit trees in midsummer. How many of these poor devils did I stew in stinking hot jam jars as a child? There are better ways of keeping caterpillars and good ventilation is one essential, so find a large tub and use black nylon mesh to secure it, or invest in a proper larval rearing cage from a specialist supplier. The Alder Moth caterpillar is at first sight a bird dropping, a neat coil of washy white and brown and then, after a moult becomes one of the real posers of the larval league, black with conspicuous bands of yellow, each leading to a weird paddle shaped hair. But best of all, and every child's dream discovery, is the Elephant Hawk Moth caterpillar. Okay it's beige, but it's big, as thick as your finger and adorned with glaring false eye spots above its humble head. In a cupped hand you can even feel its strength as it thrashes and flicks, trying to offer defense against its captor. And best of all, when you watch them eating their favoured Rosebay Willowherb, you can see the leaf disappearing, slice after slice into their little jaws. Later they produce droppings which are relatively massive and a great source of amusement to their young captors.

Left: *Frankly bizarre, the Eyed Hawk Moth larva displays an extraordinary design for what is essentially an eating machine, a growth stage whose vulnerability has taxed evolution and produced a brilliant array of adaptations.*

COMMA

Another bird dropping mimic is the Comma larva. Principally black, it is strongly banded and barred with orangy brown and has an assortment of similarly coloured hairy spines, with the exception of the top rear half of its body which is splodged with white. In a six-week life, these caterpillars can reach up to 3.5cms long and are generally found on nettles, hops, elms or willows. June and August are their peak times of appearance and the southern half of England and Wales their haunts.

PEACOCK

The Peacock caterpillar is a real black beauty which can reach up to 4.5cms in elongated length. Between its tufty spines it is finely spotted with white and has yellowish brown pro-legs, those being the four pairs of sticky footed limbs that sprout from the rear part of the body. These larvae live in a white silken web for up to a month before they disperse to pupate and, like many of the other Vanessids, are Stinging Nettle specialists. Late May and June all over the U.K. with the exception of northern Scotland. Watch your fingers if you worry about nettle rash. Red Admiral larvae actually occur in several colour forms. Dark grayish black with black prickly spines ringed at their bases with reddish brown and a band of yellow patches down the side, or pale greenish grey, or yellowy brown with pale spines. Whatever, the head is always black and they invariably occur singly on Nettles, occasionally on Hops. They pupate shortly after reaching a maximum length of 3.5cms and typically hide by rolling leaves around them.

BRIMSTONE

For about a month the caterpillar of the Brimstone is the ugly duckling to the beautiful swan of the adult insect. But then camouflage is its objective, and it achieves this by being yellowish green below and a peculiar, almost day-glo glossy turquoise green above a neat white line which runs down each side of its body. Its head is green too, and it is very finely dusted with black spots all over. During May a trained eye can spot these caterpillars resting on the midrib of Buckthorn or Alder Buckthorn leaves where their counter-shading gives them the appearance of a shadow. They reach just over 3cms before they pupate, usually in early July, and the chrysalis appears incredibly similar to the folded leaf of the food plant.

SPECKLED WOOD

The Speckled Wood's larvae has a bluish-green head which precedes a yellowish-green body with a white bordered, dark green stripe running down its back. The skin is covered with minute white warts, each giving rise to short grey silky hairs. Ask yourself, did I really need to know this? I am asking myself, did I really need to tell you? It has two whitish points at the tail and is almost impossible to spot when resting amongst the grasses on which it feeds. May is the peak month for the first brood, whilst the second may overwinter in a tussock whilst still small and complete their growth the following spring. Common and widespread and up to 2.5cms long, if you find one I'll give you a pound!

GARDEN TIGER

No rewards for Garden Tiger caterpillars which are fairly regular stars of children's palms and altogether more attractive than the 'greenies' above. 'Woolly bears', as they are appropriately known, grow up to 6cms long, are chestnut brown/black and covered in a rich pelage of black and rich reddish hairs. The spiracles, or breathing tube openings, are bright white and the head shiny black. They'll eat almost anything; nettles, docks, any weeds they can find. The larvae hibernate whilst tiny and are only encountered when they emerge to feed the following spring, or when they flagrantly sun themselves on summer mornings.

PALE TUSSOCK

Pale Tussock caterpillars are the real glamour pusses of the larval league. Quite fabulous, even flashy, with their ostentatious brushes of yellow, black and red hairs. When disturbed they curl up and reveal black bands on their back to warn any potential predator that they will be unsavory in the extreme when it comes to a snack. Birch, Oak, Hazel and Elm are food plants and the caterpillars munch between July and September. Monsters can reach 4cms and were once a pest of hops.
.

CINNABAR MOTH

Cinnabar caterpillars should require no introduction or description. These bright yellow and black banded larvae swarm over ragworts in midsummer and can be found everywhere from meadows to roadsides to wastelands. So obviously aposomatic — that is, endowed with bright colouration to warn anything hungry to go elsewhere, I can only imagine these things must be highly distasteful. I have never tried one, but I bet some of you have because these are amongst any young naturalist's top ten jam jar fillers and you know how curious kids can be.

ELEPHANT HAWK MOTH

It starts yellowish white with a green tinged head and a black horn. It ends up brownish grey, marked with a black and ochre spots and a series of increasingly large pink tinged eyes. It ends up 10cms long. It is the wonderful caterpillar of the Elephant Hawk Moth and whilst Rosebay Willowherb is its favoured natural diet, Fuschias might lure them into your garden. They feed at night and play the larval Godzilla in July and August. Of course, they are completely harmless and can be handled without any problems. It is said that they like to sun themselves around four o'clock, but it's more likely that you'll have to grub about to find one. Well worth the search — one of Britain's super bugs.

MOTHS
NO CANDLES NEEDED TO SEE THE LIGHT

Crazed satellites crashing, burning up in arcs and buzzing and ending with a terminal thud and a dazed crawl into a dark corner. A myriad sparks whirring, as electrons around an atom, blinded and confused, tiny flies and midges with no names make up the firework crowd that the meteoric moths pass through as they gravitate into the trap. A mercury vapour lamp moth trap is the entomologist's master stroke. We place ours in an open area, switch it on at dusk, and its bright light immediately begins drawing moths, many from several kilometres away. They fly in, tumble into the funnel and hide in the bucket below, seeking shelter under the cups of cardboard egg cartons. By night it's the hottest disco in town, after sunrise the hangovers have set in and all is still. The anticipation is palpable. We wake before the alarm, drawn to the magic box to see what secrets it holds. The perspex cowl is lifted off and each egg tray examined; those 'special' species and a multitude of unknowns are coaxed with a paintbrush into plastic tubs ready for identification. The trophies are soon in a tray on the bottom of Mummy's bed and she is rudely awakened to find a Buff Tip or Poplar Hawk Moth centimetres from her moth-shocked nose.

These traps are ridiculously overpriced, the single most expensive piece of any naturalist's kit, but worth every penny. Buy, beg, steal or borrow one, and you'll see what I mean.

If not, build your own, using plastic tubs and bottles. Construct a funnel and holding chamber and place it under any garden light, the brighter the better. To increase its luminous appeal you can set the contraption on a white sheet to maximize the size of the beacon.

Generally, however, a more effective alternative to the MV trap is sugaring. This lure has been used since the Victorian age and recipes have three

Above: *Don't tell me that we've no exotics, Eyed Hawk Moth showing off its 'eyes' and looking totally tropical.*

essential ingredients; a sweetener, an aromatic attractant and some alcohol, intended to stupefy the moths. Try simmering real ale with brown sugar and molasses for about ten minutes. When the brew is cold add some rum or red wine and experiment with flavourings such as mashed bananas or apples. Pour the concoction into a bowl and leave a knotted towel or plaited cotton sheet to soak in it all day. Come the evening peg or tie it on to a tree, fence, wall or washing line at chest height and paint some of the remaining mixture onto any nearby tree trunks or fence posts. Check with a torch throughout the night. I tried sugaring several times as a child and not a single moth showed. Then a few years ago I joined a party of lepidopterists for a night in the New Forest, and clouds of insects appeared. I think my mum had been a bit mean with the rum.

Left: *Home-made moth traps will focus the locals but fail to draw in animals from any great distance. I'm afraid that if you catch the 'mothing' bug you'll have to spend out.*

1 WHITE ERMINE

The White Ermine moth flies from late May until July with an occasional second generation in the autumn. This moth is a beautiful creamy white, variably spotted with dark chestnut and have the rear of their abdomen coloured yellow, something that is invisible when they are at rest. It can be found on walls, fences and trees but is normally noticed attending lights of all kinds. For me it's the 'Hamster' of the moth world, small, furry, quiet and sleepy.

2 HEART AND DART

Oh dear, the Heart and Dart. Hopeless and Dreary would be a better name if it weren't for the inconspicuous spots on the forewings of this moth which are allegedly heart and dart shaped. If a little brown moth that's been blown to bits crashes on your hall carpet to die anytime between the beginning of May and mid-August, it will almost certainly be one of these.

3 HERALD

The Herald is one of the last moths of the season. It flies from late July into November and again after hibernation when it 'heralds' spring, emerging in March and flying until June. Woodlands and gardens are its haunts and it is common everywhere except Scotland. Ivy blossom, ripe blackberries and light take its fancy, although you may find it hung up in sheds, barns, or the loft where it overwinters.

4 BRIMSTONE MOTH

In the south adult Brimstone moths are on the wing from April through to October, while in the north the principal flight time is during June and July. They can be found all over the UK, including most of the Scottish islands. They fly at dusk and are always drawn to lights, often in great numbers.

5 CINNABAR MOTH

The Cinnabar Moth, a real dapper flapper, has vermilion hindwings and red spotted velvety grey forewings. Take care not to confuse this species with the day-flying burnet moths, which are similarly hued.

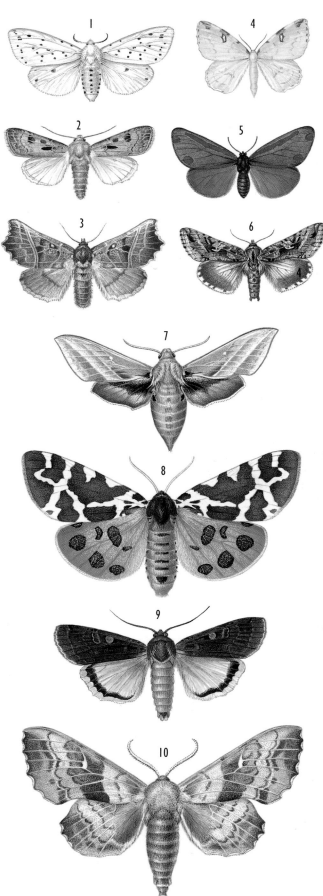

6 SILVER Y

Guess what the Silver Y has on its forewing? These are day flying summer visitors that arrive from late spring onwards and by late summer, when a British generation emerges, they can be extremely common. At rest the fragmented patterning and sculptured abdomen make this moth a triumph of concealment.

7 ELEPHANT HAWK MOTH

Both honeysuckle and rhododendron are said to attract Elephant Hawk Moths when they are on the wing between May and July. Freshly emerged from the pupae and in prime condition they are contenders for the most beautiful of the British moths.

8 GARDEN TIGER

These bright, spotty and funky moths are very variable in colour and were once selectively bred by collectors to produce even more extreme variations. They are widespread and drawn to lights during July and August.

9 LARGE YELLOW UNDERWING

If anyone says, 'there's a whacking great moth going crazy in my kitchen/conservatory/toilet', tell them immediately that it's a Large Yellow Underwing. When they say, 'it hasn't got yellow under its wings', tell them it is actually difficult to see the rich ochre on the hindwings, because it's quite invisible at rest, and their wings beat too fast to see it in flight. Between July and September these moths are common and often vast numbers of migrants join us from the continent too.

10 POPLAR HAWK MOTH

Britain has nine resident and eight migrant hawk moths on its list and in terms of size they are certainly our most exciting species. The Poplar Hawk Moth is one of the most widely distributed and a moth which comes readily to light sources between May and July. At rest its pale brown, striped silvery grey wings act as perfect camouflage on any light bark or leaf debris. But if threatened it will jerk its forewings to reveal to dark crimson splashes on its underwings.

SPIDERS

Above: *Who'd choose to be a fly upon re-incarnation? Spiders are super predators. Some use sticky webs, some chase and pounce, others jump. Some even parachute around the countryside and many are extremely beautiful. Don't just spare them, spare them some time.*

I live with arachnophobia nearly everyday of the year. Not me, of course, I've liked spiders all my life, but my girlfriend is rather severely afflicted. Now, in a spider-less environment this wouldn't present a problem, but very few such places exist. As a group the Arachnids have colonised virtually the entire globe, and our houses and gardens are no exception. At home we do little more to attract these creatures than leave our windows open, but this is invitation enough to a rich resource for foraging and breeding, and some species have made a niche for themselves behind the TV.

There are more than 80,000 species of spider worldwide, but fewer than 25 are known to be poisonous to humans and only a non-literal handful can be described as aggressive. None of the 350 larger species found in Britain fall into this category. I've been bitten by two of our resident spiders and said 'ouch'. Nothing more happened. All spiders are venomous. Being fragile, they use toxins rather than brawn to subdue their prey, but their venoms have evolved specifically to immobolise or kill that prey. Because none eat humans, few can do us any harm. They are a fabulously diverse group of animals of

which many are extremely beautiful and have fascinating life histories, so it is a pity that they are so widely vilified. Apparently it's their fast, scuttling movement, or their long, hairy legs (which also accounts for the reasons many people don't like Manchester United I suppose). Whatever you think of them, they are at – or near – the top of the invertebrate food chain, and thus, if you are not a fan of flies and most other things creeping and crawling, they will prove to be a valuable asset to your house or garden. There are many species of birds who are partial to spiders and a healthy population will prove a bonus to your Dunnocks, Robins, thrushes and Wrens. So, all in all, it's worth encouraging spiders with patches of overgrown garden and a ban on insecticides. You can't have all of those pretty predators without their multi-legged prey.

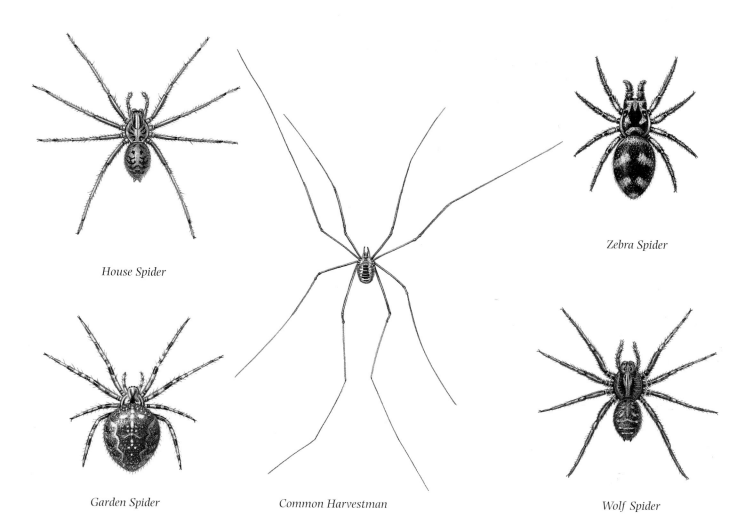

House Spider

Garden Spider

Common Harvestman

Zebra Spider

Wolf Spider

HOUSE SPIDER

I read some time ago that our common House Spider was the fastest spider in the world, able to sprint at up to four metres per second. It is a pursuit predator capable of making a meal from almost any invertebrate beneath your bookcase. The smaller males appear in early summer before giving way to the larger females, which mature in the autumn and can live for up to four years. Both are highly variable in colour, ranging from yellowish through to chocolate-brown. They are one of our largest spiders but like so many things their actual size is always exaggerated!

GARDEN SPIDER

Fat and fertile, hanging like a rich mouldy grape in the centre of her web feasting on the last of the season's fare, the female Garden Spider will prosper until the first hard frost cracks her plump body. September is her prime time, having long ago mated and deposited her batch of eggs ready to hatch in the spring. Patterned with bands and patches of ochres and reds, freckled with spots of chestnut and black and studded with diamonds of white she moults into a final coat of great finery, always reminding me of Henry VIII's brocaded waistcoats.

ZEBRA SPIDER

The black-and-white Zebra Spider can be commonly found on house walls, larger rockeries or occasionally on the trunks of mature trees. It is one of over four thousand jumping spiders and has exceptionally acute vision. Zebra Spiders stalk their prey to within a few centimetres and then leap onto it, readily capturing anything their own size. Males have an elaborate courtship dance which they perform for the female, but can be induced to dance with themselves if you place a mirror in front of them.

WOLF SPIDER

Wolf Spiders are, as their name suggests, large, robust predatory animals which roam over drier grassy areas at night. They don't howl! But they do excavate dens in which they secrete their white egg sacs and in which they remain until those eggs hatch. Males are smaller than females and both are active throughout the year.

COMMON HARVESTMAN

Leiobunum rotundum is probably our most common and widespread harvestman. It can be found in virtually any habitat between mid-summer and late autumn and, whilst males are smaller and reddish brown, the females are twice their size and generally lighter brown or beige with dark chestnut bars, spots and bands. Harvestmen are easily distinguished from most other spiders because their body parts are fused into one central oval node and they have absurdly long legs.

FLIES AND BEES

Left: *A great pretender. This hoverfly is using the warning coloration of the wasp to fool potential predators into thinking it has a sting, when of course it hasn't. A common trick among such orders of insecta.*

Iam sure you have the general gist by now. I am a man who, in an almost Jainist manner, respects all animal life and quite literally wouldn't hurt a fly. I know this may be going too far for even the most dedicated naturalist, but then how many of us in some unoccupied moment have not focused on the antics of a group of houseflies gyrating like tiny scorched satellites about the room light. This electric sun and its cording becomes their focus of their activity as they speed senselessly on strict isometric courses, tracing triangles, squares and pentagons against the stark desert of the ceiling. At the apex of each line they imperceptibly pause before an extraordinary acceleration whips them through another phase of their insane journey. Occasionally one hangs up its wings on the lamp shade for a 'time out'. Another may join the party and be relentlessly attacked, the combatants combining magnetically and vanishing in a Kamekazi plummet to the rug miles below. A few seconds later, one resumes its course and so, hour after hour, this dainty display continues. More than once I have been relaxed by the tiny dancers and wished I was among them blasting my tiny airframe about that tatty old lampshade without a thought in my ephemeral little mind.

These darting cadets are males of the Lesser Housefly, and if spared for a few hours, or even indefinitely from chemical assault, their behaviour is free to enjoy from the comfort of your armchair. I appreciate that such charity maybe difficult because these animals are universally loathed. Their ability to spread diseases, including such treats as typhoid, cholera and dysentry has not made them many friends. Neither are their breeding habits very appealing to humans. Dung, sewage, preferably decaying, and rotting foods or flesh are the favourite environment in which houseflies abandon their eggs. On hatching, their larvae frolic in the ferment and grow rapidly so that in only a few days they are treading this stuff over your tables, food and forearms. Unsavoury maybe, but successful certainly, because, along with a few other 'pests, houseflies have spread the world over, amusing some and poisoning others. I can stop these animals from soiling my foodstuffs for a few pence, so in order to enjoy their madcap fly-pasts I'll spare them all summer long. For me they are far more entertaining than those busybodies that buzz amongst the Pegonias.

Above: *The Honey Bee, probably everybody's favourite non-native with a sting. Strange how we forget fear for the price of some sweet stuff, but then it is a pollinator* par excellence *and so mild mannered that such violent eventualities are very rare.*

ROBBER FLY

Asilus crabroniformis is one of Britain's most impressive flies, a quite imposing, even fearsome creature, which is completely harmless to humans. Not so to insects, which it seizes in a short capture dart from its perch on twigs or stones. Grasshoppers, beetles, bees and wasps are all despatched and sucked dry. At rest its pose suggests that of a crouching cat, long legs folded for instant speed. Tiger Beetles and various hunting wasps get the better of them.

HOVERFLY

The *Volucella* genus of hoverflies are speedy and splendid, large, quite striking and obviously harmless. *V. zonaria* was once quite a prize for fly collectors, but recently has become common in the south and can be seen feeding on late summer blossoms, particularly bramble and ivy. However, it's actually the larvae which are most impressive — they inhabit the interiors of wasps', and bees' nests. Here they roam about unmolested until they squeeze inside a cell with a developing grub and excite it to secrete its excremental juices which they promptly eat. Now that's what I call wildlife.

HOUSE FLY

There are more than 450 species of this family of flies The true Housefly *Musca domestica* has a yellowy buff abdomen and various peculiar details in the veins of the wings. Females lay about nine hundred eggs and these can hatch in just eight hours and the larvae can mature and pupate in just under forty-eight. The main brood emerges in June or July and continues until September. As you depress the aerosol button, remember that if there wasn't a job for flies to do they wouldn't be there.

Robber fly

Hoverfly

House fly

Honey Bee

Bumblebee

HONEY BEE

There is not a better known insect on Earth, with a library of books available on this species' behaviour, ecology, physiology and management. The three castes, queen, drone and worker, are easily distinguished, although it is only the worker that is typically encountered. A good colony can have more than fifty thousand bees, all of them workers, and these rarely live more than a few weeks in a busy summer season. During the winter the drones are ejected because they don't do anything and the colony settles down to rest, feeding on the stored pollen and honey. Isn't it amazing how we all love 'busy bee' because it gives us honey, yet the poor old wasp is a pest?

BUMBLEBEE

The bumblebees or 'humble bees' are also social, building their far smaller nests under ground. Only the queens survive the winter to start a new colony by making a small tablet of 'bee bread' from pollen and nectar onto which they lay ten to twelve eggs. All hatch to become workers and they take over the task of feeding the forthcoming grubs for which the queen builds the cells. At the end of the summer males and females emerge, mate, and then the males die. There are fewer than thirty British species, typically named after the colour of their tails. Imaginative, eh?

THE PESTS' PERSPECTIVE

Pest – an abbreviated dictionary definition is as follows: 'a thing that annoys by imposing itself when it is not wanted, any animal that damages crops or injures or irritates livestock or man'.

Perhaps we should add: 'those species which out-smart and exploit us, those which are actually far more successful organisms than *Homo sapiens* and have the gall to shove the fact in our faces'.

Consider the cockroach, probably the most successful animal on the planet – ever. Highlights from their impressive CV include: having evolved 250 million years ago and to still be going strong after virtually no re-designing; the ability to fast for three or four months and go a month without water; to be able to run rapidly, even over extremely hot surfaces; to produce egg cases that can survive boiling, and to taste food before eating – thus avoiding poisons with ease. Oh yes, and to be able to eat almost anything. Why don't we just give up on the cockroach? Sit back and say we've lost. They're better than us. Stop wasting millions trying to kill them. If we all used tupperware boxes to stop them pinching our food and, after all, that's all it takes to keep them out, there wouldn't be a problem.

Still, winning converts when it comes to tolerating cockroaches is a tall order, so I'm not going to outline plans for a 'cockroacharium' for your kitchen here, merely reiterate the plea I made in the introduction concerning some of the other 'pest' species. They live with us and we with them. We are different species in the same place at the same time, both functional members of an active dynamic community. If they are too abundant, if we feel they're out of balance with the way things 'should be', consider this: the rat, mouse, wasp, ant, slug and snail have only responded to our changes, not instigated them in an aggressive attempt to aggravate us. If you fill your garden with fresh, crispy greens you've made 'slug heav-

Above: *Glistening with slime, the fat slug slowly surges towards your carefully provided salad. Ask yourself, when did you last turn down a free meal in a gourmet restaurant?*

en'. Expect an influx of hungry slimers. If you're careless with your waste foods, expect opportunist rodents to arrive smiling just as you do when you behold all those fully stocked shelves at the supermarket. If you've got a nice dry loft or if you're attracting aphids in their billions by growing roses say hello to wasps and ants. Nature is not one for reserved contentment, these are all boom-time-bioforms. They know cabbages don't last for ever, and most over-abundant food sources run out so they eat quickly and breed quickly to take advantage. Ask yourselves honestly, when you see an opportunity don't you take it? It's how life itself works. So why not think, 'good on you, go on sluggy, tuck in to my luscious marigolds, I would if I were you!' Be at one with those species that share your community, live in harmony. Peace to all pests – man. And if you can't outwit caterpillars, molluscs and mice without killing them – then shame upon you.

WASPS

One of the most innocent and yet unfortunate questions that I get asked is, 'What are wasps for?' I try not to say 'well, what are you for' because that appears to be a philosophical rather than biological retort. Life exists because it can. If there's a gap, something trying to avoid competition fills it. And in nature the system works. Nothing does the job too well too quickly, nothing goes bankrupt overnight, because apart from us nothing is able to exert such an immediate and destructive effect on that balance.

Wasps are principally insect predators. They're carnivores, intent on gathering protein to rear their young. Of course, they're happy to top themselves up with neat energy and thus they won't say 'no' to sugary stuffs – naturally nectar, these days beer, lemonade, jam and ice-cream. A worker wasp's job is to supply and service the nest. Workers are sterile females so they forage and build hard for about twenty to thirty-five days before burning out. Their objective is to get a really healthy crop of fertile males and then prospective queens out of the nest by the end of summer.

The only complication is that a nest full of tasty grubs is a ready-made meal for predators, principally birds and mammals, such as bears and badgers. So to counter the menace wasps have evolved stings to attack such marauders and bright yellow and black bodies to warn non-marauders to leave them alone. I've been stung by wasps and I'm not dead and it didn't hurt as much as when a lion bit me in the face or when I dropped a fridge on my foot. Thus, I consider an extreme fear of wasp stings fairly irrational and I bolster this attitude by knowing that they are almost always avoidable. A wasp is a simple animal programmed to react in very predictable ways. Away from the nest it will not want to sting you. What's more it can't actually sting you if you don't move. Its tiny mind won't say 'sting' unless you move. So there – stay stillish and you are perfectly safe. Near the nest this becomes imperative – any vigorous movement is interpreted by those workers on guard duty as a threat. They will emerge, investigate and react. When a wasp stings it releases a chemical scent into the air which says 'sting immediately' to all the others in the area. In an enclosed space this is annoying, multiple stings are not so easy to dismiss. My advice is to avoid conflict – leave wasp nests alone.

All right you've got a nest in the loft, you're cool about that, but they're always in the kitchen and this is annoying the family, what do you do? Well, make it easy for both parties – feed the wasps. Offer them a bonanza of blackberry jam at the quiet end of the garden. They'll soon locate this feast and leave your friends and family to argue over the lemonade without the need of first aid.

Disclaimer – if you attempt to squash a wasp either deliberately or accidentally it will try to sting you. If you attempt to squash me I will too. If you get stung by a wasp and die it's not my fault and probably not the wasp's either.

COMMON WASP. It's pretty sad when summer's public enemy number one is an insect this size. Take a closer look at their exquisite design and patterning, so Art Nouveau.

HORNETS. Simply the best. These beautiful insects have an even worse reputation yet are actually far more passive insects because even fewer populate each colony — thus their individual lives are more valuable. Never common, as they need old woodland.

GERMAN WASP. Makes its grey and smooth sided nest in bushes. Look before you trim or else you might lose on penalties!

ANTS AND APHIDS

If there is one animal that we have all encountered in our gardens it is the humble ant. Have you squashed them, poured salt onto them, drowned them, cursed them, or marvelled at their antics; perhaps as one worker struggled to carry his wounded nest mate through the crowded matrix of giant grass stems? On a safe bet I would say there are ants in every British garden, under every other British stone, or I suppose at worst, in thirty million larders. Have your jams been plundered, your fruit bowls infested, or your sugar bowls hijacked? I expect so, and yet so many naturalists know so very little of these tiny rogues. Their ecology, physiology and behaviour are ignored at the expense of a few hours in the garden with a hand lens.

Above: *How much is spent on the development and production of ant assaulting chemicals? How many people died of ant or ant attack? How many people die falling from ladders? Ever get the feeling we get things badly wrong sometimes?*

There are more than ten thousand species of ant world-wide, but only about fifty occur in Britain, and perhaps surprisingly many of these can easily be identified by those who are interested. A key to success in this department is to look closely through a hand lens at the petiole or waist between the thorax and the abdomen. This often has swellings or nodes and these, the head shape, colour and degree of hairiness can separate the few commonest species. Size is not often such a good guide, because the 'sexuals' (males and females) are often larger than workers and their sizes overlap with other species. To be honest the ant which you are most likely to encounter is *Lasius niger*, the common Black Ant.

This medium-sized, four millimetre long, grey-black ant is particularly fond of siting its nest in cracks or holes in paving, drains, brickworks or rockeries, and its workers

can be seen all over the place, hurrying maniacally about their chores. If a 'Red Ant' is encountered it is most likely *Myrmica scabrinodis*, *M. ruginodis*, or *M. rubra*. These species live in smaller colonies, numbering only a few hundred workers, and possess a sting that will shoot formic acid at any intimidating fingers. They are also more predatory than *Lasius*, tending to favour more insect food than the honeydew gleaned from aphids. For many other species, though, aphids provide a rich harvest.

Aphids feed on the sugary sap circulated through the stems of plants and obtain all of their essential sugars and proteins from it. A problem they face, however, is that this 'cocktail' has a far lower protein than sugar content, so

aphids need to imbibe far more sugar than they need just to get enough protein. The resulting excess is excreted in a solution called 'honeydew', and it is this substance the sweet-toothed ant finds impossible to resist. In fact, ants treat aphids with extraordinary care, and the relationship is an example of symbiosis, whereby both partners achieve a mutual benefit. The ants protect their batch of aphids from predators (ladybird larvae, lacewings, etc) and also keep them very clean, a habit which results in an increase in the aphids' rate of reproduction. In return the ants receive a continual nutritious source of energy, mined by the huge army of hungry aphids. Consequently this relationship has led to the evolution of some adaptive features in both sets of species.

Above: *Aphids – for gardeners the devil incarnate. For ants a sweet siphon of nectar. You won't stop either so why not just live and let live?*

Aphids that are not tended by ants have two protuberances from their bodies known as cornicles. These deter predators by producing an unpleasant sticky wax, but in ant-favoured aphids these structures are reduced or even absent. Further, these species retain the drops of honeydew on the tips of their abdomens so that it remains easily available to the ants. Non-ant-aphids flick the solution away. The ants' contribution to adaptive co-evolution simply consists of reduced aggression. Most ant species can be ferocious predators, but in the presence of aphids some chemicals are produced which inhibit their brutal urges and maintain a peaceable exchange of benefits. However, being so devoid of protein, ants cannot survive on this nectar alone and consequently they boost their diets and especially that of their brood by collecting other insect prey, a task tackled entirely by the worker caste.

Worker ants are sexually immature females; always wingless, they play no role in the reproductive cycle of the colony. In some species they vary in size and show a division of labour, for instance, some collecting honeydew while others search for insects and/or tend the brood. Queens, sexually active females, are always larger than workers, and have a swollen thorax, necessary to hold the flight muscles used to disperse them from their nest of origin and find a new nest site of their own. Males are sized midway between workers and queens, have visible genitalia and also are winged to ensure dispersal and prevent inbreeding. These air-worthy 'allates' usually emerge well into summer with a complement of many nests discharging over a few fine days. Thus millions of ants reach for the sky at once, and although most are gobbled up by birds, a few survive to mate. The males then die, as do all the workers left in the nest, while the queens shed their wings and hibernate, using their now redundant wing muscles as a food source to reach the spring. They then use the males' stored sperm to fertilize the many thousands of eggs they lay over their five to fifteen-year life span. One aspect of the ant's life that is not fully understood is how the queen lays a queen egg, a male egg, or a worker egg to demand. It seems that the speed of laying, climate and size of egg are all factors, but the precise mechanism is unknown.

Years ago, when I first became interested in wasps and Hornets I was dismayed to find that the bulk of written knowledge about these insects dealt with how to exterminate them, not their ecology or behaviour. I suspect that the ants have been treated a little more kindly, they don't sting after all, but I wouldn't be surprised if, with a little patience, a little more naturalist nosiness and a notebook you could find out something new about ants.

SNAILS
SLIME OR SUBLIME?

If the madcap meanderings of fifty ant species does not set you ablaze with enthusiasm every time you walk up the garden path, try rolling over a stone or log to look for one of the more than ninety species of land snail that slime their way over the surface of Britain. Once again, identification is fairly straightforward, unless you try it on with tiny immature snails whose shells have yet to attain adult characteristics. However, there is one species you are most likely to meet in town, *Helix aspersa*, the Common Snail. This animal's shell has a browny yellow base colour, flecked with paler patches, is slightly wrinkled and has up to five spiral bands. This shell grows to about 3 cm in diameter, and gardens are a familiar habitat, especially further north, and they are quite tasty. Yes, tasty! The Common Snail was probably introduced along with its larger, rarer relative the Roman Snail by the Romans as a food item. While today we leave it to those gastronomical Gauls across the channel to specialize in the consumption of these land molluscs, snails of course provide the non-human residents of the garden with a very valuable source of nutrition, Hedgehogs, Slow-worms and Song Thrushes being familiar predators of these species.

Snails are molluscs, an eighty thousand strong group of soft-bodied animals, which are often crammed into shells. This group also contains Cuttlefish, Squid and the Octopuses, and outnumbers chordate (back-boned) animals, such as mammals, birds, reptiles, amphibians and fish, by no fewer than forty thousand species. Many molluscs are marine, but land snails like the Common Snail, which evolved from these forms, have developed lungs. Nonetheless they still face a big problem which limits their success on land – dehydration – and in order to move over any dry surface they require the consistent use of slime. Thus snails secrete a thick layer of sticky mucus to glue themselves to any surface, rough or smooth, and such a secretion proves very expensive in terms of body moisture, a problem not helped by a moist skin, which is in no way waterproof. Faced with this

Above: The White-lipped Banded Snail shows profound somatic variation. That is to say its shell pattern varies greatly, from yellow multi-banded through to pink unbanded, a strategy to ensure survival in different habitats and despite different predators.

threat of desiccation, snails prefer to slime about at night or on still moist days. In dry weather, hot or cold, they will search out a damp shelter and remain quite inactive. Of course it's not that snails aren't successful or in any way fascinating, indeed many children are charmed and fascinated by their sticky slitherings and often colourful shells. It is their cosmopolitan herbivorous diet which brings them into conflict with so many garden owners, and sadly sees both themselves, and their close relatives the slugs, firmly ensconced in the dreaded 'pest' category.

SAVING PRIVATE SLUG
THE TRUTH ABOUT GARDEN WARFARE

At this point I felt compelled to seek assistance, to invite a recognized member of the gardening fraternity to offer an alternative perspective on 'pests' and to come up with some advice on deterrents rather than chemical controls. In a way it was a conscience thing, a way of letting that lobby react to my ideologies. And they did, two of them, they reacted by declining to be interviewed. So, undaunted, I visited a garden centre where I spent an hour reading the expensive books and came home with three cheaper ones that all related to 'pest' control. As a result, I'm pleased to remain the ecological dictator, because the people who wrote them are mad. Here's why.

'Integrated battle plans', 'chemical warfare' and 'terminal solution' were all phrases that appeared to flout respected conventions; 'fantastic kill rate', 'total death toll' and 'extermination potential' seemed more appropriate to violent arcade games and I was worried by 'the Blackbird is often a serious pest', 'repulsive maggots' and a warning that I 'beware of the Cockchafer'! When woodlice and leafhoppers are described as 'pests' you know you're dealing with poor biology but when in one book a section suggests taking 'a more relaxed view' and later worries about dogs, particularly bitches, causing brown patches by urinating on the lawn and suggests immediate flushing with water to dilute the urine you know these people are in trouble.

More serious and insidious were sections on the use of biological controls. Most books seemed to be of the opinion that resident birds, frogs, toads, hedgehogs or bugs could help but not 'completely control' the 'pest'. (Of course not – no predator is designed to eat all its prey.) So it is necessary to import an army of outside help; ladybirds, parasitic wasps, nematodes, mites and even bacteria can be bought and released. Some of these species are not even native to the UK.

Obviously, while I'd like to promote anything other than 'chemical warfare', biological controls are unlikely to be effective outside the closed greenhouse. Local climate, the pest population size and natural desires to disperse will almost undoubtedly mean that your money will be wasted. I learned that *Bacillus thurlingiensis* kills all butterfly and moth larvae indiscriminately as it spreads a toxic protein to the larvae which causes death through septicaemia. Apparently, you can spray it specifically on plants where 'pest' species are active and the rest will all be okay.

A few sections consider deterrents such as grit pavements to keep slugs and snails away from flower beds but others described traditional beer traps for those molluscs as unsightly and unpleasant. I have to say that one author did offer advice on Song Thrush conservation – put a few rocks around the garden so they can use them to smash open snails. King of Conservation – I think not.

Apparently many people are squeamish about killing animals. A solution is to drop them into a tub of soapy water. So that's nice and easy then. But get down and watch them drown, watch their little legs aching as they whip up a froth and wriggle in the searing liquid as they try to survive. Try to imagine that miserable death; that, cowardly gardeners, is the difficult job, and when it comes to 'knowing your enemy' might I suggest that ignorance and fanaticism should be the first targets on your list.

Above left: *Natural selection. The balanced biological control in action, Hedgehog eats 'pest'. If you attract the former, you'll control the latter and enjoy both benefits, hogs and whole lettuces.*

PONDS

HISTORY OF PONDS

It strikes me as sad that today most of us regard ponds as 'ornamental garden features'. We forget how important a role they have played in our social history and how at one time they were an essential centrepiece for each human community, not just a refuge for invertebrates. Defined as a small body of still water, ponds are normally man-made features. Water is essential to any human settlement and natural hollows were probably 'improved' by being lined with puddled clay and topped with flint to prevent animals hooves puncturing this sealant.

Farmers dug 'farm' and 'field' ponds to water the grazing stock and drain their land; many a monastery or mansion had its 'stew pond' where fish, typically carp, were farmed to provide an alternative to meat on fast days. Ponds formed where any excavation was made; clay, gravel and peat pits all filled with water and may have acted as flighting ponds attracting wildfowl which were caught in elaborate decoy nets. Roadside ponds refreshed travellers and their horses and served to swell their cartwheels which otherwise shrank and shed their iron tyres. Those guys aboard Constable's Haywain hadn't lost control on a tricky bend and skidded in to that famous Essex waterhole – they'd parked it there deliberately.

Mill ponds, designed to hold a good head of water above the mill stream to power water wheels, which in turn turned the stones over the corn, were also common. But all this is history, and first to go from the village was its pond. As soon as piped water stretched into the countryside, the marginal vegetation grew unchecked and a circle of rushes was all that remained, even that now buried beneath a wider road or a new estate which covers the old green. The field ponds were filled to make mechanical farming easier and wayside water is not a motorway necessity. And now, like the ponds, we've neglected the village store, the post office and the pub, and all paid the price socially. Without

Left: Size really doesn't matter. However small, the garden pond is a genuine oasis for life to colonize. Any effort will be rewarded.

focal points how can any human community function in a friendly way?

Some rural areas seem to have fared better. I once climbed to a castle perched high over Cheshire in pursuit of Peregrine Falcons and as the sun set I watched hundreds of pools glow gold in the surrounding fields. In the last few years the problems facing our desiccating countryside have been brought to the fore and conservationists regularly liaise with the newly privatized water companies to reduce abstraction from rivers, waterways and subterranean water tables. There are too few reservoirs, and our most essential resource just drains away. We lobby for reason, but everyone is thirsty and wasteful, and unfortunately our ponds and streams are vanishing. So, as usual, it's down to us as individuals to take control. Garden ponds rarely need planning permission, so if you want one you can have one. If you have the will you can make a little corner of Britain wetter. And keep it wet – no infilling, no abstraction – and it will make a difference because so many species of plant and animal need only a small body of water to thrive or survive. Some are already dependent on garden ponds, so sharpen the spade – your species need you.

Right: Staying alive is thirsty work, especially to highly active animals such as birds. Here a sparrow sips in the shallows.

91

A BUCKET FOR LIFE

Here is an enchanting idea – buy a plastic bucket and start life on Earth. Ingredients required: only water. As we all know, the rainy wet stuff is essential to all life, and life therefore seeks it out, even in the most harsh environment. A yellow plastic bucket filled with treated tap water may not seem a particularly hospitable habitat but if you place one on your windowsill or doorstep and check it once a day you'll see it transform into a remarkable little microcosm. Okay, initially it will be very slow and you'll need a microscope to see the pioneers – simple animals such as amoebae and ciliates, single-celled organisms which can arrive in raindrops or be blown in dust or on fragments of leaves too tiny to see. Their meagre nutrients will fatten an army of equally minute predators that follow them in. Flies, bees and wasps, craneflies or perhaps slugs and woodlice will amble by in search of a sip and, with characteristic carelessness, will topple in, drown and quickly decay, freeing their mixture of bodily molecules to enrich the primal soup. Algal spores will blow in and prosper and as the sides of your bucket darken with green slime, legions of little herbivores will arrive to graze on this new salad.

Above and left:
Metamorphosis is always close to miraculous even when it involves mosquitoes. In just a few days these tube-breathing larvae will emerge as winged adults and not every species will be flying straight for your jugular.

I admit that *Monads*, *Choanoflagellates*, *Rhizopodes*, *Heliozodes* and *Loxodes*, collectively protozoans, are not big news in the wildlife terms. But bigger things soon follow, notably worms (wow!). Flat worms, ribbon worms, round worms, horse hair worms and segmented worms will all wriggle in the sediment as *Tardigrades* and crustaceans paddle in the middle depths. Then what about mosquito larvae? The floating boats of eggs hatch into rapidly growing cylindrical larvae. These spend most of their time hanging on

Left: *Water louse. Not as exciting as a Tiger but commoner and equally valuable in the web of life. Without them we'd have ponds full of dead leaves.*

the surface with their breather tube while filter feeding with their brush-like mouthparts. A tap to the rim produces an immediate antipredator response – they dive with a violent wriggling action. The mobile, comma-shaped pupae do the same. Watching these humble creatures in an old baby bath was my introduction, aged three or four, to the incredible phenomenon of metamorphosis. To this day I can't resist aggravating a larva and recently sat with another fascinated four-year old and watched a pupa peel apart and the adult mosquito emerge. We were enraptured by a little thing appearing from merely water to play its role in the great scheme of things. To witness it for the price for a plastic bucket should, in my opinion, be mandatory for all because when you come down to it, all you need for a miracle on your street is a mosquito.

Microscopes

Microscopes are not out of the question. My father bought one for four pounds at a car boot sale recently. It was crude, a mirror-operated affair fabricated somewhere in the Russian federation. But it worked; we looked through

it and all saw things that we couldn't see with our naked eyes and whether you're five or forty-five that's what's important. We watched *Daphnia* the size of cars, forests of algae, some *Hydra* and some fat ciliates buzzing around with their pretty rainbows of swimming hairs and by teatime we'd all had more then four pounds' worth. Shop secondhand and see a little world bigger.

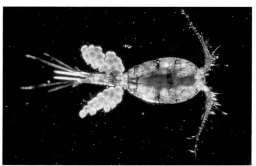

Above: *'My newt's bigger than yours.'* *'I caught the diving beetle.' 'Your tadpole has only one eye.' 'It's not a dragonfly nymph, it's a dinosaur larva.'* *Familiar pond-side banter recalled.*

Left: *This tiny symmetrical organism is Cyclops and is common in almost all waters. All you need to explore the extraordinary mini-fauna of a puddle is a cheap microscope – don't miss out.*

POND DESIGN

atching life colonize a bucket is a neat experiment but I am sure you will want to do more and one of the most fundamental ways to improve your patch as a wildlife resource is to put a pond in it. An old bath sunk into the lawn will be used by all sorts of animals, but its steep sides and small size will preclude others and inhibit its value. For instance, frogs may well choose to spawn in it when it's deep and brimming with water in March, but the emerging froglets will have real trouble scaling its sides in the summer. When it comes to ponds the rule is that big is better. As a guide, most big exciting dragonfly species require a pond of at least 40 sq m while some of the smaller ones can cope with 4 sq m.

A few factors you should consider include the presence of trees, firstly because ponds need a sunny aspect, and secondly because of the build up of leaf litter in the pond. Unless this is regularly removed, something which invariably disturbs the whole ecology, it leads to enrichment and stagnation. Shelter from prevailing winds is desirable, perhaps a wall or fence can achieve this, or you could make a bank from the soil you remove in the process of digging. Siting the edge of your pond on the very boundary of your property is counter-productive. It makes access difficult for cleaning and exploring, and it limits the amount of pondside vegetation that might be available, a necessary resource for many creatures.

It is worth reducing the size of your pond to accommodate a marshy area, a lagoon filled with rushes and sedges saves more space for an open water section and diversifies the habitat. Always think about accessibility too, if you dig the pond right outside the backdoor you'll need a bridge to get over to the lawn, and remember that you'll need to get to the edge for a bit of pond dipping, so maybe this should be adjacent to an existing path or patio. Also bear in the mind that not all the creatures that will colonize your oasis will want to be seen every time you play cricket or have a Barbeque. Offering an area which allows them some distance and privacy from your comings and goings will be welcome.

Above: *What a beauty. I wish this pond were mine. It looks superb – a perfect example of what can so easily be achieved with a little hard work.*

A good idea is to get a long length of brightly coloured nylon rope or ribbon, or a garden hose-pipe and lay it on the ground to mark the outline of your proposed pond. Then get a beer and mull it over. Show the rest of the household and see if they have any good ideas. Try different shapes and see how you can complement the design with existing features in the garden. Think three dimensionally; steep sides or sharp corners should be avoided, if you are going to use a mechanical digger consider its access, and perhaps most important of all, to avoid major embarrassment, find out if there are any water, gas or telephone lines running beneath your chosen spot.

Next, think about depth. Remember that some shallow areas are vital. If the whole pond is shallow, less than 20 cm, it will heat up in summer, reducing the oxygen content, or even dry up altogether and in winter it could freeze to the bottom and kill everything you are trying to encourage. A gently sloping shelf, at least 20 or 30 cm out into the pond is mandatory, as many species will enjoy the warmer water. A minimum depth of 60 cm is desirable over some extensive area of the pond as a deep water refuge and 75 cm or more is better for ponds over 20 sq m. Lastly, draw some simple diagrams and attempt to calculate the actual area of the pond, as this will relate to the expense of construction. Modify your plans accordingly by expanding or contracting your hose-pipe outline.

POND CONSTRUCTION

Left & below: *How to make a mud pit. Don't be disappointed when you finish, nature takes time and a couple of years are needed for the pond to settle in. If you have as many friends as this guy, you'll be lucky.*

There are five basic types of pond, three of which are likely to be inappropriate. If you have a permanently high water table, or your garden is on impervious clay you may only need to dig a hole which will fill with water. If you have access to a huge amount of fine clay you could construct a puddled clay pond. This would be cheap but involve a huge amount of hard and messy work – something for the medieval traditionalist. There are pre-formed liners, which make fine ornamental ponds or small fishponds, but their steep sides make them unsuitable as a wildlife pond.

This leaves us with concrete or plastic- or rubber-lined ponds. Concrete ponds are difficult and expensive to install. A wire cage is needed, as is an expert at using the material, which needs to be skilfully and speedily applied in good weather. Then it needs chemical waterproofing and draining and re-filling several times to prevent any toxic residue contaminating the water. Damage due to freezing is frequent around the edges and if a more serious leak appears it can be tricky to mend. So, the best, easiest and cheapest approach is a plastic or rubber lining, and the key to success like so much DIY, is in the preparation.

Polythene is cheap and easy to fit but even a three-ply fabric will not last very long. Personally, I'd spend out on butyl rubber (isobutylene isoprene). It's normally guaranteed for at least twenty years, is at least 1.75 mm thick and is thus more resistant to puncturing. If your pond plans are on a larger scale, you may wish to compromise with rubberised plastic (ethylene propylene diene), which is cheaper and a little less flexible. Water garden centres sell these materials off the roll or in sheets and for small ponds I'd

shop around for the best deal. But if you are thinking big (20 metres square plus) I'd go direct to the manufacturer.

Now the hard part. Dig your hole, either mechanically (nice) or like a navvy (not very nice). I know it's not my place to say it, but watch your back. Next, rake the surface and remove all stones, twigs and roots. Don't economize here, get down on muddy hands and knees and pick over the entire surface. Coat the entire area to be covered with the liner with at least 6 cm depth of fine sifted sand and this in turn with wetted newspapers, carpet felt, or underlay or old carpet itself.

Now measure up. A fair guide for the length of liner required is equal to the actual length, plus twice the maximum depth, plus 50 cm. Width equals actual width plus twice maximum depth, plus 50 cm. Remember to add more if you plan for marshy lagoons.

The lining is then laid, not stretched, over the hole and gently moulded to fit by pleating in creases. If it goes wrong lift it out and start again, repairing any damage. When you are satisfied, secure the sides either by topping off with stone slabs or by digging a trench about 25 cm from the intended edge and burying the outside edge of the liner, to be later covered with turf. Only at the very end cut away any wastage.

Fill the pond at a trickle to allow the weight of water to stretch and adapt the lining to the bottom and leave it standing for two or three days to allow for chlorine levels to diminish before plants or animals are introduced.

PLANTING YOUR POND

Left and below: *Lilies, white and yellow, are a favourite with both the aesthete and the invertebrate. Do not allow them to swamp the entire pond. Grub out annually.*

Standing in the mud, looking at the crater you've spent ages designing and digging, nothing could be more disappointing. Its bland, primal nakedness, its wretched trampled rim, the scummy soupy water are so different from your daydreams of a verdant, clear pool buzzing with life. But then any fool can dig a hole, the skill is in crafting it into a reality, and that means a good planting plan.

The vegetation of ponds can be divided into a series of zones, each suitable for distinctly different species. The skill is to meld a mix of species from each of these zones that will provide for the greatest diversity of other, i.e. animal, life. In a natural system the first colonizers would be submerged waterweed. Next floating weeds appear and shade out those below and thus begins a gradual process of silting. Simultaneously, emergent swampy species will get a grip, and slowly constrict the perimeter of the pond. Marsh plants at its rim will exacerbate this and eventually a swamp will exist where once there was open water. Bushes and trees follow *en route* to dry land. This phenomenon is called succession, and to keep a pond a pond you'll need to dredge and dig out the encroaching swamp. However, that's a few years away from your bombsite. Let's first consider which green bits should grow where.

Canadian Pond Weed can be purchased from any water garden centre and despite being an alien species is a good starter. When it first appeared in 1840 it grew rampantly, clogging waterways country-wide, and when you plant a few stems in your pond it will invariably do the same. However, it will soon die back to manageable levels and is worth having because of its oxygenating qualities. Root it in spring; it will overwinter as shoots and begin flowering the next summer. Despite these blooms, it always develops vegetatively.

Water Milfoil, either spiked or whorled, is a similar species that enjoys more alkaline waters. They too will proliferate if conditions suit and overwinter with specialized buds or rhizomes. The smaller starworts, of which there are a few species, are another group to add to this bouquet. A mix of species is the best option so try to gather a little material, a plastic cup full each time you visit a neighbour's pond. For these sorts of species harbour no

guilt – they are capable of rapid growth and will not notice your pruning.

Next are plants rooted in the bottom mud but with floating leaves, the most obvious of which are the water lilies. There are two common species, the white and the yellow, and both produce dense rhizome root mats in the mud. If you're up to it (and it can be a grimy struggle) then cut out a few short sections of this, preferably with a few buds in spring time and pin them down in your pond bottom. String tied to a stone will do the trick. In summer long flexible stems will sprout the waxy water repellent leaves and the characteristic and attractive flowers. Seedpods are the result and these too can be harvested to help colonize your pool. Fringed Water Lily is a similar species, with neat round leaves. Water Crowfoot can provide a beautiful veil of white flowers to cover the surface in May to July, Arrowhead with its distinctive leaves and spikes of purple and white florets and the Broad-leaved Pond Weed which can smother the surface, are all suitable species to try. Some will run riot – don't be afraid to cut them back as your aim is to create a habitat mosaic with as many different species as possible. All are suitable species to hold egg masses or larvae or colonies of smaller animals, some of which may be species specific – without the plant, you won't get the animal.

Next are the floating plants with unanchored roots. Water Soldier is rare in natural ponds and should therefore be sourced from garden centres, where it is always available. Frogbit is a mat-forming species with leaves like a miniature water lily, which needs tight control along with the duck weeds, which are likely to arrive of their own accord. The latter group with their tiny bi-lobed leaves often form a rich green layer across the entire surface. This is an indication that the water is too rich in nutrients, or polluted, and such growth is as undesirable as that of the algae, *Spirogyra* and *Cladophora*.

The fringing vegetation of your pond is important on several accounts; it is more visible to you, essential for those species that need to climb in and out of the water and for all those semi-aquatic species that need the water only occasionally, such as the amphibians that return there to breed. The swampy species which tolerate partial immersion include bulrush, reedmace and the common reed. These look great, indeed few self-respecting ponds sit proud without a clump of these poker-headed plants at their side, but they produce such an abundance of leaf litter that consolidates among their dense rhizomes each winter, that unchecked they will soon suck your pond dry. Aggressive grubbing is needed each year, and if you slack for a season then cutting out the resultant mat becomes hard and muddy work. Take heed. Branched Burweed, Water Plantain, Water Mint, Bogbean, Marestail and Watercress all occur in the marshy fringe, along with sedges, irises and marigolds. Many of these plants have showy flowers, the Kingcup for example, and as such they're a must for the fauvists.

There are two prime considerations when planting a pond. Firstly, there is no need to overspend or overcollect

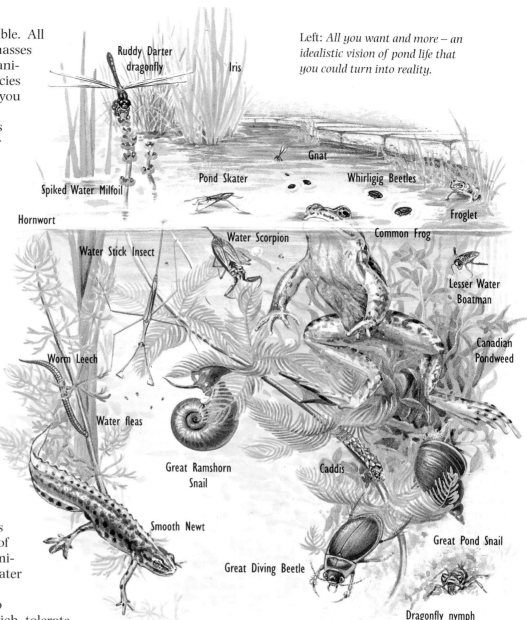

Left: *All you want and more – an idealistic vision of pond life that you could turn into reality.*

when you start. It is easier and more satisfying to add material than it is to take it out. Secondly, don't expect to get it right straight away. Your pond will need time to settle down, you may get a bloom of Duck Weed, the Canadian Pond Weed may appear to threaten your life and your water lilies may all die. The nutrients of the system will need to equilibrate and the first few species to get a hold will have a stabilizing influence. Unfortunately, you may have to sit back for that first summer and endure trophic anarchy and it could be two or three more years before your pond begins to match the fantasy in your mind's eye. Nevertheless, when your first spawn ball appears or when a brilliant blue damselfly first zips over the fence and onto your oasis, it will all be worth the wait.

97

SPIROGYRA
GREEN SLIME FROM HELL

It comes from outer space or Frankenstein's laboratory, or from Dr Who circa 1965. It appears without warning and then, in just a few days, swells into a bubbling mat which swamps your once lovely pond and encrusts it in a foul green counterpane that fades to a sickly yellow in the sun. It envelopes everything and surges onto the shore. It is ugly, toxic and resistant to attack. If you try to dredge it out you'll pull out snails, bugs, newts, fish, frogs – the lot. Face it, you've been 'Spirogyred', you've been slimed, and no pond in suburbia is safe from this hellish menace.

Sci-fi aside, *Spirogyra* is the best known of the green algae and its curse lies in its rapid rate of growth and reproduction. Seen under a microscope, the process is apparent and will occur before your very eyes. The cells grow in unbranched strands and their nuclei divide and separate, a new wall of cellulose forms between them and each new cell expands, thus lengthening the thread. Multiply this by hundreds of thousands and it's no wonder that a slippery mess is on the cards. Adjoining filaments fuse, fertilize and germinate into new strands. Multiply this by hundreds of thousands too.

Blanketweed appears superficially similar, a dark green clogger of ponds and streams, but beneath the microscope the filaments of *Cladophora* are branched. This algae enjoys polluted waters and is even used as an indicator of oxygen-starved conditions. Another choker of ponds, or perhaps 'souper' of ponds, is *Clamydomonas*, a tiny pear-shaped single-celled plant that can swim! Yes, armed with two wriggling tails called flagellae, it is able to thrash into areas of more light. It even has a light sensitive organ to help it.

As plants, algae are primary producers, the 'grass' of the pond's ecosystem and therefore essential for that system to support any higher life. Algae also contribute to the amount of free oxygen in solution, oxygen therefore available to animals of all sizes, as a by-product of their photosynthetic practices. But they get greedy, if conditions suit them they boom, in fact bloom, and bust. *Spirogyra* proliferates to the extent that it fills the surface water volume with filaments, often to a significant depth, and thus restricts or prevents the movement of many animals. Its dense mat of fibres filters sunlight, plunging the lower levels of the pond into darkness and, being such a rapidly growing species, it can consume large quantities of essential materials and nutrients and starve other species accordingly. And it looks ugly too. So what do you do to prevent, restrict, or abolish this scourge?

Above: *As yet there have been no accounts of human fatalities but this hideous canker has certainly frayed a few nerves and depressed a good many pond managers. I'd rather be bodysnatched!*

Well, the most frequently touted technique is to immerse a 'bale' of barley straw in the pond. The size of the bale depends on the volume of your pond, but typically a nylon mesh potato bag stuffed tight with straw and a heavy stone is said to do the trick. As ever, you can find commercial pre-packaged 'bales' at garden centres for about five pounds and the process should be considered an annual, springtime chore. I tried a bale of some magnitude in a badly infected pond once and it made no impact other than increasing the mess, so perhaps this is more of a preventative treatment than a cure.

WEB OF LIFE

Perhaps because they seem self-contained, ponds, and all the plants and animals that live in, on and around them, are often chosen to illustrate the fundamentals of ecology. And when it comes to constructing simple food webs to identify the inter-relationships between species and their food chains, the pond is an ideal test tube. So whether you are a student or merely curious, why not spend a week with your net, a couple of small tanks and a sheet of paper, and get to grips with what is eating what in your pond?

Ecology is the study of life in relation to the environment in which it lives. The inter-relationships between a community of species in a given habitat are governed by a continuous flow of energy through that system and a functional cycling of materials. In simpler terms, sunlight streams in and sets the plants producing organic compounds, which in turn become food for herbivores, which grow into food for carnivores. Finally, everything dies and is broken down by the decomposers into the simple chemical compounds used by the plants in the first place, and thus the cycle is complete. The transfer of energy in terms of food between each level links the various individuals in a food chain. Of course, these are rarely simple or linear as few species feed exclusively on one other species. Omnivores feed on both plants and animals, often many different species, and waiting and watching to see which will be necessary for you to construct the food web for your pond.

At the very bottom of the chain are algae and without a powerful microscope, complex guides and a great deal of patience, identifying these to a species level is impossible. I wouldn't bother, I'd lump them all together under the 'microscopic algae' heading. At this end of the chain or web there is a necessary abundance of tiny things to support the decreasing number of slightly larger things that eat them. Consequently, as you rise through the web the plants and animals become easier to identify and there is less of an excuse to be generic. Let's face it, if you can't tell a Pike from a Perch in your guide to freshwater fish, well, don't take up angling. Anyway, if you put a Pike in your pond you also won't have much of a food chain left because a trophic imbalance will ensue – too many predators, not enough prey equals catastrophe!

What I hope you will appreciate through the drawing of your food web is that even in your humble pond there is an order. Here is a community of plants and animals that exist in dynamic harmony. They come, they go, they grow old or kill each other and it all works. It's balanced, it's functional, it's perfect. It's as if the village post office still stood open adjacent to the pond and, although Billy Bumfit and Mrs Ratface don't like each other, as a whole the community gets along. The only danger is Jack Pike in the 'Boatman's Arms' as he's thinking of selling out to an international brewing conglomerate and if he does, it will be like you chucking an Octopus, nay Piranha, into your pond – it just won't work, and don't we know it.

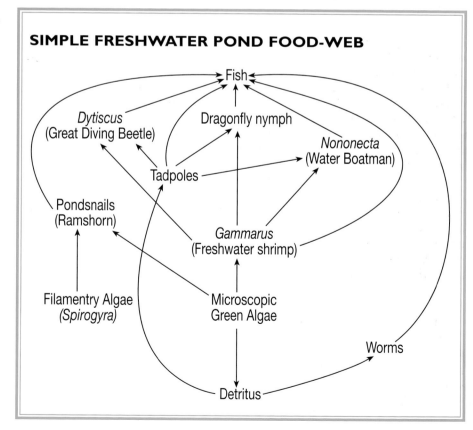

SIMPLE FRESHWATER POND FOOD-WEB

BEST BUGS

IN THE POND NO ONE CAN HEAR YOU SCREAM

Some of our most bizarre, formidable and savage predators hunt on or beneath the waters of our ponds. To appreciate the vital aspects of this phenomenon you once again need to negate scale. Of course a Siberian Tiger stalking you through the crescent or waiting to pounce from behind next door's ridiculous topiary is scary because it's big, because it can kill and eat you. When you crouch beside your pond or squint into the jam jar at your captives try to think small. Imagine you are a little beetle or a bug, a tiny herbivore, go on – be a tadpole. (I know you can do it, I have regularly after too many glasses of Chard'.) Then look again at any one of the following creatures, see how fast they move, how big their jaws are, how keenly they chase their prey, how wonderfully they've evolved to kill you – tadpole!

POND SKATER

The tips of their six legs have pads of water repellent hairs so they don't break the surface of the water. The rear legs help steer, the middle two propel, and the front limbs grasp their prey. Pond Skaters are extremely sensitive to movement so the desperate vibrations generated by a drowning insect, gyrating in its death throes on the surface, are keenly received and the bug skates confidently to its helpless prey. Out comes its sharp beak, called a rostrum, and from out of it the needle-like stylets are plunged into the soft flesh of the prey before its life is literally sucked out.

WATER BOATMAN

Replicating the role in a mirrored image beneath the surface are the water boatmen. They can be seen resting upside down with their tails poking through the surface film. Their hind legs are 'oar-like' and when rowed vigorously fittingly bestow the creature with its name. These bugs can swim maniacally and the adults, up to 1.5 cm in length, will attack animals far larger than themselves, including small fish. Their rostrum packs a toxic saliva and if carelessly handled they'll pump some into you. It's a shocking pinprick to the palm, which will make you jump, but leave you no more than embarrassed. Water Boatmen readily fly, especially on warm humid nights and will quickly populate any new pond.

Above: *Forget Crocodiles and Great White Sharks, Water Scorpions are the scariest hunters of the underwater world. Brilliantly camouflaged, they can attack and consume prey much larger than themselves – even small fish such as Minnows and sticklebacks.*

WATER SCORPION

Using stealth, not speed, the Water Scorpion cripples, kills, and consumes prey of all kinds, again including small fish such as Minnows and sticklebacks. They're brilliantly camouflaged, lying in wait looking just like a fragment of decaying leaf. Their tail is not a scorpion-like sting but a highly effective breathing tube, a snorkel which sticks through the surface and sucks air down a complex of spiracles to the body.

WATER CRICKET

Another bug worthy of note is the sprightly little Water Cricket, which can crowd the surface of small 'inlets' and 'bays' on ponds or ditches. We always found them on railway soak-aways, or on really stagnant waters. Although they are carnivorous, their small size means they equate better with the shrew than the tiger.

GREAT DIVING BEETLE

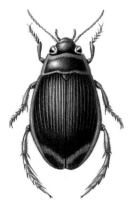

The Great Diving Beetle dives, and it's great. It's super streamlined, has bristle-fringed legs, grows to about 3.5 cm long, flies (mainly at night), and can wreak havoc in a small pond. *Dytiscus* is a Coleopteran terminator — it will attack anything and its segmented larvae are just as mad. These youngsters are armed with hollow sickle-shaped pinchers which puncture, and then suck the life from their victims. Once full grown the larvae crawl ashore and pupate in the mud. Three weeks later the killing starts in earnest, as soon as the adult has hardened its tissues it re-enters the pond. In spring the female lays eggs into the stems of submerged plants and peace reigns for a while...then....

DRAGONFLY LARVAE

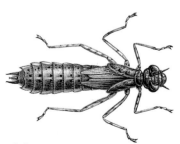

Rivalling the above 'hit men' of the pond in ferocity are the larvae of its aerial assassins — the dragonflies. Regardless of adult size and bravado, the exclusively aquatic larvae are fierce carnivores, which use a 'mask' to grasp their prey. A fabulous modification of mouthparts, this jointed structure folds under the head and flips out when anything of a seizable size passes. Interestingly, these larvae have internal gills, housed in their rectal cavities so just like the boatman and the scorpions they breathe through their bottoms.

WATER SPIDER

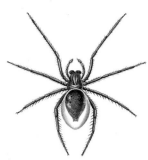

It may be alone in being solely and wholly aquatic but the Water Spider stands testament to the Arachnida's ability to diversify. They are air breathers which fabricate bell-shaped air stores beneath a web spun amongst suitable submerged weeds. Using repeated visits to the surface these spiders trap air bubbles on their hairy bodies and release them by stroking them with their legs. Once the scuba bell is built, it is fairly self-sustaining and the spider need venture out only to catch prey, which it consumes back in the bell.

FRESHWATER SHRIMP

Far further down the food chain and tediously common in ponds where there are ample decaying leaves, are Fresh Water Shrimps or *Gammarus*. These crustaceans are scavengers, can occur in huge numbers and sometimes reach 3 cm long — not quite scampi but food for many a meat-eater. In summer you often find two shrimps swimming in tandem, the bigger male hitching on the back of the female. Young are carried in brood pouches by the female and emerge as miniature versions as the adult. Interesting, eh?

CADDIS FLY LARVAE

Caddis flies score points because of their resourceful nature of using under water debris to form their protective and camouflaged cases. As soon as the larva emerges from the egg, it begins to wind a sticky thread around itself, attaching particles from its environment until it is covered. As it grows it adds new material to the head end. Each of the nearly two hundred British species can be identified by their case construction. Stones, sand, twigs and plant stems are all utilised and the larvae dwell within for up to a year. Then the pupa cuts itself free and wriggles to the surface where it splits and the adult fly emerges. Ask yourself, have you ever seen an adult caddis fly? My answer is — no. Apparently they look a bit like moths.

WATER LOUSE

It says in some books that *Asselus* can grow to 2 cm in length as an adult. Well may be 'Dr Fifties Sci-fi, black and white super louse' might but I've never seen anything beyond about 8 mm. Like Gammarus it frequents the leafy bottoms of ponds and streams where it acts as an aquatic Woodlouse, a detritivore breaking down leaf litter into fish flakes.

DRAGONFLIES
DEATH IN THE AFTERNOON

Some people are fortunate enough to have some really fab gadgets in their gardens. Some park sports cars or land helicopters, most of us can wander about with camcorders or portable CD players or other triumphs of technology, but none, not Sony, Ferrari, Bell or Westland, can hold a torch to one of nature's most enduring and perfect gadgets – the dragonfly

Having evolved nearly three hundred million years ago, dragonflies are superbly adapted to their environment and lifestyle. Okay, during the Carboniferous period they grew to have 70-cm wingspans so they may not be quite so flash today, but they remain every bit as brilliant and as beautiful. There are about five thousand species at large in the world and they are extraordinary machines. With a top speed of forty miles per hour, they are able to fly backwards and can hover and bother bees, flies or any airborne bug with the most diabolical deadliness you'll find in the world. Forget tigers in the jungle, lions on the plain or sharks in the sea – imagine you're a bluebottle over that pond and your little blue backside flashes iridescence towards the giant compound eye of a Broad-bodied Chaser, or worse a Southern Hawker. It's curtains, baby, you're over, caught, cut up and your dull bits discarded with ease in the breeze and as your dismembered legs settle on the lily leaves the Emperor is already looking for another target.

And dragonflies are in vogue too. Until relatively recently the scientific names had to be used simply because there were many species without English names and those that had them frequently had more than one. Birders looking for an interest to fill the mid-summer

Above: *Oh yes, all the better to see you with, and look at the ancient technology of those wings. It may look like the Wright Brothers' first attempt but it's Mach 1 all the way.*

lull, and in fact all self-respecting naturalists, have in recent years taken a keen interest in keeping records of our Odonates, so that all species now have well-established English names.

So jump onto the biological band wagon or better still build a home for some of these burnished beauties and when it comes to banter over the garden fence blow away your neighbours, not with talk of United's latest tedious victory, but with your most recent sightings of hawkers, darters or skimmers.

As with many metamorphoses you'll have to cater for a couple of life stages. The larvae have specific requirements while in the pond and fanatics construct special dragonfly ponds at the expense of all other species. One consideration is whether you wait for natural colonization or collect larvae from another pond. If you choose the latter option you face a major problem – identifying the species you've got in the pot. Keys are available but they are complex and difficult. However, one of your best bets is to collect nymphs from a pond, which is situated in a similar, general environment to your own, and offers the same depth and the same types of vegetation that you have available. It's a bit hit and miss, but as long as the larvae are well fed, they will emerge and if the adults don't like what they find they will disperse to somewhere more suitable. No nature reserve raids, please. A fellow pond enthusiast with a more established environment is the best option.

1 GOLDEN-RINGED DRAGONFLY

Normally this striking insect prefers faster flowing rivers to garden ponds, hence its western distribution in the UK, but it's a wanderer, especially for the two weeks after the adult first emerges. Females are the biggest dragonflies in Europe and have a strong, direct and purposeful flight. But when they hang up they are relatively easy to approach, just take it slowly and avoid any sudden movements. Of course they'll see you — just don't appear predatory! The larvae spend a minimum of three years and a maximum of seven or eight in the water depending on its temperature and the richness of the food supply.

2 COMMON DARTER

This species vies with the Broad-bodied Chaser to be our most common dragonfly as it is happy to inhabit all types of still or slow-moving waters. The males are quite aggressive, regularly attacking each other or any other large dragonflies, and they are strong flyers often straying a long way from water when foraging. Females are less aerial and spend more time perched in vegetation. The larvae live among weeds in shallow water and their development takes place in less than one year.

3 SOUTHERN HAWKER

Of all the hawkers this is the species most likely to occur around garden ponds but it is equally at home in ditches, water tanks or slow-moving streams. It is also a pioneer and will appear as soon as the silt settles — a just reward for all that hard work. Southern Hawkers are inquisitive, often flying right up to you, stay on the wing until well after sunset and don't seem to mind flying in dull or damp weather. They settle for long periods, are easy to approach and will roam into towns far from water.

4 BROAD-BODIED CHASER

My favourite. The plump, blue males are regular on garden ponds and their aggressive antics make them highly entertaining. They will take over a small pool and defend it fiercely using the same perches day after day. They like smaller ponds with lots of fringing vegetation and a fair degree of shelter, and the larvae skulk among the bottom mud or debris. The brown-and-yellow females spend more time away from water and wander widely and will soon find your pond. They are on the wing from mid-May through to August.

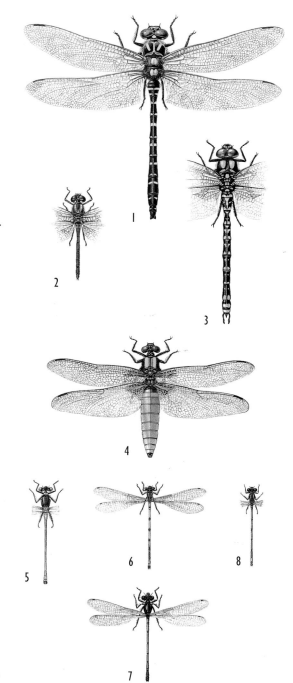

5 EMERALD DAMSELFLY

Between June and September this species can be found anywhere there is clean, still or slow-moving water, sheltered by good marginal vegetation, so it's an easy target for the amateur enthusiast. However, aside from its subtle good looks it's a passive animal with no flamboyant characteristics. It flits from plant to plant and egg laying takes place as a pair, the female often completely submerging for up to half an hour to deposit her eggs into the stems of plants.

6 AZURE DAMSELFLY

The weed-dwelling larvae are probably the commonest in the pond dipping net and generally develop in less than a year. The adults deposit the eggs together in a wide variety of habitats so long as there is plenty of vegetation. Indeed, they will venture far from water so long as there is lush growth and thus this species enjoys overgrown gardens. They fly slowly, settle frequently and may be confused with a number of other small blue damselflies.

7 LARGE RED DAMSELFLY

From late April all through to September this robust and variably coloured insect can be found around any waters except those that are very fast flowing. The commonest damselfly in the UK, its larvae take up to two years to emerge as adults. It's a slow-moving insect which is easily approached, and pairs in tandem, the females sometimes even pulling the males beneath the water's surface as they lay their eggs. As with so many species, when they first emerge the young adults spread widely into other habitats before returning to breed after a couple of weeks.

8 BLUE-TAILED DAMSELFLY

These distinctive little beauties rarely stray far from waterside vegetation and fly from mid-May to mid-September. They will colonize temporary pools and still waters of all kinds and unlike some species can actually tolerate a degree of pollution. They are common all over the UK and the females lay their eggs alone into aquatic vegetation. The larvae grow very fast, two generations may mature in one summer season and they can frequently be found when pond dipping among weeds.

POND SNAILS

A brief perusal of the most popular animal posters will probably reveal a preponderance of wolves, dolphins, tigers and eagles. No sheep or cows or goats. It's not that we don't like sheep, cows and goats; just that they lack the essential 'it' to engender superstar status. Imagine Esso promoting petrol to fill the car with a cow cavorting in slow motion through snowdrifts. Who would want to put a cow in their tank?

In the pond, the sheep-cow-goat role is played by the snails, another group of animals without 'itness'. But these animals are not only essential but ever so slightly interesting! Do you know how a snail's shell grows? Well, it is secreted as a paste by a crease in their body called the mantle and formed in three separate layers. The outer skin is a material similar to that found in insects' bodies, the thicker middle layer composed of a hard calcium carbonate (lime) and the inner layer equally hard nacre or mother of pearl. All three are added to a shell around its lip as the animal grows, gradually producing more whorls to expand and lengthen the spiral. Fascinating.

The most common pond snail in lime-rich hard waters is the Great Pond Snail, which can grow to a length of 5 cm. It's a grazer and on the underside of its foot, the term given to the flattened bottom of this gastropod's body, it has a coarse tongue, the radula. This scraping organ is rowed with teeth and acts as an abrasive file to scour any surfaces of their algae. Rocks, mud and leaves are hoovered by this snail in feeding mode. These animals and their close relative, the Wandering Snail, need to return to the surface to breathe as they lack internal gills, having lungs beneath their shells.

Another easily identifiable species is the Ramshorn Snail. Guess what? It looks like a ram's horn coiled into a flat spiral – in the case of the Great Ramshorn, the shell is over 2.5 cm across. These snails are also air breathers but because they have the highly efficient oxygen carrier

Above: Ramshorn Snail: a species never seen on T-shirts; a species without a fan base; a species utterly devoid of charisma.

haemoglobin, the same red blood pigment as us, they need to rise to the surface only occasionally. River Snails have evolved proper gills and also a hard circular plate called an operculum which they can close tightly over the shell's entrance when predators probe, conditions becomes dry or the snail needs to hibernate. This species will live in ponds and has round shells up to 3.5 cm in diameter. Like almost all of their aquatic relatives they are olivey, browny and blackish. Not thrilling.

A pond without snails is like a field without sheep. No fun for wolves or tigers. You need snails but don't worry; Great Pond and Ramshorn snails lay their eggs in tough gelatinous masses onto weeds of all kinds, so the hitchers will hatch and hey presto! By contrast, River Snails give birth to live young; this means you transporting live animals from A to B. There's no need to go mad, they are long-lived and fecund, so three or four popped into your pond will usually do the trick. These are among a whole group of animals that are said to travel pond to pond on birds' feet. Well, I've seen a lot of birds' feet – Don't ask!

NEWTS

Smooth Newt

I know it's not fair but I cannot hear the word 'gormless' without thinking of a newt. It's a legacy of frustration, of sitting for years expectantly before a tank while the amphibian ponders a wriggling worm. Its fixed grin, its bland bulging eyes, its endless hesitation, its endless hesitation, its...

Kids love newts, they like catching them in nets, letting them crawl stickily over their palms and plop into jam-jars. In 'Monty Python's Holy Grail' John Cleese is allegedly turned into a newt. He recovers but chooses the newt as a symbol of significant derision. Kids grow to recognise that newts are as near characterless as you can get. They get bored waiting and in the end, if the end ever comes, the worm stops wriggling and the newt just keeps grinning and grinning. Then the kids go and play football, or learn to read, or fight and their interest in pond dipping lies in ruins. My advice is take kids to catch newts but never allow them to watch them in tanks – it could kill fascination in natural history stone dead.

If you have a family and an interest in the amphibia, keep your tanks in a locked shed and visit them secretly to make your observations. Don't inflict the tedium on others.

Actually newts can be 'fun' for a few months of the year when males attempt to excite the females with a range of displays. Typically, the male approaches the female and she rests still. If she paddles off he'll pursue her until he can position himself a few centimetres in front of her head at an angle of about forty-five degrees to her body line. Then he curls his tail round so it stretches down the side of his body and trembles it vigorously, finally climaxing in a single violent flap and consequent repositioning and repetition of the whole process. This behaviour wafts a series of chemical stimulants from him to her, to bring her into condition to accept his gift. The latter takes the form of a spermatophore, a translucent capsule of sperm, which he drops onto the ground beneath her. If she wants it she picks it up with her vent. Between April and July she lays her eggs singly within the folded leaves of water plants. Newtpoles emerge and in a few weeks their feathery pink external gills make them clearly discernible from frogpoles. They leave the water from August, having fed upon a diet of zooplankton, crustaceans, insect larvae and molluscs. The adults choose larger individuals from the same menu and hibernate at the onset of winter beneath logs or stones on dryish land although some will stay under water.

In Britain, we have three species of newt. The **Smooth Newt** can grow to about 11 cm in length and the males can be quite fancy in the breeding season, having a black spotted crest running the length of their backs and tails and pale orange underparts. The female is duller with a yellowish wash on the belly.

The **Palmate Newt** is not so groovy, only having a low crest and distinctive black filament protruding from the tail tip. Its name derives from the obvious webbing of the toes on its hind feet. The adults are tentatively separated from their 'smooth' counterpart by spotless throats.

Palmate Newt

The **Crested Newt**, no longer so 'great', is not so bad as newts go, a monstrous 13 to 15 cm long and covered with a rough bumpy brown-black skin above and rich orange splatted with black spots below. Males further enhance their appeal, both to their mates and to naturalists, by growing a tall, ragged crest in spring. When they display, they arch their backs and become quite dragon-like in their state of shivering sexual excitement. Crested Newts are protected in the UK and cannot be handled without a licence. Consequently, translocating them to your pond is not allowed. It's not that they are so rare, or that English Nature and our government are so furiously keen on conserving them. It's just that they are fairly restricted in their range and specific in their subaquatic requirements. They don't often do well in garden ponds and should really be left alone.

Crested Newt

FROGS

BEST WITH THEIR LEGS ON

Frogs, however, have bigger problems than you and your children's skill in amphibian husbandry. For the past twenty years they have been in serious global decline. Our countryside management does not help, nor does the over use of suburban pesticides. Frogs need food, and if we kill it all to save our vegetable patch or flower beds then, well it's obvious. But what about the wider issues?

One such issue is exotic diseases, which our native amphibians haven't yet evolved to tackle. Of the two amphibian diseases that now occur in the UK, one can be common in

Childhood is... a jam-jar full of tadpoles. Black and wriggily in the crystal water, bumping into each other on the bottom, powering to the top and sinking slowly back. Next morning hanging on the glass side their little nibbling mouths moving. You can see their guts when they get fatter and they get golden spots too, and eyebrows, and at the other end their poo hangs out like a string of sausages. Remember? I bet you do!

And at the end of it all, when you've left the jar in the sun or poisoned them all with rotting bits of liver or chlorine loaded tapwater, when the casualty list has reached three or four figures, a minor miracle occurs as maybe five or six fragile, emaciated froglets crawl out of the disaster area. Two dessicate on the windowsill, one vanishes and with great pride you place the two survivors in the garden pond. It's one of those perfect-imperfect moments and one which no practitioner will ever forget.

some gardens. Most prevalent in the south-east between June and September, whole ponds full of frogs die over a few weeks and cause no end of distress to their pond owners. This disease, ranavirus, causes lethargy and emaciation, and sometimes the breakdown of limbs, haemorrhaging and the appearance of skin ulcers – it's not very pleasant; often there are no other symptoms than finding lots of dead frogs within a week or so. Frogs become more dependent on our suburban refuges as those in the countryside continue to disappear. If it happens to you, you should clean out the corpses before they decay too badly, then bury, burn or bag them, and be patient, in many cases once the disease has passed through the local population can make a good recovery. There is no evidence that people or pets can be affected by this disease, and it's unlikely to affect fish or other amphibians which share the same pond. Draining and cleaning the pond is also unlikely to help, unless too many dead frogs have fouled the water.

For more information or to report cases of amphibian disease please contact Amphibian and Reptile Conservation, which co-ordinates the Frog Mortality Project, on 01733 558844 or enquiries@arc-trust.org – your sightings contribute to important research into the disease.

Worse still is a disease called chytridiomycosis, in which a fungus is decimating frog populations around the world, particularly in Australia and Central America. It is thought to have arisen in mussels, where it is mildly debilitating, but in frogs it wreaks havoc. Tadpoles' teeth fall out and adults simply die. Whether other environmental factors are weakening the frogs and increasing their susceptibility is not known. One school believes that the thinning ozone layer and increased UV rays are damaging frogs' sensitive skins, but as most species are crepuscular or nocturnal this seems unlikely. Nevertheless if this fungus establishes in the UK it could be devastating to our frogs and toads.

Left: It's an orgy. There's no other word for it. These frogs have one thing on their mind and it's not eating flies.

pairs will choose to lay their eggs in the same spot, producing an enormous floating jelly mass. The spawn jelly serves not only to protect the egg from predators but also as an effective insulation, keeping a developing tadpole up to two degrees warmer than the water when exposed to sunlight. It is also not a solid mass, it allows water currents and oxygen to permeate and this ensures that all the eggs develop at the same rate. Frogs do croak, but only if they are in abundance, and even then it's not a great noise, audible perhaps no more than fifty metres from the pond. Unlike toads, frogs' short hibernation period can be spent underwater, usually by burrowing into soft mud at the bottom of specially selected hibernating ponds. Frogs are eaten by a great many predators: hawks, owls, crows, gulls, ducks and above all herons amongst the birds, and hedgehogs, otters, and rats among the mammals.

For all the amphibious answers you could wish for see www.arc-trust.org or contact Amphibian and Reptile Conservation on 01733 558844 or 01202 391319 or by email at enquiries@arc-trust.org.

Frog Biology

Common Frogs are extremely variable in colour, ranging from white and yellow through to black. They do not have habitual hiding places as toads do and will be found in any of the less well tended parts of the garden. They are not strictly nocturnal and regularly bask in sunshine. Frogs are far more timid and excitable than toads and when captured rarely settle down in the hand. They can be tamed, though it requires a lot of patience. Foodwise they are big on snails, but not so fond of ants and less catholic in their range of items taken, Beetles, caterpillars and woodlice coming second to the molluscs on their menu.

Frogs can breed in far colder conditions than toads and can even sometimes be seen swimming about beneath the ice. Thus tadpoles can be found as early as February in the south and exceptionally during January or earlier in Cornwall. Frogs also prefer to spawn in pools that have water flowing in and out and will return to the same part of the same pond year after year. Unlike toads they rarely spend more than twenty-four hours in union and often several pairs or even several hundred

Above: Common Frog, spawn and tadpole. The adults vary greatly in colour but never get as green as the Edible Frog.

Left: The exotic Edible Frog is popular, probably because it's more froggy, greener, more vocal and a greater jumper – if it manages to keep its legs.

TOADS

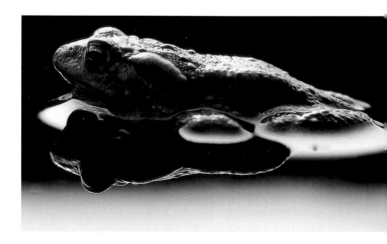

These days, come Halloween, the recipe is becoming a little more tricky. 'Wing of bat' is not on – all the British species are protected. 'Spiders' legs' should never be too difficult, but there's bound to be an arachnophobe in the coven, so that just leaves 'the toes of toad' to complete the witches' brew. Of course, a visit to the pond won't be too productive, as by mid-October most Common Toads have hibernated. Dry banks, mammal burrows or cavities under sheds and garages are all favourite spots and often small groups will all hide away together.

Males generally emerge first and make for the pond of their choice. Their homing instinct is phenomenal and immediate. If you remove toads from the spawning pond and take them off some distance beyond sight of it, they will instantly orientate themselves to start back, and nothing will stand in their way. Walls, fences, streams, fields or roads will be scaled or crossed at whatever cost.

Above: *Many male amphibians are great croakers, but Common Toads are not. You'll generally struggle to hear their feeble croaks.*

Some female toads will arrive at their pond of choice carrying a mate, others have but a minute's peace before a male clasps her across the back. If there's an unfortunate shortage of females huge 'toad balls' may form around an unfortunate maiden. I once pulled eighteen males from a single female, a none too easy task as they were extremely slippery and reluctant to let go. Remarkably she was still alive, but often such females are long dead! Males will also call to attract females, a short plaintive bark, enough to direct a lonely female, but hardly a tropical chorus.

The eggs are laid in a haphazard string around submerged weeds, usually over a period of twenty-four hours. The strings measure 1-2 m in length, and have up to four thousand eggs. After about two weeks the jelly disintegrates and the tadpoles swim free. Under exceptional circumstances their metamorphosis may take two seasons, but typically it lasts 60-85 days. Toads have always been firm favourites with gardeners. The source of this familiarity is their prodigious appetite. Any living, more importantly moving, animal of swallowable size is

Above: *Warts and all, the Common Toad is a splendid creature which remarkably can live for up to forty years.*

fair game. Ants, beetles, caterpillars, woodlice, worms and molluscs, are common prey, but newts, frogs, young grass snakes and even small mice have all been recorded in their diet. Bees and wasps are rejected on account of their stings, hairy caterpillars on account of their prickly hairs.

Toads have poison secreting glands all over their bodies. Particularly noticeable are the paratoid glands on their neck. From these a thick, white, acrid secretion is produced if this animal is attacked. The substance is a violent irritant and really upsets any dog which foolishly mouths a toad. However, toad predators include crows and Magpies and rats, as well as Hedgehogs, Stoats and Weasels. In suburbia the maulings of moggies are a demise caused by humans: a shame because, unmolested, our humble little toad can live for up to forty years. Toads tame easily and will even come when called if rewarded with a tidbit such as a mealworm. They even seem to appreciate being gently handled and thus make far more charming and enduring companions than frogs or any gnome or plastic flamingo which might decorate your pond.

Above: *In this photograph it's easy to see the huge paratoid glands behind the toad's eyes with their diagnostic horizontal pupils. The mouth is large too – for swallowing large things no less!*

SLOW-WORMS

The Slow-worm is one of the 2,500 species of lizard that currently scuttle over the globe, except that in this case, slither is more appropriate. It is a member of the widely distributed Anguidae in which we see a descending scale of lizard-likeness. Some, such as the American genus *Gerrhonotus* have well developed and functional limbs, others have an elongated body, reduced extremities and fewer digits. In the Slow-worm we see the definitive legless lizard. Vestiges of pelvic and pectoral girdles remain, however, along with other lizardy things like eyelids, external ear openings and a coarse, blunt, flat and feebly forked tongue.

The Slow-worm's skin and scales also differ markedly from its British cousins, the ubiquitous Common or Viviparous Lizard, and the rarer Sand Lizard, an inhabitant of heathlands. In these species an array of scale types ranging from smooth to sculptured are found over the body, while in the Slow-worm the series of small smooth and uniform scales are laced in rows of twenty-six the entire length of the body. Underlying these scales are small bony plates known as osteoderms, and these are united to each other with a flexible connecting thread so that the whole body is enclosed in a sheath of bony armour. Such osteoderms do appear in the heads of the Common and Sand Lizard but the skull, teeth and penis of the Slow-worm also differ. With so many profound physiological differences it's not surprising to find ecological dissimilarities as well. Slow-worms favour dry habitats such as heaths, hedgerows, woodlands and gardens, often appearing most common in coastal sites. They are hardly ever seen in daylight, except in spring when mating or in late summer when the females bask in the sunshine. Instead they prefer to hide under large stones, logs, leaves, metal or in holes in the ground. In fact, they are adept burrowers and spend a good deal of time probing under loose soil to a depth of 30 cm. Here they rest until dusk when, quite unlike the sun-loving lizards, they emerge to feed.

Worms, spiders, woodlice, insect larvae, and particularly slugs form their diet, the small white slug being a firm favourite. The

Above: Not necessarily slow and not a worm, the legless lizard it is. Note the eyelids and extremely numerous and smooth scales which are characteristic of the species.

Slow-worm slowly slides towards its victim, flicking its tongue incessantly, searching for every last scent molecule. Finally it seizes the slug centrally and just holds it for several seconds. Sometimes they're chewed from end to end before swallowing, but more often they are simply 'one-ended' and swallowed whole.

Snails too appear in their diet and these are seized in the same manner as slugs; the jaws are then shifted forward until the mollusc can be devoured head first, gradually swallowed and pulled out, indeed, sucked from its shell. That these slow-moving molluscs form the bulk of the Slow-worm's diet is no surprise because slowness is not inappropriately applied to this reptile. However, their slow, deliberate movements allow them to glide through the undergrowth, almost flowing like a liquid. Only occasionally when they are disturbed will Slow-worms thrash about madly and move considerably more quickly; most often they remain motionless and make no attempt to escape, finally loafing away in a leisurely manner to seek out some other dry, dark corner of your garden.

Left: The perfect partner for hedgehogs when it comes to scoffing slugs. The small white slug is their favourite but Slow-worms will even suck snails from their shells.

ROCKY REFUGES FOR REPTILES

Above: *Not everyone's idea of the perfect rockery, but certainly mine. Reptiles require plenty of seclusion. They are generally nervous and difficult to observe without extreme stealth and lots of patience. In summer, early morning is best – before it gets too hot and they retreat to the shade. Can you the spot the amphibians here?*

Creating a suitable habitat for Slow-worms couldn't be easier – simply throw some rusting corrugated iron and a pile of hardcore onto your lawn and let it grow rank. Nice feature? Well, admittedly, it won't look great and, unfortunately, it won't work either, despite the profusion of safe hiding places and the dramatic increase in invertebrate food, Slow-worms and for that matter Common Lizards are notoriously poor at dispersing into new habitats, particularly if they have to cross 'deserts' of open concrete, lawns and car parks crawling with cats. So let's begin with developing the right environment for these species to prosper.

As reptiles are endothermic ('cold-blooded') animals a nice warm sunny spot will be required, preferably south-facing to take advantage of all-day rays. If any trees cast shade, particularly in the early morning, choose a different location or fire up the chainsaw. If it's a hundred-year-

old oak, go for the former, if it's a tatty cypress then consider the latter. Clear an area, a minimum of 5 m by 2 m, and pile up a mound of loose soil, mix in some leaf litter or peat substitute, and then cover this with a collection of large rocks. Now, each stone should be large enough to be too heavy to be displaced by foxes, dogs or cats, and the whole lot arranged in a very loose structure, leaving small cracks and crevices. Don't infill these gaps with soil; they are the bolt holes that will save your reptiles' lives. Within your 'honeycomb' of stones both species of lizards will sleep, hide and hibernate. To further increase security you

should encourage a loose tangle of bramble to cover this cairn, and in the meantime cover it with a web of broken branches. Make sure your Reptile Rockery remains well drained, and that emergent vegetation doesn't shade it too much. Encourage coarse grasses to grow either side of it and leave them long. This will discourage cats and encourage a range of invertebrate food.

One last tip, if your Reptile Rockery is adjacent to a lawn, always rake that lawn before you mow it. I've seen too many dismembered Slow-worms that suffered more than 'bovver' beneath the Hover.

Inviting any of the other British reptiles to stay is very difficult. If you have young children or dogs, Adders are not suitable free-ranging residents. If you do wish to watch and study these beautiful animals then watching them in the wild is by far the best option. Grass Snakes need water as they source a lot of their food from around or beneath it. Frogs, toads, newts, and fish are all readily consumed by this opportunistic carnivore, but unless you have a huge pond, or live amongst the right marshy habitat, then the best you might hope for is that one of these exquisite creatures decides to stop over for a few days.

Right: The beautiful Adder – a master-piece of art and design who packs quite a potent nip. Its venom has evolved to affect its prey, primarily small mammals. So it does have an effect when it bites larger mammals, like us. Fatalities are very rare but you should never try to handle them.

Above: *Common Lizards* (left) *can, through gentle familiarity, become tame, even accepting tit-bits from fingers. A young pencil-sized Grass Snake* (right) *hatches from its leathery egg, here exposed. Small frogs beware.*

One last item of note. Since the 1930s a few naughty herpetologists have released small numbers of Wall Lizards, a beautifully marked species from continental Europe which varies greatly in colour but is always longer-legged than its common cousin. A number of colonies have established themselves, and three or four continue to prosper. Not surprisingly these lizards like drier, less grassy habitat. They climb swiftly and actively and don't mind people.

PLANTS

GREEN BITS

In terms of ecological fundamentals this should be page one. Plants of all kinds are classed as primary producers. They use the sun's energy, and water, to assimilate carbon dioxide from the air and convert it into sugars, thus releasing them from a need for an external source of carbohydrate. Animal life cannot do this and therefore nothing can exist without plants somewhere in its food chain. So why are the 'green bits' buried in the middle of this book? Simply because most of us perceive birds, mammals, insects and all the rest to be more interesting than the likes of grass, moss or algae. Despite the wonders of their blooms, the inventiveness of their seed dispersal mechanisms or the diversity which permits plants to grow almost anywhere on Earth, plants seem destined to be firmly rooted at the foot of any naturalist's interests.

Not long ago, I had the good fortune to visit Cuba and enjoy two great botanical moments. Firstly, I stood in a hot and humid orchidarium and witnessed one of the most remarkable examples of biology I've ever seen.

A rather dull but elaborately constructed orchid flower had a tiny see-saw plinth at the mouth of its nectary. It was not only a guard but also a selecting mechanism. Flies fancy a sip of nectar and are attracted by a specific scent, but if they are too big or too heavy, the fulcrum flips quickly and they fail to get in. If they are too small or too light, it won't flip at all and the nectary remains closed. Only one species of fly has the exact right size and weight ratio to see-saw into the nectary where it effects the pollination of the orchid as a by-product of its hunger. We stood and watched a little red-eyed green jewel do just this. In a great big rich and distant jungle we saw one fly interact essentially with one plant and all took our sweaty hats off to evolution. It made me feel small, inconsequential and the perfection of it was almost embarrassing.

If that was good biology, I also encountered great romance. I visited a garden full of exotic trees which had been initially planted over a hundred years ago. The daughter of its founder still lives there in a charismatic and cluttered cottage, the walls of which were papered with magazine photographs. I peeped around and saw

Above and left: *The awesome Military Orchid* (left) *is a national rarity that sprouts at secret locations and is strictly wardened. The striking dandelion* (above) *probably grows on your lawn (given the chance). Never allow familiarity to breed contempt. Beauty is in the eye of the bed-wetter.*

Sophia Loren and a young Kirk Douglas yellowing above her bed. The old, indeed ancient, lady courteously showed us around and patiently forgave my pidgin Spanish as I asked her about each of the beautifully tended plants and trees. At last she stopped by a real giant, stretched out a wizened hand to its less crinkled bark and gazed up into the mistiness of its high canopy. It was a beauty and I asked her how old she thought it was. 'Eighty-two,' she replied instantly. She had planted it with her father, aged eight, in 1917. How many of us could plant a tree with our children and know they'd still be loving and caring for it eighty years later, indeed how many of you older readers can boast this today? Surely few. Our world moves too fast for trees today, the measures we make in our gardening plans are more dot.com than decades and as a consequence we forsake the chances of our roles in such fairytales.

WANTED-WEEDS!

Shrivelling and pathetic she was, wobbling between the 'Flowerpot Men', whittering on in a puerile voice about nothing of consequence. 'Little Weed' was the least enigmatic of the trio.

Botanically, 'weed' doesn't mean weak, fragile, insignificant or ineffectual at all; it refers to anything 'that grows profusely amongst cultivated plants, depriving them of space or food etc'. It is a survivor and it's a telling paradox that we have had to spend countless millions developing and using horrible herbicides to obliterate the perfection of nature. The downside is that in our insane desire to do so we have ruined the countryside.

'Weeds' use various strategies to succeed. They produce vast quantities of tiny and mobile seeds which can lie dormant for many years (poppies). They germinate first or produce rapidly growing shoots that outperform other species and stretch up into the light before shading out their competitors (nettles). They are tolerant of extremely poor soils and prosper where others struggle (groundsels and ragworts) or they spread vegetatively using the strength of the 'parent' plant to swamp any other struggling seedlings (bracken, thistles). Non-natives can run riot in an ecosystem where the conditions for their growth are identical to their own but where no regulators such as herbivores or diseases have evolved (valerian and aubrietia). Some are resistant to trampling (plantains, silverweeds), others resistant to grazing because their essential growing points are so low or protected in the very base of the plant (the grasses). Whatever the secret of their success, 'weeds' are useful because of their sheer volume – they produce a huge amount of edible material very quickly and fill the stomachs of an army of herbivores. Nectar, seeds, shoots, leaves or roots are all gleaned by an extensive diversity of species.

Left: *Tolerance doesn't necessarily mean lack of control. Some species, here Golden Rod, will run amok if left unchecked. Every couple of years re-appraise the situation and make the cuts.*

Above: *Purple then prickly, Teasels are an attractive species which feed insects and then finches. When you've had enough, give them to granny for one of her dust-collecting, fire-hazard flower arrangements.*

Consider the thistle; a spiky and ferocious competitor to us but a salad for snails, a 'pub' for insects and a seed centre for finches. Tolerate a few in your garden and you'll make a lot of little things happy. And that's what it's all about, tolerance. You won't be farming in your garden; you don't need a crop. Why not a spattering of daisies and plantains on your lawn? Both are tolerant of mowing – that's why they're there. If you want to smash nature completely you could lay an 'Astro-turf' lawn? You won't need to weed, water or mow and it will be uniform for ever, perfect for the eco-fascist, a 'final solution' for all of your gardening worries.

Meanwhile, why not go organic and reject the use of chemicals in the garden? You can put weeds in their place by planting species which outcompete them to such an extent that manual control, 'pulling', will suffice. I have met a few keen gardeners who haven't used chemicals for years and their gardens look superb. But then if you enjoy wildlife these are unnecessary directions; you will want weeds because you will want what naturally comes with them. We rave about glades of foxgloves, groves of bluebells, beds of primroses, even verges of ox-eye daisies and we can with a little effort and planning have versions of all of these and more on our own patches. Think about it – I bet it will grow on you.

WEEDS YOU WANT

RED VALERIAN

This Mediterranean refugee has long escaped from our gardens and naturalized itself in Britain as far north as mid-Scotland. It likes dry, even stony soils and produces a great show of flowers between June and August. It is the perennial that anyone can grow, a fantastic nectar source for butterflies and moths and will add an immediate splash of colour to any garden.

MICHAELMAS DAISY

A native of the Eastern US seaboard that was introduced to Britain around 1710, it occurs in more than seventy different cultivars and is a perennial that flowers from August right through to early November. Thus it provides a superb late summer nectar source for wayside and garden butterflies. Like Valerian it prefers poor, well drained soils and is easy to establish and maintain. No garden should be without it.

FIELD SCABIOUS

Pollinated by bees and butterflies, this perennial favours chalky soils and would be an arable 'weed' were it not poisoned out of existence almost everywhere it tries to grow. It hangs on to road verges, hedge banks and areas of rough grassland. It flowers from July to September and is another favourite of butterflies, particularly the whites and browns.

FRAGRANT EVENING PRIMROSE

Another invader, this species has colonized roadsides, verges, waste grounds, sand dunes, and railway embankments as far north as Yorkshire. A biennial, it flowers from June to September and adds a flamboyant splash of yellow while supplying nectar to night-flying moths.

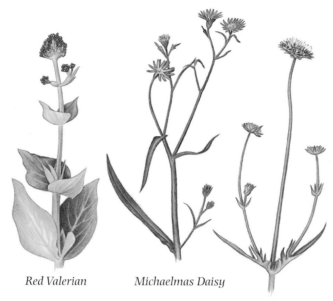

Red Valerian *Michaelmas Daisy*

Field Scabious

Common Knapweed

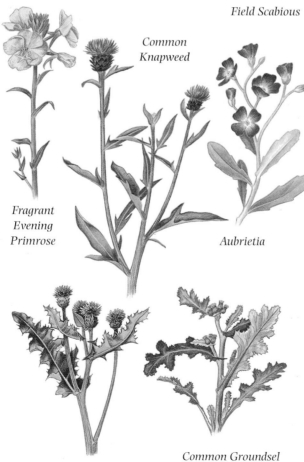

Fragrant Evening Primrose

Aubrietia

Creeping Thistle

Common Groundsel

COMMON KNAPWEED

Otherwise known as 'hard heads', this species occurs all over the UK on heavier and wetter soils. It favours meadows, rough grasslands, pastures and roadsides where it flowers from June to September and attracts a wide variety of larger insects — hoverflies, bumblebees and butterflies being the most obvious. It is a member of the thistle family but as it is not too aggressively armed it makes a good addition to the garden's edge.

AUBRIETIA

A native of the Eastern Mediterranean where it is an alpine species favouring rocks and scree, this species is commoner in gardens than out, although it has escaped onto a few dry wasteground sites. It's a perennial that flowers early in April and May and thus is a great early nectar source for overwintering adult butterflies and is very easily established in any open sunny location.

CREEPING THISTLE

This plant is common all over the UK and was included in the Weeds Act of 1959. It spreads by means of creeping lateral roots and requires thousands of tons of herbicides a year to control its spread onto any fertile arable fields. It thrives on meadows, roadsides and waste grounds where it flowers between July and September and attracts a magnificent array of insects. Best in a large garden where frequent strimming, not chemicals, can control its vegetative energies.

COMMON GROUNDSEL

This 'weed' likes heavier soils, where it is common and highly successful. It is an annual that flowers throughout the year and its small tufty flowers attract a range of smaller, perhaps less interesting, insects. Indeed the plant itself is not much of a looker so it's best included in an arable 'weed' scrape rather than actively encouraged all over the garden.

WILDFLOWERS
MEADOWS OR METRES SQUARED

Over the years I might have seen more wildflower 'meadows' than most. Squeezed into school grounds, the side of carparks, and the corners of tiny gardens, most were more metres than meadows but all worthy of merit. Sadly, quite a few people fail to realize that meadows don't remain meadows without mowing or grazing or ploughing, without annual management. Nevertheless, if you fancy recreating a little patch of an increasingly ancient landscape pick up your rake and turn your hand to your land.

As with most things, planning and preparation are essential. I spoke to the Landlife charity whose prosperous corporate partner Landlife Wildflowers is one of the few reputable merchants of seeds and flowers in the UK. Gill Watson, one of fourteen full-time staff, told me that strictly native stock are sourced and cultivated on their thirty-five hectare site near The National Wildflower Centre at Knowsley near Liverpool. Landlife share research with Plantlife and work with other urban charities such as Groundwork, but also offer fabulous packages for the wildlife gardener with their carefully selected seed mixes. Gill says that many people initially have the wrong ideas about meadows; they imagine it's all about cornflowers, corncockles and poppies, basically all the glamour, when of course it's as much about grasses and less flamboyant flowers.

In a garden context I'm sure that most people will be keen on a bit of colour and there are plenty of mixes available to fill a small palette. It is unlikely that your 'field' will be fallow so the first task is to dig out all the existing vegetation. The majority of urban soils will be too fertile. You will need to remove nutrients and clear the site, so try covering the area with black polythene for a season, perhaps lifting it a couple of times to allow the natural seed bank to germinate and then replacing it to kill the seedlings. If this is not enough to sterilize and de-fertilize your soil you can remove it, or at least remove the fertile top layer, or use herbicide. Glyphosate-based chemicals are approved by Natural England as 'eco-friendly' herbicides; 'Tumbleweed' and 'Roundup' will kill off the less tenacious weeds, 'Broadshot' will hit thistle and docks harder and 'Klout' or 'Fusillade' will remove unwanted grasses.

It is essential that the soil is worked into a fine, dry crumb structure prior to sowing and that it is rolled after-

Above: *Monet would have loved this. Ox-eye daisies dominate a small meadow, and make me wonder who dreamt up the ridiculous idea of lawns in the first place. Answers on a postcard please.*

wards to ensure a good soil-seed contact. Sowing rates vary between species and mixes but one thing is for sure, although this is not a financially expensive undertaking, to work properly it requires good preparation and careful and continual management. Not all mixes will instantly burst into colour, some will require two or three years, some longer; for instance bluebells may need six years to produce a flowering bulb. If you are sowing by hand, mix the seeds with sand or sawdust so you can see where you have scattered.

Once plants are established, cutting regimes and timings are critical; many mixes/swards require only one cut late in the summer. As a non-gardener, I must with honesty refer you to other texts at this point:. *Wildflowers Work – A Technical Guide To Creating And Managing Wildflower Landscapes* by Lickorish, Luscombe and Scott is published by Landlife and appears to be just the job for larger scale projects. If your meadow is more of a patch than a field *How To Make Wild Flower Habitat Gardens*, is an excellent guide in Landlife's commercial catalogue. Seed mixes and advice are available for a range of soil types and shade conditions and the potential results look spectacular. Even I may be tempted to pick up a spade.

BUSHES TO BEAT ABOUT

Left: Fully loaded Hawthorn; the thrushes can't wait.

Below left: Honeysuckle blossom and berries. Bees, butterflies, caterpillars and birds will all benefit, and Dormice even strip the bark to make their nests. Of course the scent is subtle, but divine.

What your garden really needs is spatial heterogeneity. It is one of the key ingredients to a rich biodiversity; rainforests have huge amounts of it and it isn't difficult to come by, but what is it?

You walk on a heath, across a meadow or through a wood – the difference is profound. Spatial heterogeneity translates to the filling of space using different physical means. A meadow may be rich in species but few grow above waist height, which is a waste of sky. Because nature doesn't suffer 'waste' easily we have bushes and then trees, growth forms that have evolved to exploit the lowest part of the sky. So to get some spatial heterogeneity you need bushes and trees.

My favourite bush is the **Elder**. It is found throughout the British Isles. It is a pioneering shrub and will colonize any broken sandy ground, often occurring on dunes and around rabbit warrens. It also prospers on fertile calcareous soils, particularly if there has been some nitrogen enrichment. Thus old rubbish dumps, bonfire sites and riversides are frequently covered in dense elder growth. It is a deciduous species which produces dense umbels of flowers in June and July, these have been used for wine and champagne but are better exploited by a huge diversity of insects, notably flies, hoverflies and beetles. Remember, even if you're not a fly fancier, many birds are.

Elder can grow to 10 m in height but is best kept lower and bushier, say around 4-5 m maximum. This ensures that its rich foliage provides better cover for a huge range of nesting birds which may include Blackbirds, Song Thrushes, Robins, Wrens, Greenfinches, Chaffinches, Bullfinches and Goldfinches, plus a range of warblers and doves. It also readily 'hollows', so I've also found hole nesters such as the tits and even Tree Sparrows ensconced within its rotting trunks. In August and September its berries ripen to black and the bush becomes a bonanza. Thrushes predominate, but birds such as Blackcaps can be found picking through the clusters and come nightfall no Wood Mouse or Bank Vole in the area forsakes this feast.

A close second in the Best Bush Awards is the **Hawthorn**, only its slower growth rate preventing a dead heat. Also known as 'May tree', or 'white- or quickthorn' it is similarly widespread and produces an abundance of blooms in May and berries, and haws in September. Both are a great draw for pretty much the same spread of species but the hawthorn's foliage is eaten by a few more larvae, including those of many moths.

Holly planted near to the house may ward off lightning but it is also slow-growing and not so productive on the berry front. **Cotoneaster** is in fact a native berry-bearer, but exotic varieties are more popular and, along with firethorn, are richly fruiting and provide good nesting cover at the expense of being vegetatively inert – nothing eats them.

Although not a bush by any means, **Honeysuckle** can be a fantastic bonus. It tolerates all kinds of soils but likes them well drained and produces attractive 'hands' of richly scented flowers as it climbs. These are pollinated by night-flying moths, including the hawkmoths and by bumblebees. Prune it hard to produce dense nesting cover.

Above: Elder – winner of the best bush award, here drooping 'umbels' of tasty berries. Try to leave some for the wildlife.

BUDDLEIA AND NETTLE SPECIAL

There is something so 'Disney' about a buddleia bush in July. The vulgar colour, bulbous blooms, sickly smell, and reeling chaos of crassly coloured butterflies, really smacks of a come-to-life-candy-castle in a cartoon. It's all so gaudy, so childish, so summery and definitely rude. I bet if Red Admirals could talk they'd be goin' "Aw right mate, look at the wings on that tortoiseshell", the tortoiseshell meanwhile dancing around the mauve cone – like a disco dolly around a white patent leather handbag. "Oh yeah, that admiral bloke's a bit of alright, ain't he?". Every now and then a gang of drunk lads comes wasping around going " 'ere we buzz, 'ere we buzz, 'ere we buzz". By half past eleven in the morning they are all nectared out of their brains and trying to sleep off the debauched riot in the shade of some brickwork. Those dollies who got lucky are off laying their future families in the multi-storeyed nettles, and only the more debonair Honey Bees are mad enough to go out in the midday sun. Once in a while an Englishman and his dog passes by the bush, as it drapes over the fence and into the street.

But ridiculing the aesthetics of the buddleia bush and its vortex of sunshine activities is really unfair because this native of north-west China is an invaluable asset to garden insect life. It was discovered growing on shingle beds and scree by a French missionary, Père David, who sent seeds back to Europe and named the species after an English clergyman, Bishop Buddle.

Arriving at Kew in 1896, this colourful shrub soon found favour with Victorian gardeners, and its wind-borne seeds ensured its presence on any broken ground.

Above: *This appears to be an ideally suited bush in terms of all day sunshine. In stronger breezes and wind most butterflies prefer a little more shelter, so you might try filling any shielded suntraps with this species to ensure maximum appeal.*

Buddleia's thick lilac flower trunks are rich in nectar, and attract a great diversity of butterflies, moths, hoverflies, bees, flies and beetles. Very few of these visitors can find any more use for the plant though. Only a few moth larvae can eat the leaves, so like many non-native species it is ecologically inert.

What buddleia needs is a good strong bed of stinging nettles as a complementary food source. Here the larvae of butterflies such as Peacock, Red Admiral and Small Tortoiseshell frolic and feed in safety, relying on the fiercely barbed leaves to ward off rash-wary predators. However, the ferocity of nettle is not only directed at the hands of gardeners, blackberry pickers and a host of herbivores. It is one of the most aggressive and competitive plants in Britain, inflicting cruelty on other plants through some extraordinary adaptations.

That the nettle is an effective competitor on its favoured nitrogen-rich soils is undoubtable. Carefully peer into the canopy of one of those dark green, spreading beds of the species at the height of the summer. The soil below the stems will be almost naked, decorated with a few scraps of last year's detritus. No other plant can stand this rude barbarian. It is a light hog,

which outcompetes other plants for this valuable resource, enabling rapid intake of nutrients under crowded conditions to produce lots of leaf material. The design of the leaves, their arrangement, shape, thickness, and the distribution of the light-hungry chlorophyll in the plant tissues enable it to maximize its use of light and grow, grow, grow. Everything else is left to decay in the shade.

Above: *What a combo. More colourful than you could shake a very colourful paint set at. Red Admiral* (top) *and Peacock* (bottom) *all dressed up for a summer's fling. A trifle gaudy, but firm family favourites, both species are on the wing throughout the milder months and hibernate as adults. With only a modicum of stealth you can pry into their privacy and watch their proboscis probing. Nice.*

TOP TREES

Quite how complex and how great a role trees play in the management of the Earth's ecosphere we shall never fully appreciate. Our weather patterns, the winds, the rains, and the temperatures are intricately linked with the world's forests. Trees produce soil, draw up nutrients and stabilize erosion; forests act as great coolers, emptying humid air of its moisture and then holding that water in their tissues. Deforestation is the most dangerous environmental threat we have as a species. Forget nuclear war, ask the flooded refugees of the Ganges or Bangladesh or the Far East, or the survivors of South American mud slides or the drought-stricken farmers of the Cape Verde Islands, the Sahel or Afghanistan, ask them what they think of the felling of our forests. In the watersheds that once protected these regions the answer is to plant more trees. In our safe suburbia it is to protect those that we already have. If you do this you won't save the planet but you might save the world for some of your local wildlife.

Always think native. Native species have an existing fauna that has evolved over hundreds of thousands of years to exploit some aspect of each tree. Since the retreat of the ice that covered much of Britain up until ten thousand years ago, a succession of trees has colonized our islands.

Left: Birch catkins heavy with pollen which, when sudden winds blow, sheds in small yellow clouds. A sneeze on a breeze for some, but a feast for a few too.

Left: Birch in full glory; a magnet for a million miniature things that will grow on the poorest soils, and quickly too.

Those that have been here longest tend to support the greatest diversity of other life. For instance, pollen studies show that birch arrived in Britain just after oak, about 9,500 years ago, but it is a short-lived pioneer, that is to say it appears en route to the oak forest which in many places will be a natural climax vegetation. Thus oak supports a greater diversity of life in the long term. Which is precisely what we haven't got, we impatient twenty-first century naturalists. No, we want it all now, and when it comes to species that take one hundred years to mature and can live for four hundred more years that's a real problem.

This is why I prefer **birch** trees. There are two native birch tree species, the downy and the silver. They are hardy and able to grow on the thinnest, rocky, gravelly soils, thanks to fungus partners in their roots. So long as they get plenty of light, birch will flourish and begin flowering between five and ten years old, producing masses of tasty pollen and huge numbers of equally valuable seeds that birds, particularly the tits, will enjoy. In fact, birch can support up to 334 herbivorous invertebrate species, which puts it third to oak and willow. Insects from Winter Moths to weevils, to a massive range of gall-producing wasp species flourish and in turn attract a greater array of predators, including the top-of-the-pile Sparrowhawk that eats the caterpillar-scoffing, bud-nibbling tit!

Birch is not long lived, rarely passing eighty years south of Scotland where the trees grow more slowly, but it is very fast-growing. Its roots are very delicate and need careful transplanting so it may be worth buying saplings from nurseries rather than raiding the local thicket. These trees are cultured in root bowls, making them more hardy, and they are also relatively inexpensive compared with other species. Buy as big as you can fit and afford.

Next are the **willows**. Quite how many British species there are is difficult to say because of introductions and the group's prodigious ability to hybridize, perhaps eighteen with as many as twenty-six confusing hybrids. Those you might think about finding space for include the bay, goat, white, crack, grey, almond and dark-leaved willows. All are extremely palatable to insects and no fewer than 450 herbivorous species are associated with these trees, including 162 butterflies and moths and 104 bees and wasps, mostly gall-forming parasites. Big deals include the Puss Moth and Eyed Hawk Moth and a few neat longhorn beetle species. Willows regenerate vegetatively and thus can be grown from cuttings. Whether you prune a local willow of a few small branches or select a cultivated seedling depends on your patience and budget, but at least with the former you know exactly what you're going to get growing in the end. Many of the species, white and to some extent the riverside crack willow being exceptions, are rapidly growing but not over tall trees – an important consideration when planting.

Left: *Willow catkins; great for wildlife, but not what you want dripping sticky nectar onto your car. I'd avoid planting anywhere near where you park.*

I read in a book that planting native trees can seriously damage nature conservation interest, even if they are planted in areas where they grow naturally, because it confuses local genetic variability. Apparently stock for planting should be obtained from individuals no further than ten miles from the site of planting. Rubbish. This small-minded scientific twaddle could not be more counter-productive to the arboreal enhancement of suburbia and to the ethos of conservation in general. The British countryside bears no relation to a natural system. It's the planting that's important not the genetic purity; it's damage limitation that we're involved in. Get a life and plant a tree.

A few thoughts on this practice; firstly and obviously, think tree not sapling. That is to say if you plant at the edge of the patio in a few years' time you won't see the greenhouse and no light will enter your dining room. And trees are not easily moved. Secondly think neighbours, because for similar reasons, as trees mature they will exert an influence over their houses and gardens too. If your garden is small and cannot take a full grown forest or even a single tree, then successively plant several trees, say every five to eight years. Then when the first gets too big you can fell it (keeping the logs on site as a valuable dead wood pile) and the others will come on to take its place. Lastly, and most important of all, please don't think your gesture is a solution to the neighbourhood or national problem of woodland conservation. The animal species that suffer most are those that which need mature or ancient trees and those which need dead trees. Even if your saplings survive to reach an ancient age it will not help. What is needed is to care for those trees that will 'soon' become ancient and those that already are. In short, look after your neighbourhood trees. Fiercely protect them from felling for whatever reason and campaign for their better management. There are many 'tree societies' and most councils have qualified tree officers. Seek their help and advice whenever vandalism, legal or criminal, threatens your community's trees.

Right: *Trees have prescribed forms, shapes and characteristic profiles. Each 'design' has evolved to maximize the tree's performance. Try to recognize and respect this and prune or cut carefully to maintain the proper look.*

THREE MORE TREES

They are sacred trees; to the Greeks, the Norsemen and the Celts, trees of thunder and lightning, trees of great nostalgia; **oaks** provided the timbers that built the British empire-building fleets, the branches that hid King Charles II, the leaves that enhanced the honours of military and civic worth. An ancient oak has an aura, not only of age, but of worth, and to stand beneath its canopy of drooping boughs all crusted with mosses, lichens and ferns, to look up and listen to that orchestra of buzzing beetles, bugs and flies and wait for the chatter of a woodpecker or hoot of an owl is a wonderful thing. A reason for summer, and it only takes a modicum of fantasy to become a Beowulf, a Bruce, or a Bronte, clasped by its great verdant embrace. If you have such a tree in your garden you are immeasurably lucky; if you'd like one – forget it. It takes between 350 and eight hundred years longer than you've got.

There are two native British oaks, the pedunculate and the sessile. Strangely, they are pioneers, flourishing on infertile and acidic soils and eventually ceding to lime, elm or beech. They leaf late, from early May in the south to mid-May in the north and only begin to produce their acorns after forty years. Every six or seven years a 'mast' season occurs and a super abundance of acorns are produced – a great bonus for Jays, woodpeckers, squirrels, mice and all their fruit-fancying friends. Those that germinate do so vigorously the following spring and will soon sprout in shaded areas. In the invertebrate diversity awards oak is the number one tree with more than five hundred species associated with it. Many moths, the Purple

Right: A parkland oak, something special, something that we should strive to protect at virtually any cost to enjoy a rich reward.

Right: Acorns in unadulterated form. So many are afflicted with spangle gall, sometimes an entire tree's crop corrupted into these cankered sticky growths.

Hairstreak butterfly, spiders, beetles and bugs occur as does the greatest diversity of fungi, many of which will grow on oak and no other tree. So this tree is a treasure house for British wildlife and is a perfect example of a species that will benefit more from protection than from planting. By all means sow a few acorns to see a few bushes, but don't worry yourself waiting to see them fruit.

My parents had a large **rowan** tree in their front garden and a couple of its offspring grew in the gardens that stretched up the hill. In summer these and a few other trees gave the modest thirties estate a pleasing continental feel. They took the pinch out of the pebbledash and put a splash of green before the grey and red brick. The tree died years ago and was replaced by a sycamore which, sadly, now stands as the only tree in the street, a street all the more cold, shabby and sorry without its trees. Trees enclose a space, fill a volume, you peer round them, walk under them, they're a great aesthetic enhancement to any area and that the fear of their roots damaging foundations or them falling on cars or children has been so absurdly fostered is a great shame for suburbia.

And if it's a little brightening you're after then rowan could be the answer. It's not great in the biodiversity awards, with few species associated with it, but scores points for its fabulously scented flower cushions which provide ample nectar for an array of insects and for the resulting berries, a great boost for the local Blackbirds and their cousins the Fieldfares and Redwings. Note also that many less scrupulous texts advise the planting of rowan to attract Waxwings, those top ten dandies which dribble our way during hard winters in Scandinavia. But they are so rare, such infrequent visitors, that it's unkind to build up hopes. Imagine you planted a rowan and lived to see a Waxwing eating its berries. Now, I'd listen to you bragging about that.

These trees rarely exceed 15m grow at a moderate pace on modest soils and the autumnal show of gold and scarlet make them a must for those who fall for 'The Fall'. A host of folklore exists about these wizards' or witches' trees, both good and bad, providing a wealth of cursed tales to tell the kids.

Left and above: A wizened and wicked old Rowan, maybe the carrier of curses, but certainly the bearer of a berry booty of some magnitude.

Limes are lovely but the aphids that cloud them will drip sticky honeydew over everything – not a great bonus for the car or the garden furniture. Beech are nice but mature quickly and cast such a thick shade that they become almost a monoculture and thus are only good for great big gardens. Scots pines may amass up to one hundred and seventy-two invertebrates but they require awful soils, a related fungal root partner and are not as well favoured by southern aesthetes. So that leaves us ash as the last consideration in the 'tree for you' category.

Ash grows fast and well on moist well drained soils, so long as it sees the sun. Don't put it in the lee of a wall, fence or other tree because it will struggle, a picture of frustration. It comes into leaf late in May, produces huge quantities of wind-dispersed seeds and supports sixty-eight 'invert' species of all kinds. The seeds or keys are a great source of food and survive well in urban settings where there are generally fewer 'rodents' gobbling them up. As a consequence, after a few years of fruiting you'll discover seedlings sprouting all over the garden to either pull or replant as you fancy. Ash produces an open canopy and is well suited to the encouragement of ivy which often naturally scales its trunk. It produces the hardest of our hard woods and has traditionally been used for making spears, oars, wheel rims, and perhaps most notably, the

Right: Ash holes well, and when it's mature it becomes a great source of nesting niches for birds such as Little, Barn and Tawny Owls, Kestrels and Jackdaws.

The Facts about Foundations and Tree Surgery

The tragic storms of 1987 and 1990 had few benefits for British trees, but one was the unique opportunity all the fallen trees afforded to study their usually hidden root systems. Tree experts discovered a great deal. Firstly, and emphatically, no tree roots, even those of the so-called 'mighty oak' ever directly damage foundations. The purpose of the roots is to secure oxygen, water and to anchor the tree but when they meet anything as solid as bricks or concrete they cannot insidiously grow into the material and then swell up to dismember it. In fact roots grow around such structures, embracing them until they can find space to again spread into free soil.

A problem can occur, however, albeit rarely, when a root ball absorbs water from the soil into which the foundations are sunk, causing shrinkage and thus subsidence. The problem is worse in clays with a high moisture content, and non-existent on sandy well drained soils. If you know your soil type you can quite realistically assess the potential of any problem you might have but then the National Housing Association has guidelines for foundation depths for all soil types and if they are properly adhered to then these problems shouldn't occur anyway.

British Standard 5837 (Trees and Development) stipulates how close new houses may be built to existing trees, generally the distance the crown stretches from the trunk or half the maximum height of the tree. This tenet is also designed to protect the roots of course, but despite stipulation at the planning stage, only about five per cent of developers or builders stick to the guidelines. These rules also outline the need to care for roots during construction in terms of avoiding compaction, toxic spillage or suffocation and also caring for the bark of the trunk with appropriate cladding. Councils simply lack the resources to monitor this problem, and although I'd not be the one to advocate a 'nosy neighbour' policy, if a hundred and fifty year-old oak was being abused I'd play that role without any qualms.

A paradox of the root/foundation legend is that more often it is the felling or removing of a tree which causes problems through a phenomenon known as 'heave'. When the tree is felled, the soil refills with its original moisture and the foundations in the near vicinity lift up. Shallow structures such as patio tiles may be lifted by invasive roots purely through their physical increase in size but that this only occurs near the trunk of the tree. If you remain worried about these matters, an excellent series of leaflets is published by the Tree Advice Trust. They have a tree helpline, 09065 161147, lines open from 9.00 a.m. to 5.00 p.m. weekdays, answerphone service operates at other times. Calls are charged at £1.50 per minute. See www.treehelp.info or the information at back of book for more details.

Tree Surgery

If a man knocks on your door to inform you that a tree at the front of your house 'could do with a bit off the top', or that it's a 'hazard to pedestrians, politely tell him to go away. The country is littered with the carcasses of trees that have been unnecessarily butchered, and the result is the sad waste of a potentially beautiful resource.

Of course proper tree surgery is sometimes essential, so what should you do when searching for a practitioner? First try the Yellow Pages, where you will find various companies with a range of qualifications and affiliations. The qualifications are serious, and indicate that tree surgery is a real skill – not something that anybody like you or I could do. The affiliations are a bit more tricky: there's the International Society of Arboriculturalists, The Forestry Contracting Association, the National Arborist Association, The National Association of Tree Officers, and the Arboricultural Association. I spoke to Nick Eden, a spokesman for the last, and he had the following advice.

Forget doorsteppers, they are an unregulated blight on the industry. Instead, ring the AA headquarters in Romsey, Hampshire and request their list of approved tree surgeons in your area. These companies have been fully examined by the AA and meet not only recognized standards of arboricultural skills, but also business practice and good service. With more than two thousand members and thirty-five years of experience the AA has a good reputation. If when your chosen company staff arrive you still have doubts, ask them one simple question – to which British standard do they plan to cut the tree? If they suggest anything other than British Standard 3998, send them away.

Finally, remember, tidiness is the arch enemy of nature. If your tree is not a hazard to any human life, leave it. In the centre of our garden is a full-sized dead oak. It doesn't overhang our neighbours' gardens nor the areas where we regularly walk. Thus it remains untouched, left to be ravished by time. I am endlessly asked what I'm going to do about that tree and the answer will always be the same – nothing, because I like to lie in bed listening to woodpeckers drumming.

Ivy

I vy is abundant all over the British Isles with the exception of parts of the Scottish Highlands. It is an evergreen, woody climber which attaches itself to trees, walls or rocks with its 'cohesive roots', short, densely packed extensions which sprout all along its stems. Ivy flowers late, from September through to November, and its small yellowish green florets are thus a great draw for many insects, particularly wasps and flies, which are probably the most important pollinators. Spherical black berries then develop and despite being mildly poisonous to humans and other mammals, they are a favourite with many birds, especially Blackbirds, thrushes and pigeons.

Butterflies that overwinter as adults, such as Small Tortoiseshells, Peacocks, Red Admirals, Brimstones and Commas, are all frequently seen on ivy flowers, snatching a last meal before they hibernate, some even finding shelter in the plant's leaf cover. However, one of our most delicate and lovely species, the Holly Blue, has a greater need for ivy – the summer brood of this insect lays eggs onto the unopened buds of the ivy blossom.

Ivy is extremely shade tolerant and thus has a habit of growing up the trunk and main branches of trees, particularly those with slightly more open canopy or those growing singularly in hedgerows. Thus, beneath the dark canopy of beech forest it is uncommon but can frequently be seen cloaking the trunks of stand alone ash trees. For some reason it has become popular belief that ivy 'strangles' trees. This is nonsense. On a mature tree with a full canopy it could never compete with the tree at all and quite how it is perceived that it may harm the trunk, a structure of such obvious fortitude, I cannot imagine. In fact ivy greatly enhances the tree as a resource, offering evergreen shelter for many species.

Similarly a fence or wall covered with ivy provides a nesting haven for Blackbirds, Robins, Chaffinches, Wrens, pigeons, doves and even Jays, a species which seems deliberately to seek the seclusion of an ivy-covered cleft. When a thick web of fronds forms the plant begins to accumulate its own litter which soon becomes an ideal habitat for many invertebrates and in turn a foraging resource for small mammals, particularly the more arboreal Wood Mouse.

So ignore its pagan associations with death, forget the nonsense about its murderous abilities, recall that its rash-inducing qualities are not nearly as developed as its poisonous American namesake and actively encourage ivy wherever possible. If it does it for me, then I'm sure

DEAD WOOD

I t's so human. A grand old oak, or beech or chestnut or elm takes between one hundred and three hundred years to grow and die and then we feel compelled to bury it. Cut it up into little pieces and lay them all out, or worse cremate it, turn it all to carbon and a pile of ash. All that effort, all those years of struggle to strain nutrients from the soil and form a giant, cut and burned away in a morning with a chainsaw and a box of matches. A sorry, criminal atrocity. You see, although dead, a tree like that has only served a fraction of its worth in the community in which it stands when it dies. It will be another hundred years before it fully decays, all the while providing a refuge and food for an extra range of species, a specialized set of more than a thousand creatures for which life without death is a misery if not impossible. We must lighten up and leave the dead trees

Left: More forgotten fauna: beetles. Whilst we all recognise ladybirds and stags, the majority remain unknown in home and habit. Strange, given their extraordinary success across our planet.

Above and below: Life thanks to death: a fantastic array of creatures thriving upon decay, many becoming rarer due to our blinkered attitude regarding tidiness in the environment. Log piles aren't the answer, but they're an interesting way of helping.

be. "Oh," say the councils, "they'll fall on people and we'll be sued." "Well," say I, "fence them off and stick up disclaimers." Frankly, it is ridiculous that in such an ecologically enlightened age our parks and gardens are devoid of dead wood. I think it's a hang-up, arising because most of us are frightened of death and don't want to be reminded of it, and that's ridiculous too. When you're born there's only one certainty, that you'll die, and me, well, I don't mind recycling my nutrients, I might be part of a Sparrowhawk or Stag Beetle. Smart, eh?

So, if you haven't got any dead wood, go and get some. Make a log pile in the corner as big as you can, with logs as big as you can carry or drag or wheel. Or crane? Where should you get your logs? Well, there's no point in pinching them from the local countryside where they'll already be doing their good work. Instead get them from a wood for fuel merchant. Wood burners are back in fashion (we have one, it makes our house so hot we can't live in it so we hardly use it), and thus 'logs for sale' signs adorn the roadsides and the cheap ads country-wide. Take a trailer and get a range of sizes from a range of species before they're cut and split. Stack them neatly, leaving a few access gaps for larger species to crawl in and then forget about it. To be honest, a lot of the life you'll provide for will be invisible, gnawing and burrowing behind the bark and into the rotting timber, and if you expose it with a blade or chisel it will die. True, some fairly exciting species will pop by, quickly and secretly, to lay their eggs and leave, but a lot will be 'grubby' or 'slimy' or 'scaulky', things that love cool dark damp decay – not the light of day. It doesn't matter; when you put a pound in a pot in the precinct, you don't see the good it does in Africa, but you feel good about it. So, now you've installed a log pile, sit back and feel good about having provided a home for woodlice.

In fact the first pioneers to reach your woodpile may be bark beetles, the females of which bore a tunnel in which to lay their eggs. When they hatch the larvae produce beautiful radiating patterns which loosen the bark and allow other species to creep underneath. Woodlice, centipedes and millipedes sneak in as well as the larvae of longhorn beetles. The adults of these are amongst the most tropical looking of our British species and feed on nectar so your best chance of seeing them will be elsewhere in the garden. But in the core of the logs larger beetles' larvae will thrive although they often wait until it has begun to rot. A Stag Beetle grub as big as your little finger may spend up to five years chewing in this damp and dark world before pupating to emerge into ours. Britain's largest insects, the males weighing up to 5 g, they are also our most spectacular, armed with horns fit for the jungle. A host of less exciting species also benefit including the click beetles, Cockchafers, and the larvae of various flies and hoverflies.

Left: *Fungal fruiting bodies such as toadstools can be a brief but highly attractive feature. Few are actually deadly poisonous, but all are highly specific in their requirements, and thus difficult to cultivate.*

While the insects are at work on the inside of the log pile, the molluscs get busy beneath it, with a host of slugs and snails helping to speed the processes of decomposition. However, the true masters of decay are the fungi and many species will soon set about your rotting wood. The trouble is that for most of the time they are less than spectacular, persisting only as hyphae, thin transparent threads which creep through the timber. These strands are normally microscopic although they occasionally aggregate into visible white 'doilies', still quite unidentifiable. It is only when fungi produce their fruiting bodies that they may be separated into species. Toadstools, mushrooms and brackets come in all shapes and sizes and often have highly specialized environmental needs in terms of tree type and position. The larger, more flamboyant fungi tend to occur during the early stages of decay when there are still plenty of nutrients available in the log, and thus need logs of a larger diameter. If you want fancy fungi you'll need to forklift in some substantial trunks.

One word of caution – try to moderate your curiosity. The habitat requirements of many of the species in rotten wood, especially the insect larvae, are precise and peculiar and rarely include exposure to the air and light. As such, if you pry open rotten wood you destroy the habitat you are creating. Patience is required; perhaps have one log that you 'investigate' throughout the course of its decay while the others remain intact. I once broke open an old tree stump beneath a bush and four almost mature Stag Beetle larvae fell out. I tried to push them back into crevices in the crumbling wood but doubt that they survived their violent introduction to the outside world. Five years of eating dead wood in the dark down the pan. I still feel rotten about it now.

Right: *A plethora of detritivores working away at dead material means that there's ample opportunity for the predatory niche to be diversified. Centipedes and beetles, in adult and larval form, all do diabolical things in the damp and dark.*

127

PHOTOGRAPHY

BASIC PRINCIPLES

These days wildlife photography is extremely popular, with a great many professionals and amateurs taking advantage of a superb range of easy-to-use equipment – in fact there are few technically limited challenges left, now it's all down to the subject. And as a subject what could be a greater, richer and a more enigmatic and widely appealing resource? Not even the nude! So why is it that as a genre wildlife photography is still in the artistic doldrums? Why is it that the fine art establishment ignores its very finest practitioners as 'hicks who chase animals' while exhibiting and printing mediocre snaps of most other subjects?

I believe it's the legacy of the past, a past blighted by the embarrassing acclaim we bestowed upon those who merely captured their subject, irrespective of photographic, let alone artistic, quality. We all said 'wow' just because it was rare, shy, difficult, sharp or properly exposed, and frankly none of these matter an iota. What counts is that the subject has been uniquely interpreted and presented in an interesting or invigorating manner. That the photograph has communicated something to us, something personal, some idea we haven't had or seen or dreamt of. As you can tell this predicament irks me and many others. I've long been an advocate of taking a hard line on the mundane replication of reality and banishing those imperfect photographs which we enjoy just because the animal is doing something unusual. Dump it. 'If it's not art, don't even save it' was a maxim that I adhered to for years. My library is not extensive!

But I have become a little more tolerant. I don't quite like wallpaper yet, but I'm happier to accept that not everything has to be perfect, or say something or be 'high art'. Some things can just be nice, easy to live with, happy or curious. And they can be all these things and still be a very good photograph, maybe even a picture. But I still can't imagine why anyone would bother to pick up a camera if they didn't at least start with the inten-

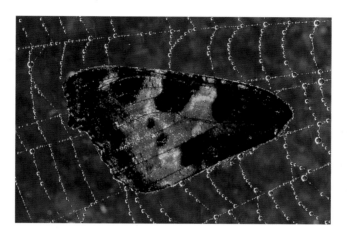

Left: Pattern can be useful in picture making. Here a small tortoiseshell's wing held in a spider's web incorporates its veins into the spangled structure to tell a story of fragility and predation.

tion of taking a good photograph. So it's on this account that I implore you to aim high. You have a pair of eyes connected to a mind that has never been before nor ever will be again and everyone is capable of taking a great picture or two. Don't be lazy, look at a few fundamentals such as colour, texture, balance, composition, as well as photographic technique and integrate them into your ideas and photographs. Aim to take shots that you might want to hang on your wall, or better still that others might wish to hang on theirs. Be hard on your results, be ruthless, draconian. Prune and cut and discard until you're on the brink of having nothing left and then ask yourself again how your picture could be better.

Lastly, if you ever take a picture that you really think is perfect, throw all your equipment into the sea and give up. Actually, mail it to me because I haven't got there yet and hopefully never will. Perfection is personally unobtainable, reality is invariably horrible so achieving any satisfaction should take all eternity.

Above: Be alert to interesting patterns and motifs; here the repeated curved shape of a chewed leaf and the culprit make a little something out of virtually nothing.

YOUR GARDEN STUDIO

For the budding wildlife photographer the garden is the best studio available, and it doesn't matter how big your garden grows because our wildlife is all relatively small – no elephants, rhinos or herds of Wildebeest, and foxes, squirrels, frogs and insects can fit into the most conservative spaces, if not into a conservatory itself.

There are many benefits of working at home but privacy is probably top of the list. You see, if you decide to build a set or wish to leave your tripod out for an hour, it won't be interfered with, unlike anything you try to do in our over-populated countryside.

So you've designed a masterpiece and constructed your set. Now, because you are at home you can keep trying until you get it right. Time and privacy are great luxuries but there is also one unfortunate enemy of this cosy home practice, the dreaded handicap – familiarity. There is no doubt at all that at worst it breeds contempt, and at best laziness.

There is nothing so invigorating as the exotic, and if you take photographs and have travelled with your camera you'll know exactly what I mean. So here's the challenge: take the subject on your bird table, buddleia or back windowsill, and look again. Generate a new photographic excitement about those most accessible, convenient and

Left: *House spider on blown lightbulbs. A curious set maybe, but the bubbles are better than a dusty garage floor. As usual, a little artistic licence goes a long way.*

easy subjects which you have previously overlooked, and then come up with something that no one else has seen or photographed before.

Years ago, when it hadn't apparently been done, I took a photograph of a fox through the bottom of a dustbin. For some time afterwards acquaintances would remark that they had seen it in magazines or books to which it had never been sent. When I looked I found that other photographers had replicated my shot and some of their pictures were better. Good luck to them – it's the picture that counts.

Okay, you've researched the competition, you've readied the camera, it's time to take control. You've got to get to grips with the light, the colour, the texture, the composition and the position of the camera and its lens and your subject.

Let's consider a Robin on the bird table. Firstly, in front of the camera the bird table is not a bird table, it has become a photographic platform. I don't care whether Conran or Chippendale created your feeding station, neither I, nor most people, would wish to see it in the picture – we all like birds to look as if they are in the wild. And to fool us is easy, just nip down to the woods and pick up a nicely sculptured piece of moss and lichen-covered branch, preferably windblown, and G-clamp it to the table top. Only momentary confusion will grip Robbie Robin before he pitches on a far more picturesque perch. You don't have to go 'au natural' either – rusty pipes, car bonnets and a huge pile of empty but brilliantly coloured paint tins have all been at times attached to my bird tables to provide a more interesting backdrop than my neighbour's out of focus garage door. And remember, if the light is not right, you can always reposition everything into the shade or into the sunshine, and a new or novel background can be pinned to your fence, propped up against the pagoda or painted on the wall. After all, it's your garden.

Left: *Through the dustbin – such a simple idea, such a success, even if I do say so myself. New angles are literally everywhere, they won't all work but they're worth a look.*

CHANGING THE ANGLE

Of course you should immediately aim higher than a Robin on the bird table. Take advantage of whatever wildlife subjects you have, especially those which are least upset by your constructive changes. I once built a cemetery – lots of hardboard, lightweight tombstones and withering wreaths dotted a friend's lawn to get a shot of a fox which took food from her patio. However, not all the visitors will be as forgiving as the Robin. There's no doubt that some of the more timid will be instantly put off if they see you anywhere unusual. You will normally find that your subjects are more wary than you'd imagined they might be. As a general rule, animals rely on familiarity for security; thus as long as you are where they expect you to be, they're happy. Move outside these areas, step off the path or outside the shed and suddenly everything becomes cautious. Nevertheless, urban subjects should be quicker to adapt and it's easier for you to persevere.

I know of only one comfortable, centrally heated hide complete with tea, coffee or beer, that normally has an assistant standing by and is free to use, without booking, 365 days a year – my house. Before you consider going out into the cold or wet exploit, the indoor opportunities. Ideally, shoot from where you normally sit or stand, from your armchair in front of the patio window or out of the kitchen window over the washing up. In this way you'll stand little or no chance of terrifying your thoroughly accustomed subjects. Obviously clean both sides of the glass and try to find a scratch-free section to line up with your lens.

To minimize the risk of reflection keep the lens as close to the pane as possible, almost touching it is best. If you do need to use flash, get an extension lead to run out through the window to the gun which you've taped to a second tripod or stand and clad in a polythene bag to stop any rain getting in. This may take your subject a few days to get used and you may flatten a couple of batteries with all the flashes – but by then all but the most timid visitors will be prepared to bask in a brief lightning strike.

If your lenses won't reach, or the bird table or set can't be moved close enough to a window then you have two choices; firstly you could fire the camera by remote, trigger

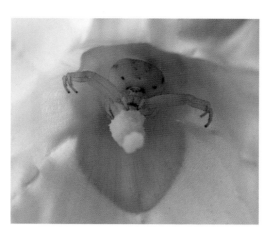

Left: *White and waiting, a crab spider poised to pounce in the tunnel of a bindweed bloom. By excluding any background I've simplified the picture and thrown all the focus onto the animal.*

cables can be bought for most cameras. Manually focus on the spot where the subject will be and lock the focus off. Using auto exposure you should be confident enough not to keep running back and forth to the camera to make adjustments. Use another polythene bag to protect the camera from Mr Moisture – secure it with a couple of elastic bands to stop it flapping in front of the lens. You can get perfect pictures using this approach but it's always nerve racking and will test the most confident practitioner. One word of caution; if Grey Squirrels are active in your garden be careful what you leave out unattended and unprotected. Irrespective of value, they will chew it and this will really upset you.

The second option is a case of moving outside yourself. Check the conservatory, greenhouse, garage, or outside toilet windows for prospective vantage points – if none are suitable build a hide out of anything. Remember it's your garden, so what it looks like is up to you; make it dry, comfortable and flap proof so that when the wind blows it doesn't startle your subject or expose you to it. Family camping tents, especially toilet tents, are easily 'cannibalized' or you can build more permanent structures from fencing panels, whatever; the choice is yours, and that of the family you have to live with. Remember they will have to barbecue, hang out the washing or play football around your structure.

Standing up straight or sitting down are among the most comfortable options, and if you have to spend hours waiting, comfort is essential. But this approach can in turn often mean that you end up looking down on your small ground-based subject, something which always appears unnatural and is therefore the mark of a lazy photographer. Get down to your subject's level; if you lie down, support the camera on a bean bag, and peer through the glass or over the pond, your perspective will make an immediate impact in a photograph. It increases the 'wildness' and reduces its domesticity.

BUILDING SETS

Above: *Not a scrapyard scene, but a set that once adorned my parents lawn all summer until a Grass Snake finally showed up and I got the shot. I paid ten pounds for the crumpled moggie minor and nailed it up to a wooden frame.*

Building small manageable sets is a great way of infinitely extending the scope of your garden – because part of it can be part of anything you like.

Generally even the tamest animals will require a little time to accustom themselves to your new ideas, so a degree of permanence is desirable. For naturally curious species, such as Grey Squirrels or Foxes, a few days or maybe a few hours will be enough to overcome their caution and jump onto or into your best laid plans. Even then the light, weather or pose may not be quite right and you may wish to repeat your shot. Hence piling things loosely together is not a good idea and nor is putting the set in the middle of the lawn.

Bolt, nail or screw your set together because this will help with the second essential – portability. Between shoots you can store it out of everyone's way and avoid conflicts about what constitutes an attractive feature in the garden. It seems that most people prefer cupids, urns or even gnomes to would-be sections of castle battlement or factory air-conditioning outlets – a couple of my realized, but vilified beauties. And because most of our British subjects are small then your set doesn't need to be that much bigger, just large enough to allow for 'shoot-off' around the subject. It's best to plan all this in advance, design your ideal picture, even sketch it and measure it out. You know, or can find out, how tall a Starling stands. Decide how big you'd like it to appear in your final photograph and extrapolate to decide how much background you need to make. Keep a camera complete with the appropriate lens handy so you can check on all perspectives and remember, the more confident you are about what you want the less flexibility you'll need to exploit.

Often there's not a lot of DIY needed, just a keen eye for opportunities. I was walking along a railway line once where the tops of all the telegraph poles had been cut off; with permission, I lugged one away and stood it up in the garden. Immediately I was standing 2 m away at eye level from a top of a telegraph pole. A trained Kestrel and a roll of sky blue paper provided me with a simple but never before seen perspective of this bird.

But now we're gravitating towards 'props' rather than full-blown sets and many of these can be natural artefacts to enhance the picture. Moss or lichen-covered branches look better than a plain fence top if you have a bird perched on them, as would natural stones, rather than paving slabs at the pond side. It is not too hard to procure and place items like this and it instantly turns a lazy snap into a better photograph. I once constructed the tail-end of a Cruise Missile out of a drainpipe, hardboard and cardboard as I wanted to get a poignant shot of a Blackbird singing from its unexploded fin. It didn't work, but only because I didn't put in enough time, but I recall that it was great to tell my mates down the pub that I'd spent the day making a nuclear weapon.

PHOTOGRAPHING POND LIFE – THE SURFACE

Not all the species that inhabit the pond live in it. Some literally live on the pond, and its surface offers a great scope for photographs. The trouble is that it's low down and I don't know about you, but I'd rather not lie flat on my belly in the damp, getting my elbows wet or risk dropping my camera into the water. The simple solution comes in the form of trays.

A few years ago I wanted to photograph frogs, toads and pond skaters on perfectly clean, simple minimizing backgrounds, something that my pond didn't offer. Overhanging trees cast reflections, pond plants protruded from the surface and the creatures, well, they all had other ideas – 'escape', 'flee' and 'hide' top of their agendas. So I went to a garden centre and bought both square and long thin plastic gravel trays, sanded their inside surfaces and painted them both matt black. I set them on a chest height bench and filled them with 3-4 cm of water. When the light is low in the sky and you are close to the surface it becomes a mirror reflecting that sky, whether blue or blustery and this makes a wonderful background to isolate any subject upon. Often your subject will be reflected too so the scope for abstract mirror image reflections is frequent and entertaining. Pond Skaters, Raft Spiders, Grass Snakes, frogs, toads, and resting adult dragonflies all make great subjects, and of course, in terms of other props, the sky is your limit as well as your backdrop.

By using trays you also make a pond portable and by gluing or taping strips of flower-arranging foam to the base before filling you can add vegetation and renaturalize your pond as required. For both the animals and your own well-being it's always best to work with an assistant. Things have a horrible habit of hopping out and away and if you have to keep moving from behind the camera life becomes pretty difficult. If you're photographing frogs and toads then place a generous amount of padding, carpets or old blankets either side of the tray table as they will unpredictably leap off and the sound of a frog flopping onto a concrete patio is sickening as well as inexcusable.

The water surface offers equally rewarding opportunities from underneath, the problem is that if you look up through a conventional tank with your camera the distortion caused by the glass becomes extreme and any pictures unusable. A special tank is required and I believe that in

Left: Simplicity shows off the superb adaptations that allow pond skaters to perform. Dimples and shadows beneath their span – superb.

the mid-1980s I was its inventor. The Third Reich have the V1, Honda has the V-tech, but I came up with the V-tank, more creative and less expensive than the latter pair, but perhaps not so popular as Churchill's V-sign!

The V-tank is less complex than the two-tank arrangement but allows you to shoot up at the surface of the water where, if any subject is lit correctly, some interesting total internal reflections appear. Placing the necessary neutral background is tricky so you'll have to experiment and work equally hard to keep the surface free of dust and hairs – a small paint brush and patience are your only real allies. Again, size of tank is dependent on the size of your subject.

The V-tank is best placed high up, as a crick in the neck is a very real possibility. I always put mine on a stout plank supported between the top two rungs of step ladders and use a third to gain access to the surface and its suspended creatures. My favourite subjects have been water beetles and boatmen, whose backside breathing technique means that they will inevitably hang still long enough for a shot, and the Great Raft Spider, which frequently pops under to avoid predators or probing paint brushes. I'm sure you could do more but I must warn that this setup requires the patience, not only of one, but of a veritable team of saints.

Right: From the V shaped tank a water boatman and its total internal reflection (top). An attempt at abstract art with a marvellous animal. Just look at its killer rostrum tucked beneath its head – all the better to stab you with.

PHOTOGRAPHING POND-LIFE TANK PHOTOS

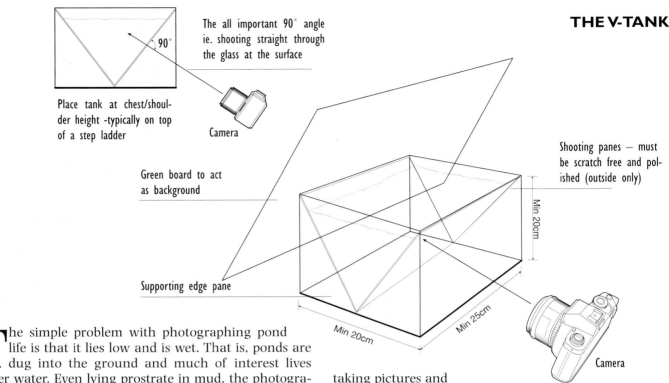

The all important 90° angle ie. shooting straight through the glass at the surface

90°

Place tank at chest/shoulder height -typically on top of a step ladder

Camera

THE V-TANK

Green board to act as background

Shooting panes — must be scratch free and polished (outside only)

Min 20cm

Supporting edge pane

Min 20cm

Min 25cm

Camera

The simple problem with photographing pond life is that it lies low and is wet. That is, ponds are dug into the ground and much of interest lives under water. Even lying prostrate in mud, the photographer cannot maximize the potential. Fortunately, there are two obvious and simple solutions to the watery dilemma – tanks and trays.

There is a real art to photographing anything in a glass tank and sadly it is rarely encountered. Buying a nearly made aquarium and lighting it with an angle-poise on the living room table is not going to rectify this. A little effort and planning will pay dividends in the final picture.

Firstly, it is always best to build your own tanks. Have a glazier cut the glass to your requirements and ensure that at least the front pane is scratch- and blemish-free. You will make a mess of the silicone seaming but it doesn't matter – these receptacles are for work, not for displaying on the mantelpiece. Secondly, build or cannibalize a heavy duty workbench which will support the base of the tanks at chest height. There is nothing worse than kneeling or craning down to peer into a camera when you have plenty of other distractions and irritations to contend with. Comfort always helps with concentration.

Now, a couple of tricks of the trade. Build a large 'background tank' which you fill with substrate, weed, debris, etc. but never any of your living subjects. Construct it as deep as possible while considering the weight of water it will hold and the stability of your supporting table. Once complete, this tank will need a couple of weeks to settle down, for the silt or sand to clear from the water and for all of the vegetation to recover from its uprooting and transplanting. Make any future adjustments well in advance of taking pictures and with care but aim to make this tank look as real as possible – so use lots of debris, not a smooth, gravelly or sandy base. Also because this permanent set will be the background to all of your tank pictures, a little diversity of light-coloured texture from right to left will provide more scope for a variety of shots.

Next construct a series of 'subject tanks', up to the same height as your 'background tank' and of adequate width to hold the relevant subject, i.e. if you're photographing a dragonfly larva it doesn't need to be as deep or as wide as a tank used for a shoal of Minnows. Fill this with clean, fresh water and nothing else. As usual, allow it to stand for a couple of days to de-chlorinate and also for all of the air to come out of solution. Initially, the glass sides will be coated with thousands of tiny silver bubbles, which if you dislodge will only reappear again. The benefit of this two-tank technique is obvious – your subject can never disappear into the weed or silt as soon as you introduce it and lead you to angrily poke it about while churning up a mess and wrecking the set. In your 'subject tank' use minimal and clean natural supports – single strands of weed, twig or stones – and gently coax your subject to pose on these rather than against the glass. From the front it will look as if that subject is actually in the rear tank amongst the natural set. In fact, it is held in a highly controllable environment where it can be coaxed into position with a long handled soft paint brush or removed without any distress or damage.

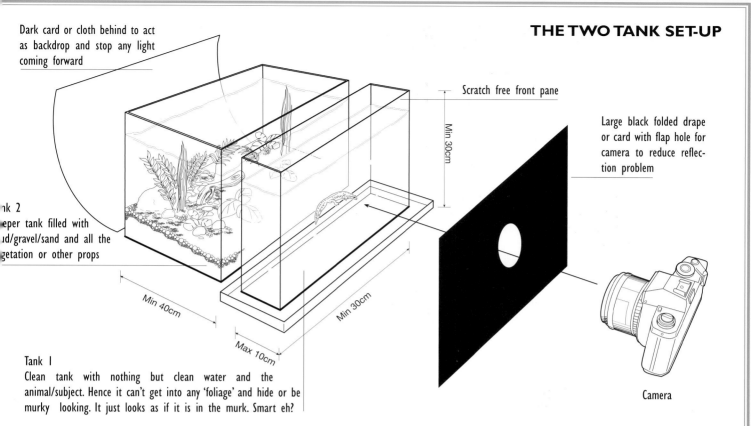

Dark card or cloth behind to act as backdrop and stop any light coming forward

Scratch free front pane

Min 30cm

Large black folded drape or card with flap hole for camera to reduce reflection problem

nk 2
eper tank filled with
ud/gravel/sand and all the
getation or other props

Min 40cm

Min 30cm

Max 10cm

Tank 1
Clean tank with nothing but clean water and the animal/subject. Hence it can't get into any 'foliage' and hide or be murky looking. It just looks as if it is in the murk. Smart eh?

Camera

Left: *Spawning Common Frog photographed in a set up similar to that illustrated above. Here a little unreal back light has enhanced the simplicity. Reducing colour and a lack of weed or other detail helps in a similar way.*

Poor lighting is what ruins most tank pictures, normally because there's too much of it. Consider reality, if you were submerged in a pond all the light would come from above – thus shield the back and at least one side of your tanks with dark paper or card. Then begin the difficult task of reducing reflections by shading yourself, your camera and everything behind you from any bright light. I hang several metres of black drape on stands, wear black, throw another drape over myself and the camera, loosely wrap the material around the tripod and for all this trouble completely solve the problem.

Another tip is to make your 'subject tank' slide-able, especially if you're photographing a macro subject. It becomes easier to gently slide the tank and subject toward or away from the lens rather than to refocus the camera or shift the tripod back and forth. I put a layer of cloth (felt) on the bench top and put the tank on top of a stainless steel tray.

Lastly, make sure your glass is clean, inside and out – magnetic aquarium cleaners, lint-free cloth and a tiny carefully applied amount of window cleaner will do the trick. Use as shallow a depth of field as you can get away with and always shoot at ninety degrees to the glass. Flash works well if it is heavily diffused but it's best to shoot a few test rolls and keep note of your experiments. I prefer to use softer, natural light, and remember you can always boost that or localize it by using a mirror to reflect light onto the subject. A patient assistant is invariably a necessity for this method of lighting. One last comment; photographing a subject in a tank is obviously not something you do in ten minutes before tea. By the time you've cleaned the tanks, prepared your set, collected the subject, or several of them, hung the drapes, readied the camera, waited for the light and waited for the animal to swim into the right position, several hours will have passed. And it's a frustrating business directing a shoot with a cast of Caddis Fly larvae or Common Frogs, so to avoid insanity I'd allocate a whole afternoon if not the best part of a day.

CATS – THE NOT-SO-PHANTOM MENACE

Throughout this book I have struggled to refrain from pre-empting what you are about to read. Few of the creatures about which I have enthused are immune from its horrible and unconstrained impact. Thus I will now attempt to deal, in a fair and rational manner, with the role that the domestic cat and its feral partners play in shaping the ecology of our urban and suburban wildlife.

All cats are sly, greedy, insidious murderers. There, I've failed. Oh dear, I've said what so many urban naturalists know, but are too afraid to say for fear of ostracizing themselves from friends and family who are too fond of felines.

Some simple science – cats are top of the food chain predators and as such should be relatively rare. In a 'natural' situation they would have a home range of in excess of ten square kilometres each and yet in a typical neighbourhood there can be as many as two hundred cats in one square kilometre. Cats are superbly evolved animals; stealthy, quick, keen of sight and sound, whiskered for nocturnal prowess and relatively clever animals. With such a super over-abundance of super predators nothing else stands a chance. Nothing. Not Robins, Slow-worms, moths, mice or newts. Even bats end up on the sickening 'trophy mat'. To qualify this I once spoke to one of Britain's most eminent ornithologists, the late Chris Mead of the British Trust for Ornithology, a man with a vast and detailed knowledge of our garden bird populations.

Chris told me that there are more cats than dogs in Britain, a staggering seven and a half million, and each year they account for the direct death of sixty million songbirds. SIXTY MILLION SONGBIRDS and three hundred million small mammals and an unknown amount of other garden wildlife.

Above: This time a Greenfinch on the feline menu? It's just not fair. Not right, not sound, not acceptable. It's just not, contrary to what most people dismissively claim, nature. In nature, and in my dreams, cats would be rare.

Not all cats are equally destructive; those house-bound pussies at the top of tower blocks are virtually exonerated of blame whereas their feral relatives are no less than mass murderers. The typical suburban cat equates to a serial killer. Notorious examples include a Hebridean pet that had a compulsive attraction to baby Corncrakes, and another with a fondness for Redstarts. Imagine waking on a crisp May morning to find your neighbour's cat grinning through the patio doors with... a male Redstart hanging limply from its mouth. Where did I put my shotgun?

I asked Chris which was the most unusual species 'catted' and was astounded to hear that Lesser Black-backed Gull was on the list. It appeared that the limitations of the BTO's computer at the time was the cause of this bizarre record because the assassin was in fact a safari park Lion. No available category on the screen for 'big cat' meant the event was logged under 'mini-cat',

Chris estimated that between five hundred to six hundred million small birds die annually in the UK, thus ten per cent are killed by cats, and that their populations have learned to tolerate this depredation. However, when the problem is compounded by the increasing number of road kills, over-use of both farm and garden insecticides, and habitat loss, the actual impact that cat predation makes could be far more significant than the figures suggest.

N.B. Unlike myself, Chris Mead was not a cat hater. He was the owner of a pet cat.

CATS – THE NOT-SO-FINAL SOLUTION

The magnitude of this problem no doubt depends on your affinity for felines, but it does exist, nevertheless. So what can we do about it?

Firstly, we could choose not to have cats unless we are real cat fans. Then I personally would advocate a licensing scheme. Licences would be very cheap to prevent cat lovers of any kind from being unable to pamper pussies but only granted to those whose animals are fully inoculated. The cost of this, a surely mandatory requirement to anyone serious about their moggy, is about eighty to one hundred pounds. This might put paid to the 'kittens free to good home' situation.

Chris Mead, who I mentioned on page 136, didn't support the licensing idea; he believed that an effective neutering programme is what is needed.

Okay, what if your neighbours' cats are a problem? Firstly lobby for a collar with not one but two bells. A single bell can be cunningly silenced by the creeping cat but two normally tinkle enough to scare a few birds. Next, come Christmas, buy them a 'CatSafe', 'Cat Alert' or 'Liberator' collar. These new technological cat collars have a silicon chip that registers the pattern of the cat's movement when it is stalking and emits an electronic squeal and causes a small red LED to flash before it leaps. Some automatically switch off when the animal enters the house but even so the sound is not intrusive to humans. Chris Mead has tested these devices and believes they work well with birds but not so well with small mammals. Even so, he believes that if one third of our domestic cats were fitted with these cheap gadgets ten million fewer birds would be killed each year.

Other devices purport to recognize cats as intruders and scare them off with high-pitched blasts of ultrasonic sound. There is a wide range of these deterrents on the market; the 'Catwatch MK II' boasts a range of forty feet and emits a five-second pulse of sound at high volume, all in with a cable and mains adapter for around seventy pounds; the 'Catstop' is an entry level, battery powered black box whilst the 'Dazer' produces ultrasonic blasts ten times per second, is weather resistant, and protects an area of 278 sq m. It costs forty pounds, comes with fifty feet of cable and is apparently not heard by birds or fish. The trouble is that it,

and all the others, cannot be heard by humans either and as a consequence many people distrust these devices.

However, both Chris Mead and Trevor Williams of the Fox Project told me they had good anecdotal evidence to suggest that these can be very effective deterrents. Indeed, the one problem is feline deafness, a phenomenon that appears more frequently in white cats and some of the eastern breeds. Other stubborn mogs appear to hear these devices but simply put up with the annoyance. My concern is that these devices might interfere with any foxes, badgers and deer which you are trying to attract. However, because these are principally nocturnal visitors you could simply wire your ultrasonic deterrent to a light sensitive switch so it switches off after our feathered friends have flown to roost.

Above: *More obvious than a tabby. Some people say that white cats kill less wildlife because they're more easily spotted. You could try painting your cat white to test this (OK, don't really, but you take my point).*

ASSORTED GADGETS

If you make internal flights across America you'll often find in the seat back pocket facing you a colourful catalogue of gadgets. Similar things are produced in the UK but as usual the Americans do it bigger... and naffer. My favourites to date include a raised dog feeding and drinking table, to prevent your 'pooch' from straining its neck when it lowers it to eat and drink, and also a 'Smile Enhancer'. This ingenious device clamps to your head and various hooks and levers are inserted into your mouth. In order to smile you have to lift attached weights. Apparently through such exercise you can produce a 'broader, brighter smile'. In fact it works, because even without purchase I cannot remember when I last smiled as much as I did when I found this little gem on offer. Sadly the silly gadget market has also infiltrated the natural history department. Having already battered bat boxes and butterfly feeders I will try to be constructively critical.

Insect hibernacula. Several are available, some specifically targeted at ladybirds, earwigs and remarkably one for... lacewings. The last is a box filled with twigs that claims to increase lacewing survival from five to ninety-five per cent, a benefit of course because lacewings eat aphids and aphids are 'pests'. Look, have lacewing scientists been at work here or is this just twenty pounds worth of marketing madness? I've a good mind to buy one and test it, but I bet you a pound I'm more likely to get a bat roosting in it than a lethargic lacewing. I'm sure that after millions years of practice insects can hibernate without our help.

While we're on invertebrates, how about fifty pounds' worth of an electromagnetic and ultrasonic spider scarer. Phase-shift-current technology and dual acoustic transducers shift the electromagnetic field in alternate current wiring circuitry in your walls and ceilings to disrupt 'pests' in their nest-making activities. Sounds great, in fact probably even sounds great if you're a spider. Given that cockroaches and scorpions can survive high levels of radiation and being frozen solid in ice, and still emerge with a smile, I'm sure that spiders won't mind having their magnets manipulated.

Okay, how about a pot with holes which you hang in your garden and fill with 'safe, bug-free roosting and nesting materials' for your birds? Moss, grass and feathers not good enough any more then? Or how about another terracotta chamber with a specially designed toad hole? Yes, you invert it in the garden to offer 'sanctuary and security' to those 'slug-eating friends of the gardener'. My favourite by miles, however, is a 60-70 cm diameter brilliant yellow inflatable beach ball adorned with 'eyes' and a tinsel tassel. Suspended in your garden it is meant to scare Magpies, which it might because it certainly scares me. Who would want to ruin their garden with such preposterous flotsam?

To conclude, there is one 'gadget' not covered elsewhere in this book that might actually work and if it does may save the lives of birds, so it's worth a try. A range of bird silhouettes, usually raptors, are produced to stick onto large or french windows into which startled birds fly to their invisible death. In certain situations the glass reflects the garden and birds fleeing from feeders, perhaps spooked by Sparrowhawks or cats crash into it. Our own glass frontage has accounted for at least one Blue Tit, one Chaffinch, a Collared Dove and two Greenfinches in the last eighteen months – and we have stickers on top of stickers. I don't think the shape matters at all, anything decorative will do, but remember always to keep the curtains or blinds drawn when you're out for long periods – this works best of all.

From the ridiculous to the radical. Left: Butterfly feeders – what on earth next? Top: Bird silhouettes should be mandatory on french windows or any glass adjacent to feeders. Right: Bird proof squirrel feeder for those for whom fur is more fun than feathers.

ETHICS AND THE LAW

Ethics

Let's be clear from the start. I've spent most of my life collecting living plants and animals and modestly moving them about for my own amusement. So, I suspect, have many of you. It's not the sort of thing that a keen conservationist likes to admit to, but then at least I'm honest.

It all started years ago with a jam-jar full of frogspawn which I proudly carried from Southampton Common's cemetery lake to an old bath in the garden. Next came Grass Snakes, Slow-worms and Common Lizards. Our garden was not suitable for these animals and only the Slow-worms remained for a short while. These were acts of childish selfishness committed at a time when my parents knew no better than to always encourage my interest. But now we all do know better. I wouldn't allow such unsuitable introductions to be made by our equally keen little girl. But what if we had created a suitable resource for a given species and after all the object of much of this book is to encourage just that, then would we collect it and move it?

It would depend. There are no clear-cut rules or laws. Extremists fiercely oppose even the shortest movements on the ground of unnatural genetic mixing. I feel that on a small scale this is counter-productive nonsense. We live in the very jumbled wreckage of an environment, particularly when it comes to gardens and all the introduced and exotic flora. And in the wider countryside? Rabbits, Grey Squirrels, Ring-necked Parakeets, Honeybees... all these animals have been introduced and we have learned to live with them, even to enjoy or value some of them.

And then there are reintroductions. Red Kites and White-tailed Eagles have been brought back to tremendous popular acclaim. As I write, the Beaver looks to be the next creature to be carefully nursed back into the British countryside and will the wolf, the lynx and the Brown Bear follow? I hope so but many would not.

My point is, that when collecting for your garden, you should always consider the welfare of the animals or plants involved. Can they survive and prosper? Will the introduction upset the harmony of the resource or your garden? A metre-long Pike in the pond might, a few Smooth Newts probably won't. Be responsible and plan. Never denude a patch in the wild for your own gratification, never exploit a species, remember you are meant to be enhancing the world for these other animals. If you've worked hard to make part of your garden into a suitable habitat for a species in many instances it will arrive of its own accord, something which is always far more satisfying.

The Law

We must not forget that there are laws that protect particular species and their environment. The Wildlife and Countryside Act was passed in 1981 and the Environmental Protection Act in 1990. Both are regularly updated. Large tracts of these and other laws will never apply to us in our garden, but some sections are appropriate, particularly with regard to birds. Within the 1981 act all British birds are divided among nine schedules. Schedule One lists our most endangered species, from Avocets to Wrynecks. To kill, injure, disturb or interfere with the bird or its nest, eggs and young is a serious crime. Heavy fines can be exacted and possibly custodial sentences. Up until 1993 there was a schedule of thirteen species that could be destroyed by authorized persons at all times, but this schedule has been dropped. The term 'pest' is no longer an excuse to persecute any bird. So, if Magpies drive you mad – tough, put away your airgun.

Many other animals are protected under Schedule Five of the Wildlife and Countryside Act: Adders, all bats, Crested Newts, twenty-five butterflies and seven moths. Thus attempts to capture Purple Emperors, most fritillaries and hairstreaks and release them at home are not on. Nor is killing or selling any other reptiles or amphibian, although Smooth and Palmate Newts, frogs, toads, Common Lizards, Grass Snakes and Slow-worms can be captured and moved.

Schedule Nine has a list of animals which it is illegal to release into the wild – Wall Lizards are on it. But so are Grey Squirrels, American Mink and Ruddy Ducks, and I was under the impression that the damage, if that's how you perceive it, has been done with these species.

The list of protected plants runs to three pages but includes a host of mosses and lichens, not many, if any, species which you might feel are necessary to enrich the flora of your garden. Sadly it does not include Bluebells, Primroses, Foxgloves, etc... so in reality there is nothing to stop you removing these plants from areas which are not otherwise designated as sites of conservation interest or nature reserves. But that doesn't mean you should do it. Most of these species suffer terribly from over-collection in the wild, so behave responsibly, shop around for wild flowers which are definitely cultured 'in captivity' and spend whatever it costs to keep your conscience clean.

In our homes we are all our own judges, juries and executioners. My only absolute advice is ensure that you sleep soundly at night with your conscience as clear as your pond water.

ADDRESSES

Amphibian and Reptile Conservation
Tel. 01733 558844 and
 01202 391319
Email enquiries@arc-trust.org
Website www.arc-trust.org

Bat Conservation Trust
15 Cloisters House
8 Battersea Park Road
London SW8 4BG
Tel. 0845 1300 228
Email enquiries@bats.org.uk
Website www.bats.org.uk

Birdcam
42 Scafield Road
Langman Industrial Estate
Inverness IV1 1SG
Tel. 01463 731525
Email debbie@birdcam.co.uk
Website www.birdcam.co.uk
(birdtables and nestboxes with
 cameras.)

British Dragonfly Society
Secretary: Henry Curry
23 Bowker Way
Whittlesey
Peterborough PE7 1PY
Email bdssecretary@
 dragonflysoc.co.uk
Website
 www.dragonflysoc.org.uk

British Trust for Ornithology
The Nunnery, Thetford
Norfolk IP24 2PU
Tel. 01842 750050
Email info@bto.org
Website www.bto.org

Brunel Microscopes (BR) Limited
Unit 2, Vincients Road
Bumpers Farm Industrial Estate
Chippenham
Wiltshire SN14 6NQ
Tel. 01249 462655
Fax 01249 445156
Email mail@brunelmicroscopes.
 co.uk
Website
 www.brunelmicroscopes.co.uk

Buglife – The Invertebrate Conservation Trust
First Floor
90 Bridge Street
Peterborough PE1 1DY
Tel. 01733 201 210
Email info@buglife.org.uk
Website www.buglife.org.uk

Catwatch (cat/fox deterrents)
Unit 9, Bowmans Trading Estate
Bessemer Drive, Stevenage
Hertfordshire SG1 2DL
Tel. 01438 727183
Email main@
 conceptresearch.co.uk
Website
 www.conceptresearch.co.uk

Conservation Foundation
1 Kensington Gore
London SW7 2AR
Tel. 020 7591 3111
Website www.
 conservationfoundation.co.uk

Countryside Council for Wales
Maes-y-Ffynnon
Penrhosgarnedd, Bangor
Gwynedd LL57 2DW
Tel. 0845 1306229
Website www.ccw.gov.uk

Dazer (cat/fox deterrents)
16 Thorpe Meadows
Peterborough PE3 6GA
Tel. 01733 315888
Email enquiries@dazer.com
Website www.dazer.com

Department of the Environment for Northern Ireland
Clarence Court
10-18 Adelaide Street
Belfast BT2 8GB
Tel. 028 9054 0540
Email doe.iemonitoring@
 doeni.gov.uk
Website www.doeni.gov.uk

Fauna and Flora International
Jupiter House, 4th Floor
Station Road
Cambridge CB1 2JD
Tel. 01223 571000
Email info@fauna-flora.org
Website www.fauna-flora.org

The Fox Project
The Lodge, Kings Toll Road
Pembury, Kent TN2 4BE
Website www.foxproject.org.uk

Garden Organic
Coventry CV8 3LG
Tel. 024 7630 3517
Email enquiry@gardenorganic.
 org.uk
Website
 www.gardenorganic.org.uk

Liberator Cat Collar
Khazu Limited
The Old Chapel
Ferrars Road, Huntingdon
Cambridgeshire PE18 6DH

The Microscope Shop
Oxford Road
Sutton Scotney, Winchester,
Hampshire SO21 3JG
Tel. 01962 760228

Natural England
Northminster House
Peterborough PE1 1UA
Tel. 01733 455000
Email enquiries@
 naturalengland.org.uk
Website
 www.naturalengland.org.uk

New Forest Badger Watch
Alistair Kilburn
PO Box 2297, Ringwood
Hampshire BH24 4PH
Tel. 01425 403412
Email akilburn@
 badgerwatch.co.uk
Website
 www.badgerwatch.co.uk

Plantlife
14 Rollestone Street, Salisbury
Wiltshire SP1 1DX
Tel. 01722 342730
Email enquiries@
 plantlife.org.uk

Royal Society for the Protection of Birds
The Lodge, Sandy,
Bedfordshire SG19 2DL
Tel. 01767 680551
Website www.rspb.org.uk

Scottish Natural Heritage
Great Glen House, Leachkin
Road, Inverness IV3 8NW
Tel. 01463 725000
Email enquiries@snh.gov.uk
Website www.snh.org.uk

Secret World
New Road, Highbridge
Somerset TA9 3PZ
Tel. 01278 783250
Website www.secretworld.co.uk

Tree Advice Trust
Alice Holt Lodge
Farnham, Surrey GU10 4LH
Tel. 01420 22022
Email admin@treehelp.info
Website www.treehelp.info

Urban Wildlife Network
Website
 www.urbanwildlife.org.uk

Watkins and Doncaster: The Naturalists
PO Box 5, Cranbrook
Kent TN18 5EZ
Tel. 01580 753133
Fax 01580 754054
Email sales@watdon.co.uk
Website www.watdon.co.uk
(General naturalist supplies –
 nets, boxes, moth traps,
 pooters, etc.)

Wildfowl and Wetlands Trust
Slimbridge
Gloucestershire GL2 7BT
Tel. 01453 891900
Email enquiries@wwt.org.uk
Website www.wwt.org.uk

Wildlife Computing
6 Fiddlers Lane, East Bergholt
Colchester CO7 6SJ
Tel. 01206 298345
Website www.wildlife.co.uk
(Bird recording software for PC
 and Pocket PC.)

The Wildlife Trusts
(See page 5)
The Kiln, Waterside
Mather Road, Newark
Nottinghamshire NG24 1WT
Tel. 01636 677711
Email enquiry@
 wildlifetrusts.org
Website www.wildlifetrusts.org

The Wildlife Watch
(Contact details the same as
 The Wildlife Trusts)
Email: watch@wildlifetrusts.org

The Woodland Trust
Autumn Park
Dysart Road, Grantham
Lincolnshire NG31 6LL
Tel. 01476 581111
Email enquiries@
 woodlandtrust.org.uk
Website
 www.woodlandtrust.org.uk

Yorkshire Wildlife Trust
10 Toft Greens
York
North Yorkshire YO1 6JT
Tel. 01904 659570
Email info@ywt.org.uk
Website www.ywt.org.uk

SUGGESTED READING – BOOK GUIDE

Albouy, Vincent
Nature by Night
New Holland Publishers, 2008
ISBN 978 1 84773 114 2

Armstrong, Edward A.
The Wren
Shire Publications, 2000
ISBN 0 7478 0160 6

Backshall, Steve
Wildlife Adventurers' Guide
New Holland Publishers, 2009
ISBN 978 1 84773 324 5

Barthel, Peter
New Holland European Bird Guide
New Holland Publishers, 2008
ISBN 978 1 84773 110 4

Beddard, Roy
The Garden Bird Year
New Holland Publishers, 2009
ISBN 978 1 84773 503 4

Brooks, Steve
*Field Guide to the Dragonflies and
    Damselflies of Great Britain
    and Ireland*
British Wildlife Publishing, 1997
ISBN 978 0 95313 990 3

Burrows, Ian
Food From The Wild
New Holland Publishers, 2005
ISBN 978 1 84330 891 1

Carter, D., Hargreaves, B.
*A Field Guide to Caterpillars of
    Butterflies and Moths in Britain
    and Europe*
Collins, 1986
ISBN 0 00 219 080 X

Chinery, Michael
Butterflies of Britain and Europe
Collins and The Wildlife Trusts,
1998. ISBN 0 00220059 7

Chinery, Michael
*A Field Guide to the Insects of
Britain and Northern Europe*
Collins, 1972
ISBN 0 00219216 0

Corbet, G., Southern, H. (Eds)
The Handbook of British Mammals
Blackwell Scientific, 1964
ISBN 0 632 09080 4

Coster, Bill
Creative Bird Photography
New Holland Publishers, 2009
ISBN 978 1 84773 509 6

Dewar, S., Shawyer, C.
*Boxes, Baskets and Platforms –
    Artificial Nest Sites for Owls
    and other Birds of Prey*
Hawk and Owl Trust, 1996
ISBN 0 9503187 6 0

Dig a Pond for Dragonflies
British Dragonfly Society, 1990
See www.dragonflysoc.org.uk

Easterbrook, Michael
*Butterflies of the British Isles –
    The Lycaenidae*
Shire Publications, 2000
ISBN 0 85263 9457

Easterbrook, Michael
*Butterflies of the British Isles –
    The Nymphalidae*
Shire Publications, 2000
ISBN 0 85263 8809

Easterbrook, Michael
*Butterflies of the British Isles –
    The Pieridae*
Shire Publications, 2000
ISBN 0 7478 0032 4

Easterbrook, Michael
Hawk-moths of the British Isles
Shire Publications, 2000
ISBN 0 85263 7438

*Field Guide to Mushrooms and
Other Fungi of Britain and Europe*
New Holland Publishers, 2006
ISBN 978 1 84537 474 7

Flegg, Jim. *The Blue Tit*
Shire Publications, 2000
ISBN 0 85263 7160

Gibbons, Bob
*Field Guide to the Insects of
    Britain and Northern Europe*
The Crowood Press, 1996
ISBN 1 85223 895 X

Holm, Jessica. *The Red Squirrel*
Shire Publications, 2000
ISBN 0 7478 0022 7

Jones, D.
*The Country Life Guide to Spiders
of Britain and Northern Europe*
Country Life Books, 1983
ISBN 0 600 35665 5

Kwet, Axel
*New Holland European Reptile
and Amphibian Guide*
New Holland Publishers, 2009
ISBN 978 1 84773 444 0

Jordan, Peter
*Field Guide to Edible Mushrooms
    of Britain and Europe*
New Holland Publishers, 2006
ISBN 978 1 84537 419 8

Leach, Michael
Mice of the British Isles
Shire Publications, 2000
ISBN 0 7478 0056 1

Lever, Christopher
*The Naturalized Animals of
    Britain and Ireland*
New Holland Publishers, 2009
ISBN 978 1 84773 454 9

Morris P. A.
The Hedgehog
Shire Publications, 2000
ISBN 0 85263 958 9

Mullarney, K., Svensson, L.,
Zetterstrom D., Grant, P.
Collins Bird Guide
Harper Collins, 1999
ISBN 0 00 219728 6

New Holland Concise Bird Guide
New Holland Publishers, 2010
(New Holland Concise Guides
series published in association
with The Wildlife Trusts)
ISBN 978 1 84773 601 7

*New Holland Concise Butterfly
and Moth Guide*
New Holland Publishers, 2010
ISBN 978 1 84773 602 4

*New Holland Concise Wild
    Flower Guide*
New Holland Publishers, 2010
ISBN 978 1 84773 603 1

Oddie, Bill
Birds of Britain and Ireland
New Holland Publishers, 2001
ISBN 978 1 85368 488 3

Oxford, Roma
*Minibeast Magic – Kind hearted
    Capture Techniques for
    Invertebrates*
Yorkshire Wildlife Trust, 1999
ISBN 978 0 950 94 602 0

Packham, Chris
Wild Side of Town
New Holland Publishers, 2007
ISBN 978 1 84537 696 3

Simms, Eric
The Song Thrush
Shire Publications, 2000
ISBN 0 7478 0023 5

Skinner B.
*Colour Identification Guide to
    Moths of the British Isles*
Viking, 1984
ISBN 0 670 80354 5

Skinner G.
Ants of the British Isles
Shire Publications, 2000
ISBN 0 85263 896 5

Slater, Fred
The Common Toad
Shire Publications, 2000
ISBN 0 7478 0161 4

Snow, David W.
The Blackbird
Shire Publications, 2000
ISBN 0 85263 854 X

Taylor, M., Young, S.
Photographing Garden Wildlife
New Holland Publishers, 2009
ISBN 978 1 84773 486 0

Waring, P., Townsend, M.
*Field Guide to the Moths of Great
    Britain and Ireland*
British Wildlife Publishing, 2003
978 0 95313 992 7

Wardhaugh, A. A.
Bats of the British Isles
Shire Publications, 2000
ISBN 0 7478 0303 X

Wardhaugh, A. A.
Land Snails of the British Isles
Shire Publications, 2000
ISBN 0 7478 0027 8

Wisniewski, Patrick J.
Newts of the British Isles
Shire Publications, 2000
ISBN 0 7478 0029 4

INDEX

AUTHOR'S ACKNOWLEDGEMENTS

I would like to thank Chris Mead, David White and Chris Whittles for boosting the birdy bit, Tony Hutton, Graham Cornick, Pauline Kidner and Trevor Williams for helping to maximize the mammal potential, Nick Eden and Alexander Whish for taking the trouble to talk trees, David Cottridge for supplying most of the photographs, Jo Hemmings, Sylvia Sullivan and Mike Unwin for editorial energies, Barbara Levy for literal logistics, and Rita Packham and Joe McCubbin for taking the trouble to type all this.